A
Bibliography
of
Georgia Methodism

Edited and Compiled by
Harold Lawrence
Member, N. Ga. Conference

HERITAGE BOOKS
2026

HERITAGE BOOKS

AN IMPRINT OF HERITAGE BOOKS, INC.

Books, CDs, and more—Worldwide

For our listing of thousands of titles see our website
at
www.HeritageBooks.com

Published 2026 by
HERITAGE BOOKS, INC.
Publishing Division
5810 Ruatan Street
Berwyn Heights, MD 20740

International Standard Book Number
Paperbound: 978-0-7884-5163-8

ACKNOWLEDGEMENT

This publication was made possible through the generosity of John W. Boyd, Sr., Emory University graduate and member of The Committee of 100, Emory University. Mr. Boyd is an active United Methodist layman whose dedication and labors in the states of Georgia and Florida have benefited The United Methodist Church through the churches with which he can be identified. It is with profound thanks that this editor acknowledges his gratitude to the man who financed this publication.

This bibliography represents a compilation of most accessible Methodist materials found in the libraries of Woodruff and Pitts (Candler) at Emory University, Atlanta, Ga.; The University of Georgia, Athens, Ga.; Wesleyan College, Macon, Ga.; Young-Harris College, Young Harris, Ga.; and Erskine College, Due West, S.C.

Materials here are by no means complete, but include the major works on record concerning Methodist churches, pastors, and educators in Georgia. In 1981, efforts were made through the *Wesleyan Christian Advocate* to gain current data from United Methodist pastors. A thorough attempt was also made to locate the non-current vite of former teachers in the Candler School of Theology. Both efforts were unsuccessful, and their inadequacies represented here.

The following Conference and Conference-related records have not been located:

South Georgia Conference:
Minutes: 1867; 1978-81 (Wesleyan minutes at bindary)
Woman's Foreign Missionary Society: 1895, 1898, 1900-04, 1906, 1908-9, 1911-
Woman's Home Missionary Society: 1905, 1907, 1910, 1912-
Woman's Missionary Society: 1914, 1915-17, 1920-29, 1933-39, 1941-

North Georgia Conference:
Woman's Home Missionary Society: 1895, 1897, 1911-
Woman's Foreign Missionary Society: 1894, 1911-
Woman's Society of Christian Service: 1947, 1949-53, 1955-60, 1962-
Woman's Missionary Society: 1882, 1884-87, 1889-1910, 1927-28, 1930, 1940-

Abbreviations:

Major abbreviations for periodicals and publishing companies have not been made in this bibliography due to its narrow interest. Some materials, however, have been marked Sp Cl and the library designated to identify it as either a Special Collections item or an item unique to that particular library. Much of the information from the Woodruff Library Special Collections has been copied from their identification sheets and is the work of their librarians and not this editor.

The designation MECS will abbreviate the Methodist Episcopal Church, South in many instances and the designation (uv) will denote unverified material. (mp) indicates the number of marked pages.

In most cases, where information was available, works are listed by the author or editor and not the specific dates of a publication (as in the case of the Conference Journals). This is done to quickly identify the persons responsible for the publications—that being of more interest perhaps to Methodist and United Methodist researchers than the volumes themselves.

Contents

A.M.E. Zion Church, OFFICIAL JOURNALS, by Broadway Temple, Louisville, Ky. Candler has 1948, 1952.

Abbey, Rev. R., "A Critique on Dr. L. Pierce's View of Church Government," found in *Quarterly Review,* (H.B. Bascomb, ed.), Jan., 1854, p. 65-82.

Abney, Beth Mobley, THANKSGIVING EVERY WEEK, Southeastern Color Lithographers, Athens, Ga., 1975. (122 p.)

Adams, Charles, THE POET PREACHER, (Charles Wesley), Carlton & Porter, New York, 1859. (234 p.)

Adams, J.C., I HAVE ONLY ONE LIFE TO LIVE, Methodist Publishing House, Nashville, 1964. (143 p.).
THE BISHOP OF HEARD COUNTY PREACHES, Privately Printed, Nashville, Tenn., 1962. (160 p.)

Adams, Jewell and Adams, Decora, TEN DECADES OF LIGHT, 1877-1977, The Royston United Methodist Church, Advocate Press, Franklin Springs, Ga., 1977. (100 p.)

Ainsworth, Bishop W.N., "THE PLAN OF UNIFICATION: WILL IT WORK?" (brochure), Jan. 1925. (14 p.) Ga Room

Akers, Samuel Luttrell, THE FIRST HUNDRED YEARS OF WESLEYAN COLLEGE 1836-1936, The Stinehour Press, Macon, 1976. (160 p.)

Akin, Mrs. Paul F., ed., WOMAN'S MISSIONARY SOCIETY OF THE N. GA. CONFERENCE, MECS, 8TH ANNUAL SESSION, NEWNAN, GA., MARCH 11-13, 1918. (91 p.)
9TH ANNUAL REPORT OF THE WOMAN'S MISSIONARY SOCIETY OF THE N. GA. CONFERENCE, 1919, MILLEDGEVILLE, GA., MARCH 18-20, 1919. (92 p.)
10TH ANNUAL REPORT OF THE WOMAN'S MISSIONARY SOCIETY OF THE N. GA. CONFERENCE, 1920, WESLEY MEMORIAL CHURCH, FEB. 3-6, 1920, Tribune Pub. Co., Cartersville, Ga. (96 p.)

Alexander, Gross, A HISTORY OF THE METHODIST CHURCH, SOUTH, IN THE UNITED STATES, The Christian Literature Company, New York, 1894. (144 p.)
HISTORY OF THE METHODIST EPISCOPAL CHURCH, SOUTH, The Christian Literature Company, New York, 1894. (144 p.)
ed., JOURNAL OF THE 15TH GENERAL CONFERENCE OF THE MECS, HELD IN BIRMINGHAM, ALA., MAY 3-21, 1906, MECS Publishing House, Nashville & Dallas. (370 p.)
ed., JOURNAL OF THE 16TH GENERAL CONFERENCE OF THE MECS, HELD IN ASHVILLE, N.C., MAY 4-21, 1910, MECS Publishing House, Nashville & Dallas. (440 p.)

"Two Chapters From The Early History of Methodism In The South," *The Methodist Review*, (J.J. Tigert, ed.), Vol. 23, No. 1, Sept. Oct., 1897, p. 3-20. "Two Chapters From the Early History of Methodism In the South," *Methodist Quarterly Review*, 63, July 1914, 419-437.

Alexander, Gross, and Kirby, John L. eds., JOURNAL OF THE 17TH GENERAL CONFERENCE OF THE MECS HELD IN OKLAHOMA CITY, OKLA., MAY 6-23, 1914, MECS Publishing House, Nashville, Dallas, Richmond. (500 p.)

Allen, Charles Livingston, ALL THINGS ARE POSSIBLE THROUGH PRAYER, Revell, Westwood, N.J., 1958. (128 p.)
GOD'S PSYCHIATRY; THE TWENTY-THIRD PSALM, THE TEN COMMANDMENTS, THE LORD'S PRAYER, THE BEATITUDES, Westwood, N.J., Fleming H. Revell Co., 1953. (159 p.)
HEALING WORDS, Fleming Revell, Westwood, N.J., 1961. (159 p.)
IN QUEST OF GOD'S POWER, Westwood, N.J., Fleming H. Revell Co., 1952. (191 p.)
LIFE MORE ABUNDANT, Fleming H. Revell, Westwood, N.J., 1968. (160 p.)
PERFECT PEACE, Fleming H. Revell, Old Tappan, N.J., 1979. (157 p.)
PRAYER CHANGES THINGS, Revell, Westwood, N.J., 1964. (128 p.)
RICHES OF PRAYER, Fleming H. Revell Co., 1956. (30 p.)
ROADS TO RADIANT LIVING, New York, Fleming H. Revell Co., 1951. (157 p.)
"TAKING THE FEAR OUT OF DEATH," 1950, Grace Methodist Church, Atlanta, Ga. (16 p.)
THE BEATITUDES, Fleming H. Revell Co., Westwood, N.J., 1967. (61 p.)
THE JOHN C. CAMPBELL FOLK SCHOOL, (thesis), Emory Univ., Atlanta, Ga., 1938. (52 p.)
THE LIFE OF CHRIST, Revell, Westwood, N.J., 1962. (160 p.)
THE LORD'S PRAYER, AN INTERPRETATION, Revell, Westwood, N.J., 1963. (64 p.)
THE MIRACLE OF HOPE, Fleming H. Revell Co., Old Tappan, N.J., 1973. (64 p.)
THE MIRACLE OF LOVE, Fleming H. Revell Co., Old Tappan, N.J., 1972. (126 p.)
THE MIRACLE OF LOVE, G.K. Hall & Co., Boston, Mass., 1973. (202 p.)
THE MIRACLE OF THE HOLY SPIRIT, Fleming H. Revell, Old Tappan, N.J., 1974. (64 p.)
THE SECRET OF ABUNDANT LIVING, Fleming H. Revell Co., Old Tappan, N.J., 1980. (157 p.)
THE SERMON ON THE MOUNT, Fleming H. Revell, Westwood, N.J., 1966. (187 p.)
THE TEN COMMANDMENTS, Revel, Westwood, N.J., 1965. (64 p.)
THE TOUCH OF THE MASTER'S HAND; CHRIST'S MIRACLES FOR TODAY, Revell, Westwood, N.J., 1956. (158 p.)
THE TWENTY-THIRD PSALM, Fleming Revel, Westwood, N.J., 1961. (62 p.)
TWELVE WAYS TO SOLVE YOUR PROBLEM, Grace Methodist Church, Atlanta, Ga., 1954. (30 p.)

Twelve Ways To Solve Your Problem, Atlanta, Privately Printed, 1954. (30 p.)

Twelve Ways To Solve Your Problems, Spire Books, Fleming H. Revell Co., Old Tappan, N.J., 1954 and 1961. (64 p.)

What I Have Lived By, Fleming H. Revell Co., Old Tappan, N.J., 1976. (159 p.)

When The Heart Is Hungry; Christ's Parables for Today, Fleming H. Revell, Westwood, N.J., 1955. (159 p.)

When You Lose a Loved One, Revell, Westwood, N.J., 1959. (61 p.)

You Are Never Alone, Fleming H. Revell Co., Old Tappan, N.J., 1978. (154 p.)

Allen, Charles L., and Biggs, Mouzon, When You Graduate, Fleming H. Revell, 1972. (63 p.)

Allen, Charles L., and Parker, Mildred, How To Increase Your Sunday-School Attendance, Fleming H. Revell, Old Tappan, N.J., 1979. (127 p.)

Allen, Charles L., and Wallis, Charles L., Candle, Star and Christmas Tree, Revell, Westwood, N.J., 1959. (64 p.)

Christmas, Fleming H. Revell Co., Old Tappan, N.J., 1977. (158 p.)

Christmas In Our Hearts, Revell, Westwood, N.J., 1957. (64 p.)

When Christmas Came to Bethlehem, Revell, Westwood, N.J., 1963. (64 p.)

Allen, Young J., (1854-1924) — 43 boxes — Ga. — China. Papers of this Methodist minister and missionary to China (1860-1907) includes correspondence, diaries, notebooks, biographical data, memoranda, account books, sermons, addresses, articles, essays, and other writings, printed matter, missionary lists, clippings and papers relating to his career. Includes material on his work with the Educational, Editorial and Translation Dept., Government Institution in Shanghai; Anglo-American College; Shanghai; Chinese history, language, customs and culture and the Allen family. (A related collection is the Warren Candler Collection which contains his unpublished biography of Y.J. Allen) Sp Cl Woodruff

A Providential Door, Board of Education, MECS, 1898, Nashville. (No. 19 in Annual Report of Board of Education, 1896). (7 p.)

"Our China Mission," *The Quarterly Review of the MECS,* (J.W. Hinton, ed.), Vol. 4, No. 1, Jan., 1882, p. 34-50.

"The Changed Aspect of China," *Methodist Quarterly Review,* (W.P. Harrison, ed.), Vol. 8, No. 2, July, 1890, p. 345-363.

"The Diary of A Voyage To China," The Emory Univ. Library, Atlanta, 1943. (39 p.) (Reprint of 1859-60 diary, ed. by Arva C. Floyd.)

The Gospel Liberating China, The Missionary Training School, Nashville, 1906. (45 p.) (Training School Series No. 13). (Address delivered at General Conference of MECS, Birmingham, Ala.).

"The National System of Religion in China," *The Methodist Review Quarterly,* (Gross Alexander, ed.), v. 56, Oct. 1907, p. 627-643.

Allred, C. Robert, "Back From The Valley of the Shadow," *The Circuit Rider,* October, 1977.

"Barking Up The Right Tree," *Forward,* Vol. 1, No. 4, 1980.

"Healing From The Inside Out," *The Circuit Rider,* Nov.-Dec., 1978.

"Modifying Prejudice Through Local Chruches," *United Methodist Today/ Preacher's Supplement,* April, 1975.

"Programming: Easy as P.I.E." *The Interpreter,* November, 1979.

"The P.I.E. Process and Professional Ministry," *The Crusader,* January, 1974.

"The Preaching Event As a Change Agent," *The Preacher's Magazine,* October, 1974.

"When The Pastor Moves," *Wesleyan Christian Advocate,* March, 1978.

"Why So Many Doctors In The Church?," *Pulpit Digest,* Nov.-Dec., 1978.

Anderson, Rev. Josephus, OUR CHURCH: A MANUAL FOR MEMBERS AND PROBATIONERS OF THE MECS, Southern Methodist Publishing House, Nashville. (304 p.) (Reviewed in *Quarterly Review of the MECS,* D.S. Doggett ed., April, 1860, p. 271.)

"Recollections of Bishop Capers," *The Home Circle,* MECS Publishing House, Nashville, Tenn., 1860, p. 324. (Huston, L.D., ed.).

"Revivals of Religion"—sermon preached in Quincy, Fla., July, 1857. (briefly reviewed in *Quarterly Review of the MECS,* (D.S. Doggets, ed.), January, 1858, p. 140.

THE BIBLE CHRISTIAN, A.H. Redford, for the MECS, Nashville, Tenn., 1875. (350 p.)

"The Christian Church and the Heathen World," *The Home Circle,* MECS Publishing House, Nashville, Tenn., 1860, p. 705-708. (Huston, L.D., ed.).

"The Problem Examined," *The Methodist Quarterly Review,* (W.P. Harrison, ed.), Vol. 5, No. 2, Jan. 1889, p. 373-393.

Anderson, W. H., "Ideas—Their Nature and Uses," *Methodist Quarterly Review,* (W.P. Harrison, ed.), Vol. 11, No. 2, Jan. 1892, p. 375-387.

"Law of Limitation," *Southern Methodist Review,* (W.P. Harrison, ed.), Vol. 4, No. 1, March, 1888, p. 42-52.

"Methodise Nomenclature," *The Southern Methodist Review,* (W.P. Harrison, ed.), Vol. 2, No. 1, March, 1887, p. 216-230.

"Moral Character of Doubt," *The Quarterly Review of the MECS,* (J.W. Hinton, ed.), Vol. 8, No. 1, Jan. 1886, p. 63-71.

Anderson, Rev. Robert, THE LIFE OF REV. ROBERT ANDERSON, Macon, Ga. 1892. (195 p.)

Andress, Robert P., "Young Harris College: From Institute To College, 1886-1892," *The Wesleyan Quarterly Review,* Vol. 3, No. 4, Nov. 1966, p. 252-261.

Andrew, James Osgood, (1813-1848) — 13 items — Ga. — Oxford. Papers of this Methodist bishop, center of the 1844 controversy over whether a bishop should own slaves (Andrew owned slaves through his wife), which led to the formation of a Southern branch of the Methodist Church, the M.E. Church, South. Includes correspondence from Andrew to Bishop William May Wightman, who was director of the Southern Methodist Printing concern (1844-1848), a news clipping and a program. (A related collection is that of Robert Watkins Lovett, who married Andrew's daughter.) Sp Cl Woodruff

Andrew, Bishop J.O., "Bishop McKendree," review reflective of BIOGRAPHICAL SKETCHES OF EMINENT ITINERANT MINISTERS by T.O. Summers, found in *Quarterly Review of the MECS,* D.S. Doggett, ed., April, 1859, p. 161-170.
"Education For The Ministry," found in *Quarterly Review of the MECS,* D.S. Doggett, ed. January, 1861, p. 1-11.

Andrew, James O., FAMILY GOVERNMENT, B. Jenkins, Charleston, S.C.; Sorin & Ball, Philadelphia, Pa., 1847. (151 p.)
FAMILY GOVERNMENT, Southern Methodist Publishing House, Nashville, Tenn., 1882. (175 p.)
"Letter of Introduction," dated 7-21-1823 introducing the letter of John I. Triggs (also recorded) concerning the Chatahoochie Mission, 6-11-1823. found in *The Methodist Magazine,* (Soule & Mason, eds.), Vol. 6, 1823, p. 44-45.
"Letters on Methodist History; Methodism in Charleston, S.C.," found in *The Methodist Magazine & Quarterly Review,* (Emory & Waugh, eds.), Vol. 1, 1830, p. 16-28.
MISCELLANIES: LETTERS, ESSAYS & ADDRESSES, Morton & Griswold, Louisville, 1854. (395 p.)
MISCELLANIES: COMPRISING LETTERS, ESSAYS AND ADDRESSES, MECS Publishing House, Nashville, Tenn., 1855. (395 p.)
PERSONAL JOURNAL, 1813-14, available in typescript from Commission on Archives & History, Lake Junaluska, N.C., where original is kept.
"The Instability of Sublunary Things," in Henry Bascom's, THE CROSS OF CHRIST, 1851, p. 93-150.
"The Ministry of Young Ladies," THE HOME CIRCLE, MECS Publishing House, Nashville, Tenn., 1860, p. 257-260. (Huston, L.D., ed.).
"The Rev. Ignatius A. Few, LL.D." (a review reflective of BIOGRAPHICAL SKETCHES OF EMINENT ININERANT MINISTERS by T.O. Summers, found in *Quarterly Review of the MECS,*/D.S. Doggett, ed., April, 1860, p. 223-236.
"The Southern Slave Population," (review of an address delivered in Charleston, 8-18-1829, by Charles Cotesworth Pinkney to the Agricultural Society of S.C.) found in *The Methodist Magazine and Quarterly Review,* (Emory & Waugh, eds.) (probably Vol. 1, 1830-???)

Andrews, W.P., (review of...) Jack-Knife and Brambles by A.G. Haygood, MECS Publishing House, Nashville, Tenn., 1893, *Methodist Quarterly Review,* (J.J. Tigert, ed.), Vol. 16, No. 1, April, 1894, p. 85-102.

Andrews, W.T., ed., MEMORIAL SKETCHES OF LIVES AND LABORS OF DECEASED MINISTERS OF THE N. ALABAMA CONFERENCE, MECS, 1870-1912, MECS

Publishing House, Nashville-Dallas-Richmond, 1912. (359 p.)
MEMORIAL SKETCHES OF THE NORTH ALABAMA CONFERENCE, ME Church, South Publishing House, Nashville, 1912. (359 p.) (Contains some biog. of Ga. pastors.)

Ansley, Mrs. J.J., "Frances Willard: Educator and Reformer," *The Methodist Quarterly Review,* (J.J. Tigert, ed.), v. 54, July 1905, p. 467-471.
"William Ewart Gladstone: The Christian Statesman," The Methodist Review Quarterly, (Gross Alexander, ed.), v. 56, July, 1907, p. 488-501.

Anthony, Bascomb, FIFTY YEARS IN THE MINISTRY, J.W. Burke Co., Macon, Ga., 1937. (280 p.)

Anthony, Rev. J.D., LIFE AND TIMES OF REV. J.D. ANTHONY, An Autobiography with a Few Original Sermons, C.P. Byrd, Atlanta, Ga., 1896. (140 p.)

Anthony, Walter, "Jesus Among The Doctors—of Philosophy," *The Methodist Quarterly Review,* v. 77, July, 1928, p. 374-395.

Armistead, Rev. W.S., BAPTISMOS: BIBLE VIEW OF THE SUBJECT, Foote & Davies Co., Atlanta, 1893. (228 p.)

Arnold, M. W., "Scriptural Pharaphrases," *Scott's Monthly Magazine,* Vol. 1 & 2, Franklin Steam Print, Atlanta, Ga., 1866, p. 37. (Scott, W.J., ed.).
"Spring Is Coming," (poem), *Scott's Monthly Magazine,* Vol. 1 & 2, Franklin Steam Print, Atlanta, Ga., 1866, p. 227. (Scott, W.J., ed.).

Asbury, Daniel, "Letter to William M. Kennedy," dated Camden, S.C., 6-27-1820, found in *The Methodist Magazine* (Soule & Mason, eds.), Vol. 3, 1820, p. 355-356.

Asbury, Francis, (1800-1816) — 2 folders — Georgia. Papers of this English born Methodist minister, who was responsible for the founding and proliferation of American Methodism after serving as itinerant preacher in the U.S. for over 30 years. Includes letters, a sermon signed by Asbury, his will (1813), a note on Western Annual Conference written by Asbury at Liberty Hill, Tenn. (1808), other notes on general conferences (1808-1812), and a published article by Bishop W.R. Cannon on Francis Asbury and Georgia. Sp. Cl Woodruff
THE JOURNALS OF THE REV. FRANCIS ASBURY, VOLS. 1-3, published by N. Bangs and T. Mason, Abraham Paul, printer, New York, 1821. Vol. 1—(400 p.); Vol. 2—(400 p.); Vol. 3—(420 p.).

Asbury, Herbert, A METHODIST SAINT (THE LIFE OF BISHOP ASBURY), Alfred A. Knopf, New York, 1927. (355 p.) (Ga. Ref. — 33, 35, 36, 54, 152, 188, 219).

Ashburn Methodist Church (Ashburn, Ga.), "List of Members and Monthly

Assessments, 1906,'' (pamphlet) (12 p.) Ga Room

Athens, Ga., ''A Brief History of the 1st Methodist Church, Athens, Ga.'', Athens, 1924. (19 p.)

Atlanta Conference, Minutes of the Atlanta Conference, 1939-1952.

Atwood, Sanford S., ''New Year's Greetings,'' The Emory Univ. Quarterly Review, v. 19, n4, Winter, 1963, p. 193.

Augusta District, ''Christ, The Heart of the Church,'' District Conference Handbook, 1-14-1963, held at St. Luke Methodist Church, Augusta, Ga. Ga. Room

Austin, George F., 100 YEARS OF METHODISM IN TATTNALL COUNTY, GEORGIA, 1808-1908, Journal Print, Reidsvile. (43 p.)

Avary, Robert, (1895-1942), 4 boxes — Georgia, Atlanta. Papers of this Emory alumnus and Georgia lawyer, include a folder of church papers which relate primarily to the First ME Church, South in Atlanta. Sp Cl Woodruff

Aylin, Stanley. JOHN WESLEY. Collins, St. Jame's Place, London. 1979. (350 p.) (Ga. Ref. — Chapter 4 and p. 13; 88; 90; 96; 102; 109; 116; 124; 137; 178; 185; 199).

Bailey, J. H., THE FACTORS OF CIVILIZATION, James P. Harrison & Co., Atlanta, Ga., 1883.

Baker, Frank. FROM WESLEY TO ASBURY. Duke Univ. Press, Durham, N.C., 1976. (223 p.) (Ga. Ref. — p. 3-13; 18-23; 187; 189-191; 197-198; 202-203).

Baker, J.M., HISTORY OF THE MOUNT GILEAD M.E. CHURCH, SOUTH, (Benn Hill, Fulton Co., Ga.), 1924. (50 p.) (softbound).

Baker, John Wesley, (1877-1892), 6 diaries — Georgia. 6 diaries of this Methodist minister who served the M.E. Church, S. on the following circuits: Gwinnett, Hartwell, Morganton, Alpharetta, Dallas, Dawsonville, Belton, Etowah, Polk, and Cobb—include accounts of church activities, lists of members, financial information and church statistics. Sp Cl Woodruff

Baker, Mrs. Bonnie Taylor, HISTORY OF CAMPGROUND UMC, (104 p.)

Bangs, Nathan, A HISTORY OF THE METHODIST EPISCOPAL CHURCH, M.E. Church, New York, 1840. (4 Vols.)

Barclay, Wade Crawford, Early American Methodism, 1769-1844, Volume 1-3, Board of Missions of The Methodist Church, New York, 1949. Reprinted

1952; 1967. Vol. 1 — (449 p.) — Ga. Ref. — 14, 201, 8, 18, 27, 76, 102, 126, 287, 233-34. Vol. 2 — (562 p.) Vol. 3 — (1211 p.)

Barclay, Wilbur Fisk, THE CONSTITUTION OF THE METHODIST EPISCOPAL CHURCHES IN AMERICA, MECS Publishing House, Nashville, Dallas, 1902. (134 p.)

Barnes, Annie Maria, SCENES IN PIONEER METHODISM, MECS Publishing House, Sunday School Dept., Nashville, Tenn., 1890. (397 p.)

Barnett, Albert Edward, ANDREW SLEDD — HIS LIFE AND WORK, Emory Univ., Atlanta, Ga., 1956. (18 p.)
DISCIPLES TO SUCH A LORD, Board of Missions, The Methodist Church, New York, 1957. (162 p.)
PAUL BECOMES A LITERARY INFLUENCE, The Univ. of Chicago Press, 1941. (277 p.)
THE CHURCH: ITS ORIGIN AND TASK, National Methodist Student Movement, Nashville, Tenn., 1960. (101 p.)
THE LETTERS OF PAUL, Abingdon — Cokesbury Press, New York, 1947. (160 p.)
THE NEW TESTAMENT: ITS MAKING AND MEANING, Abingdon-Cokesbury Press, New York and Nashville, 1946. (304 p.)
THE NEW TESTAMENT, ITS MAKING AND MEANING, Abingdon Press, Nashville, Tenn. 1958. (304 p.) Revised ed.
UNIVERSITY GROUPS IN CHURCH HISTORY, (thesis), Emory Univ., Atlanta, Ga., 1921. (52 p.)
UNDERSTANDING THE PARABLES OF OUR LORD, Cokesbury Press, 1940, Nashville, Tenn. (223 p.)

Barnhart, Phil, DON'T CALL ME PREACHER, William B. Eerdmans Publishing Co., Grand Rapids, Mich., & Forum House, Atlanta, 1972. (118 p.)
SEASONING FOR SERMONS, C.S.S. Publishing Co., Lima, Ohio, 1980. (160 p.)

Barrett, George W., ed., YEAR BOOK AND MINUTES OF THE 61ST SESSION OF THE NORTH GEORGIA CONFERENCE, MECS, WESLEY MEMORIAL CHURCH, ATLANTA, GA., Nov. 23-28, 1927, Lyon-Young Printing Co., Atlanta. (176 p.)
YEAR BOOK AND MINUTES OF THE 62ND SESSION OF THE NORTH GEORGIA CONFERENCE, MECS, WESLEY MEMORIAL CHURCH, ATLANTA, GA., Nov. 14-19, 1928, L.W. NEFF, PUBLISHER, BANNER PRESS, EMORY UNIVERSITY, GA. (162 P.)
YEARBOOK AND MINUTES OF THE 63RD SESSION OF THE NORTH GEORGIA CONFERENCE, MECS, 1ST METHODIST CHURCH, ATLANTA, GA., Nov. 13-18, 1929, L.W. Neff, Banner Press, Emory University, Ga. (162 p.)
YEARBOOK AND MINUTES OF THE 64TH SESSION OF THE NORTH GEORGIA CONFERENCE, MECS, WESLEY MEMORIAL METHODIST CHURCH, ATLANTA, GA., Nov. 13-16, 1930, Banner Press, Emory University, Ga. (158 p.)
YEARBOOK AND MINUTES OF THE 65TH SESSION OF THE NORTH GEORGIA CONFERENCE, MECS, WESLEY MEMORIAL METHODIST CHURCH, ATLANTA, GA., Nov. 12-15, 1931, Lamar and Whitmore, Nashville, Tenn. (105 m.p.)

YEARBOOK AND MINUTES OF THE 66TH SESSION OF THE NORTH GEORGIA CONFERENCE, MECS, WESLEY MEMORIAL, ATLANTA, GA., Nov. 23-27, 1932, Whitmore and Smith, Methodist Publishing House, Nashville, Tenn. (137 p.)

YEARBOOK AND MINUTES OF THE 67TH SESSION OF THE NORTH GEORGIA CONFERENCE, MECS, WESLEY MEMORIAL CHURCH, ATLANTA, GA., Nov. 22-26, 1933, Whitmore and Smith, Methodist Publishing House, Nashville, Tenn. (148 p.)

YEARBOOK AND MINUTES OF THE 68TH SESSION OF THE NORTH GEORGIA CONFERENCE, MECS, WESLEY MEMORIAL CHURCH, ATLANTA, GA., Nov. 28-DEC. 2, 1934, Whitmore and Smith, Methodist Publishing House, Nashville, Tenn. (144 p.)

YEARBOOK AND MINUTES OF THE 69TH SESSION OF THE NORTH GEORGIA CONFERENCE, MECS, WESLEY MEMORIAL CHURCH, ATLANTA, GA., Nov. 21-24, 1935, Whitmore and Smith, Methodist Publishing House, Nashville, Tenn. (139 p.)

YEARBOOK AND MINUTES OF THE 70TH SESSION OF THE NORTH GEORGIA CONFERENCE, MECS, WESLEY MEMORIAL, ATLANTA, GA., Nov. 26-29, 1936, Whitmore and Smith, Methodist Publishing House, Nashville, Tenn. (141 p.)

YEARBOOK AND MINUTES OF THE 71ST SESSION OF THE NORTH GEORGIA CONFERENCE, MECS, WESLEY MEMORIAL CHURCH, ATLANTA, GA., Nov. 18-21, 1937, Whitmore and Smith, Methodist Publishing House, Nashville, Tenn. (141 p.)

YEARBOOK AND MINUTES OF THE 72ND SESSION OF THE NORTH GEORGIA CONFERENCE, MECS, WESLEY MEMORIAL CHURCH, ATLANTA, GA., Nov. 17-20, 1938, Whitmore and Smith, Methodist Publishing House, Nashville, Tenn. (143 p.)

YEARBOOK AND MINUTES OF THE 1ST SESSION OF THE NORTH GEORGIA CONFERENCE, METHODIST CHURCH, WESLEY MEMORIAL METHODIST CHURCH, ATLANTA, GA., Nov. 23-26, 1939, Whitmore and Smith, Methodist Publishing House, Nashville, Tenn. (187 p.)

YEARBOOK AND MINUTES OF THE 2ND SESSION OF THE NORTH GEORGIA CONFERENCE, METHODIST CHURCH, WESLEY MEMORIAL METHODIST CHURCH, Nov. 21-24, 1940, Whitmore and Stone, Methodist Publishing House, Nashville, Tenn. (131 p.)

YEARBOOK AND MINUTES OF THE 3RD SESSION OF THE NORTH GEORGIA CONFERENCE, METHODIST CHURCH, WESLEY MEMORIAL CHURCH, ATLANTA, GA., Nov. 19-23, 1941, Whitmore and Stone, Methodist Publishing House, Nashville, Tenn. (153 p.)

YEARBOOK AND MINUTES OF THE 4TH SESSION OF THE NORTH GEORGIA CONFERENCE, METHODIST CHURCH, WESLEY MEMORIAL CHURCH, ATLANTA, GA., Nov. 19-22, 1942, Whitmore and Stone, Methodist Publishing House, Nashville, Tenn. (143 p.)

YEARBOOK AND MINUTES OF THE 5TH SESSION OF THE NORTH GEORGIA CONFERENCE, METHODIST CHURCH, WESLEY MEMORIAL METHODIST CHURCH, ATLANTA, GA., Nov. 16-19, 1943, Whitmore and Stone, Methodist Publishing House, Nashville, Tenn. (141 p.)

YEARBOOK AND MINUTES OF THE 6TH SESSION OF THE NORTH GEORGIA CON-

FERENCE, METHODIST CHURCH, WESLEY MEMORIAL METHODIST CHURCH, ATLANTA, GA., Nov. 21-24, 1944, Whitmore and Stone, Nashville, Tenn. (141 p.)

Barrow, David C., "Box Borders," *The Methodist Quarterly Review,* v. 71, Oct. 1922, p. 693-698.

Bascomb, H.B. BRIEF APPEAL To PUBLIC OPINION in a series of Exceptions to the course and action of the M.E. Church from 1844-1848. Morton & Griswold, Louisville, Ky., 1848.
(ed.), *Quarterly Review (Methodist Review)* Methodist Episcopal Church, South, Vol. 1, Morton & Griswold, Louisville, Kentucky, 1847. (periodical)

Baskette, Floyd K., "Atticus G. Haygood's Thanksgiving Sermon," *The Emory Univ. Quarterly Review,* v2, n1, March, 1946, p. 21-29.

Bass, W.C., "A TRIBUTE TO THE MEMORY OF REV. G.F. PIERCE," J.W. Burke & Co., Macon, Ga., 1884. (16 p.)

Bassett, Ancel H., A CONCISE HISTORY OF THE METHODIST PROTESTANT CHURCH, Charles A. Scott, Springfield, Ohio, 1877. (424 p.)

Baumn, Mark K., WARREN AKIN CANDLER: CONSERVATIVE AMIDST CHANGE, PART 1, (dissertation), Univ. Microfilms International, Ann Arbor, Mich., 1976. (303 p.)
WARREN AKIN CANDLER: THE CONSERVATIVE AS IDEALIST. (290 p.)

Baxter, James Hamilton, (1876-1889) — 110 items — Ga. Minister in North Ga. Conference. Collection is mainly sermon notes and outlines. Sp Cl Woodruff

Baxter, Rev. J.H., (N. Ga. Conf.), "Santification," J.W. Burke & Co., Macon, Ga., 1886. (56 p.) Ga Room
"Sanctification," J.W. Burke & Co., Printers, Stationers and Binders, Macon, Ga., 1897. (56 p.)
TWO SERMONS ON THE SPIRITUAL LIFE, J.W. Burke & Co., Printers and Binders, Macon, Ga., 1890. (32 p.)

Bayley, John, "Bethseda, Whitefield's Orphon-Home In Chatham County, Georgia," *The Home Circle,* MECS Publishing House, Nashville, Tenn., 1860, p. 300-302. (Huston, L.D., ed.).

Belden, Albert D., GEORGE WHITEFIELD, THE AWAKENER, Cokesbury Press, Nashville, Tenn., 1930. (302 p.) Reprint, The McMillian Co., New York, 1953.

Bellinger, Rev. Lucius, STRAY LEAVES FROM THE PORT-FOLIO OF A METHODIST LOCAL PREACHER, J.W. Burke & Co., Macon, Ga., 1870. (311 p.) (Ga. Ref. —

Campmeetings in Ga. p.107f)

Bennett, R.H., "Versailles The Magnificent," *The Methodist Review*, v. 69, Oct. 1919, p. 702-707.

Bethesda Orphan-Asylum, Chatham County, Ga., (1915-1945) — 1 box; 5 reels micro. — Savannah, Ga. Records of this orphanage founded in 1740 by George Whitefield include the diaries of the Director of the school, O.W. Burroughs; the journal of Superintendent Quarterman; scrapbook of newspaper clippings (all on miro.); and material re the history of the school. Sp Cl Woodruff

Betts, Albert Deems, HISTORY OF SOUTH CAROLINA METHODISM, Advocate Press, Columbia, S.C., 1952. (544 p.) (Ga. Ref. — 12, 197).

Bigham, Benjamin H., "Political Equality," (a review of DEMOCRACY IN AMERICA by Alexis de Tocqueville), found in "The Methodist Quarterly Review," (MECS), periodical listed under Bascomb, H.B. (ed.), July, 1849, p. 364-379.
"The Consulate," (a review of HISTORY OF THE CONSULATE AND THE EMPIRE OF FRANCE UNDER NAPOLEON by M.A. Thiers, 1845) found in *The Methodist Quarterly Review*, (MECS), periodical listed under Bascomb, H.B. (ed.) July, 1848, p. 442-451.
"The Egotism of Genius," (a review of HISTORY OF THE FRENCH REVOLUTION OF 1848 by A. M. Lamartine), found in *The Methodist Quarterly Review*, (MECS), periodical listed under Bascomb, H.B. (ed.), January, 1850, p. 33-52.
"The Empire," (a review continued of HISTORY OF THE CONSULATE AND THE EMPIRE OF FRANCE UNDER NAPOLEON by M.A. Thiers, (1845) found in *The Methodist Quarterly Review*, (MECS), periodical listed under Bascomb, H.B. (ed.) October, 1848, p. 618-627.

Bigham, R.J., The American Bible Society," *The Methodist Review*, (J.J. Tigert, ed.), Vol. 20, No. 2, May-June, 1896, p. 251-258.
"The Scarrit Bible and Training School," *The Methodist Review*, (J.J. Tigert, ed.), Vol. 24, No. 2, May-June, 1898, p. 261-267.

Bigham, Robert W., "After The Battle of Swords," *Methodist Quarterly Review*, (W.P. Harrison, ed.), Vol. 11, No. 2, Jan., 1892, p. 324-339.
CALIFORNIA GOLD-FIELD SCENES, Southern Methodist Publishing House, Nashville, 1886. (283 p.)
JOE: A BOY IN THE WAR-TIMES, MECS Publishing House, Sunday School Department, Nashville, Tenn., 1889. (226 p.)
VINNY LEAL'S TRIP TO THE GOLDEN SHORE, MECS Publishing House, Nashville, Tenn., 1875.
VINNY LEAL'S TRIP TO THE GOLDEN SHORE, Southern Methodist Publishing House, Nashville, Tenn., 1878. (271 p.)
VINNY LEAL'S TRIP TO THE GOLDEN SHORE, MECS Publishing House, Nashville, Tenn., 1890. (271 p.)

WINE AND BLOOD; UNCLE VIV'S STORY, Southern Methodist Publishing House (208 p.) Nashville, Tenn., 2nd ed., 1880 review in MQR.

Birch, E. P., "The Poetry of Woman's Life," Scott's Monthly Magazine, (v.3), Franklin Steam Print, Atlanta, Ga., 1867, p. 413-418. (Scott, W.J., ed.).

Birrell, Augustine, LETTERS OF JOHN WESLEY, Hodder & Stoughton, London, 1915. (510 p.) (Ga. Ref. — 25, 57, 127, 180, 237, 310, 479).

Bishop, Mrs. Mildred, HISTORY OF THE WATKINSVILLE UMC AND PARSONAGE, Watkinsville, Ga., 1978. (49 p.)

Blackstock, Walter, "Corra Harris (1869-1935): An Analytical Study of Her Novels," FLORIDA STATE UNIVERSITY STUDIES, 19, 1955, p. 39-92. (on her writing of Methodism in Ga.).

Blake, E.L.T., "Christian Liberty and Church Organization," *The Methodist Review,* (J.J. Tigert, ed.), Vol. 17, No. 3, Jan.-Feb. 1895, p. 371-387.

Blanks, Rev. J. J., "Pastor of 4 Churches" and "History of Norcross Circuit," (pamphlet containing these and 2 sermons). (28 p.) Ga Room

Bond, Beverly Waugh, LIFE OF JOHN WESLEY, MECS Publishing House, Nashville, Tenn., 1890. (216 p.)

Bonnell, John F., "In His Steps," *The Methodist Review,* (J.J. Tigert, ed.), Vol. 26, No. 3, May-June, 1900, p. 367-378.
"Psychic Waves," *The Methodist Quarterly Review,* (J.J. Tigert, ed.), Sept.-Oct., 1901, v. 50, p. 690-705.
"Science and Society," *The Methodist Review,* (J.J. Tigert, ed.), Vol. 18, No. 1, March-April, 1895, p. 77-87.

Bonnell, John Mitchell, c. 1850 — 6 v. — Georgia — N. Ga. Conf. Sp Cl Woodruff
A MANUAL OF THE ART OF PROSE COMPOSITION, John P. Morton & Co., Louisville, Ky., 1867. (359 p.)
FIRST LESSONS IN ENGLISH PROSE COMPOSITION, John P. Morton & Co., Louisville, Ky., 1871. (206 p.)
"Palmyra," *The Home Circle,* v.1, MECS Publishing House, Nashville, Tenn., 1855, p. 214-217; 248-252. (Huston, L.D., ed.).
"Sacred Music," (a review of THE WESLEYAN HYMN & TUNE BOOK by L.C. Everett found in *Quarterly Review of the MECS,* D.S. Doggett, Ed., October, 1861, p. 498-510.
"The East India Trade," *The Home Circle,* v.1., MECS Publishing House, Nashville, Tenn., 1855, p. 12-16; 49-53; 97-100. (Huston, L.D., ed.).
"The Educational Institution," found in *Quarterly Review of the MECS,* (D.S. Doggett, ed.), January, 1858, p. 105-117.

Boozer, Jack S., "A Biblical Understanding of Religious Experience," *Journal of Bible and Religion,* XXIV (1958), p. 291-297.

"Acknowleding No One Norm of Morality," *The Emory Wheel,* Jan. 26, 1971, p. 5.

"Are Colleges Destroying Our Students' Faith," *Together,* Vol. IX, No. 11, (1965), p. 46-48.

"Art and Faith," *Emory University Quarterly,* Vol. XXI, No. 4 (1965), p. 219-235.

"Battle Evil and Perfect the World," *Southern Israelite,* Sept. 5, 1975, p. 22.

"Children of Hippocrates: Doctors in Nazi Germany," *The Annals of the American Academy of Political and Social Science,* Vol. 450, July, 1980, p. 83-97.

"Comments on 'Religion, the Id, and the Superego.' " (Review Article), *Journal of Bible and Religion,* XXVIII (1960) p. 323-328.

"Death and Truth-Telling," *Anlage,* Nov. 28, 1979, p. 3.

"Dr. Franz Lucas at Auschwitz: Torment, Compromise, Courage," *Anlage,* Vol. 12, No. 4, Spring, 1980, p. 13, 15.

"Jews and Christians: The Struggle for Understanding," *The Candler Review 2* (1975), No. 2, p. 14-17.

"Morality and the Church-Related University," *Emory University Quarterly,* Vol. XXIII, No. 2, (1967), p. 77-94.

"Paul Tillich: An Introduction to his Thought," *Emory University Quarterly,* XII (1956), p. 44-58.

"Religion and Culture: A Review Article," *Journal of Bible and Religion,* XXVIII (1960), p. 229-234.

Rudolf Otto, AUFSATZE ZUR ETHIK, ed. by Jack Boozer, C. H. Beck, Munich, West Germany.

"Rudolf Otto, Theologe und Religion-swissenschaftler," *Marburger Gelehrte* (Hrsg. I. Schnack) Marburg, 1977, p. 362-382.

"The Chaplain in the German Armed Forces," *The Chaplain,* Vol. 20, No. 1, February, (1963), p. 7-15.

(Issue ed.), "The Church-Related University," *Emory University Quarterly,* Vol. XXIII, No. 2, (1967).

"The Method is the Message," *Junction,* Vol. 6, No. 2 (1970), p. 21-25.

"The Military Chaplaincy: One Calling, Two Roles," *The Chaplain,* Vol. 27, No. 6, (1970), p. 3-12.

"The Sociological-Theological Assumptions Underlying a Ministry to the Military," a commissioned paper for the Gen. Conference of the UMC, April, 1980.

"The Relation of State and Military Authority to Religious Authority," *Chaplaincy,* Vol. III, No. 1, (1980) p. 32-47.

"Three Revolutions or One?" *Journal of Bible and Religion,* Vol. XXXIV, No. 2, (1966), p. 130-38.

"To Search Not to Saction," *Emory Magazine,* Vol. 42, No. 3 (1966), p. 8-11.

"Vantage Point: How Do We Keep Vehicles from Becoming Barriers?" *Emory College Today,* Vol. 1, No. 4, (1966), p. 43-44.

Boozer, Jack and Beardslee, William A., FAITH To ACT, Abingdon, Nashville, 1967. (72 p.)

Boraine, A.L., THE NATURE OF EVANGELISM IN THE THEOLOGY OF JOHN WESLEY (dissertation), Univ. Microfilms, Ann Arbor, Mich., 1973. (276 p.)

Boring, Jesse, "The Use and Abuse of Tobacco," *The Home Circle,* v.3., MECS Publishing House, Nashville, Tenn., 1857, p. 454-460. (Huston, L.D., ed.).

Borom, W. Robert, ed., THE JOURNAL OF THE SOUTH GEORGIA ANNUAL CONFERENCE OF THE UMC, 1973, United Methodist Publishing House, Nashville, Tenn. Part 1 — May, 1973 (39 p) Part 2 — Aug., 1973 (57 p.) Part 3 — Aug., 1974 (191 p.)
THE JOURNAL OF THE SOUTH GEORGIA ANNUAL CONFERENCE OF THE UMC, 1974, The UMC Publishing House, Nashville, Tenn. Part 1 — April, 1974 (108 p.) Part 2 — Aug., 1974 (191 p.)
THE JOURNAL OF THE SOUTH GEORGIA ANNUAL CONFERENCE OF THE UMC, 1975, The United Methodist Publishing House. Part 1 — April, 1975 (125 p.) Part 2 — Aug. 1975 (280 p.)
THE JOURNAL OF THE SOUTH GEORGIA ANNUAL CONFERENCE OF THE UMC, 1976, The United Methodist Publishing House. Part 1 — April, 1976 (167 p.) Part 2 — Aug., 1976 (217 p.)

Boswell, John W., A SHORT HISTORY OF METHODISM, ME Church, South Publishing House, Nashville, 1903. (188 p.)

Bowden, Haygood S., HISTORY OF SAVANNAH METHODISM, J.W. Burke Co., Macon, 1929. (321 p.)

Bowen, Boone M., DOCTRINE OF IMMORTALITY IN THE OLD TESTAMENT PRIOR TO THE EXILE, (thesis), Emory Univ., Atlanta, Ga., 1924. (39 p.)
"Jerico, The World's Oldest City," *The Emory Univ. Quarterly Review,* v14, n1, March, 1958, p. 1-11.
"Old Testament Bases for Authority in Religion," *The Emory Univ. Quarterly Review,* v1, n4, Dec. 1945, p. 230-237.
THE CANDLER SCHOOL OF THEOLOGY—SIXTY YEARS OF SERVICE, Emory University, Atlanta, Ga., 1974. (246 p.)
"The Crisis In The Holy Land," *The Emory Univ. Quarterly Review,* v11, n2, June, 1955, p. 83-87.

Boyd, Clarence Eugene, "The Art of Authorship Among The Ancients," *The Methodist Quarterly Review,* v. 76, Jan. 1927, p. 99-118.

Bradley, David Henry Sr., A HISTORY OF THE A.M.E. ZION CHURCH, Parthenon Press, Nashville, 1956. 2 Vols. Vol. 1— (183 p.) (Ga. Ref. — 18, 32) Vol. 2 — (500 p.) (Ga. Ref. — 63)

Bradley, H.S., "Ants," *The Methodist Review,* (J.J. Tigert, ed.), Vol. 22, No. 2, May-June, 1897, p. 238-249.

Brailsford, Mabel Richmond, A Tale of Two Brothers—John and Charles Wesley, Oxford Univ. Press, N.Y., 1954. (301 p.) (Ga. Ref. — 80, 81, 82, 90, 109).

Branch, Rev. James Orson, Sermons, Julius Magath, Oxford, Ga., 1909. (323 p.)

Bray, Vivian L., Potpourri, Pathway Press, Cleveland, Tenn., 1957. (117 p.)

Brewer, Earl D.C., "A Candler Profile," *Junction*, Vol. 5, No. 3 (April, 1970), p. 22-27.
A Chart Book of Urban Parish and Rural Parish, RRC, 1965. (53 p.)
"A Conversation on the Future," (Interview with Arthur B. Rutledge and Lyle Schaller), *Home Missions*, Vol. 47, No. 1 (January, 1976), p. 32-36.
A Program For The Local Rural Church, Department of Town and Country Work of The Methodist Church, New York, 1948. (30 p.)
A Report and Evaluation of the Crisis In the Nation, National Council of Churches, New York, 1970. (29 p.)
A Self-Study of the General Board of Education of The Methodist Church and the General Board of Christian Higher Education of The Evangelical United Brethren Church, Report One: Background Papers, 118 p.; Report Two: A Self-Study of Organizational Units, 246 p.; Report Three: Opinions of Board Members, Staff Members and Others, 87 p.; Report Four: Summary and Suggestions, 63 p.
A Sociological Study of the Methodist Church and its Membership, RRC, 1963. (114 p.)
"A Study of Employment of Women in Professional or Executive Positions in the Churches at a National Level," in Sarah B. Doely (ed.), Women's Liberation and the Church, Association Press, New York, 1970, p. 115-119.
A Study of First Methodist Church, Decatur, Ga., 1956. (56 p.) (softbound)
A Study of Mount Vernon Methodist Church, Danville, Virginia, 1955. (33 p.)
A Study of New Church Development: The Methodist Church, RRC, 1967. (289 p.)
A Study of Park Street Methodist Church, Atlanta, Ga., RRC, 1964. (47 p.)
A Study of St. John Methodist Church, Chattanooga, Tennessee, 1960. (23 p.)
A Study of the Churches and Counties of the N. Georgia Conference of the United Methodist Church, by Earl Brewer and Marie Townsend, Atlanta, Religious Research Center, Candler School of Theology, Emory University, 1975. 178 p.
A Study of the Churches Of Dade County, Miami District, The Florida Conference of The Methodist Church, RRC, 1965. (41 p.)
A Study of The Churches of the Gainesville District, The Florida Conference of The Methodist Church, RRC, 1965. (53 p.)

A Study of the Churches of the West Palm Beach District, The Florida Conference of The Methodist Church, RRC, 1965. (43 p.)

A Study of the Crusade Scholarship Program of The United Methodist Church, RCC, 1970. (118 p.)

A Study of the General Superintendency of The Methodist Church; Part II: Relation of the Episcopacy To Pastoral Charges and Special Appointments, RCC, 1963. (132 p.)

A Study of The Ministry, North Alabama Conference, 1962, RRC. (34 p.)

A Study of the Ministry, North Alabama Conference—A Supplement, RRC, 1963. (34 p.)

A Study of Trinity Methodist Church, Chattanooga, Tennessee, RCC, 1961. (29 p.)

A Study of Two Downtown Methodist Churches of Jacksonville, Florida, RCC, 1962. (69 p.)

A Study of Wagg Memorial Methodist Church, West Palm Beach, Florida, RCC, 1963. (64 p.)

"A Teacher of Teachers," *Church School,* (October, 1964) p. 12-13.

An Inventory of the Harlan Paul Douglas Collection of Religious Research Reports, (with Douglas W. Johnson), Department of Research, National Council of Churches, New York, 1970. (196 p.)

"Attitudes Toward Inclusive Practices in the Methodist Church in the Southeast," *Review of Religious Research,* Vol. 6, No. 2 (Winter, 1965), p. 82-89.

Attitudes Toward Inclusiveness In Local Methodism, (with Clyde W. Faulkner, Jr.), Women's Division of the Board of Missions of The Methodist Church, New York 1968. (57 p.)

"Bigger and Better?" *The Methodist Story,* Vol. 8, No. 5 (May, 1964), p. 3-6.

Black Pastors and Churches in United Methodism, (with Grant Shockley), Center for Research in Social Change, Atlanta, Emory University, 1976. (67 p.)

"Change and the Quality of Life," Georgia Adult Education Humanities Workshop, The University of Georgia Center for Continuing Education, Athens, p. 17-23.

"Christian Religioning and Ministering," *Candler Review,* Vol. 2, No. 1, pp. 31-37.

Christian Rural Fellowship Lectures, Department of Rural Church, Cumberland Presbyterian Church, Memphis, 1952. (43 p.)

Church Extension Strategy, Southeastern Jurisdictional Council, Atlanta, 1962. (20 p.)

Content Analysis of Selected Methodist Periodicals, (with Lance Webb and David M. White), Coordinating Council and Commission on Promotion and Cultivation of The Methodist Church, Evanston, 1963. (62 p.)

"Exploring Religion: Some Intimations and Some Indications," *Character Potential,* 6 (February, 1974), p. 200-206.

Gammon Theological Seminary of the Interdenominational Theological Center and Candler School of Theology of Emory University, Atlanta Consultation Task Force of the Commission to study the Ministry, 1974. (66 p.)

General Characteristics of the Methodist Ministry, (with G. Ross Freeman), Department of Ministerial Education of the Board of Education of

The Methodist Church, Nashville, 1963. (148 p.)

IMAGE OF THE NATIONAL COUNCIL OF CHURCHES: A NATIONAL SURVEY OF OPINIONS, (with Douglas W. Johnson), National Council of Churches, New York, 1969. (54 p.)

LIFE AND RELIGION IN SOUTHERN APPLACHIA, (with W.D. Weatherford), Friendship Press, New York, 1962. (165 p.)

"Life Stages and Spiritual Well-Being," in David O. Moberg (ed.), SPIRITUAL WELL-BEING: SOCIOLOGICAL PERSPECTIVES, Univ. Press of America, Washington, 1979, p. 99-111.

METHODISM IN ATHENS AND CLARKE CO., GA., 1955, New York, Section of National Missions of the Methodist Church, Dept. of Research & Surveys. (61 p.)

METHODISM IN SURRY COUNTY, NORTH CAROLINA, 1954. (46 p.)

METHODISM IN THE ATLANTA METROPOLITAN AREA, 1950-1970: A STUDY IN CHURCH EXTENSION NEEDS, 1960. (47 p.)

METHODISM IN THE CHANGING SOUTHEAST, Southeastern Jurisdictional Council of The Methodist Church, Atlanta, 1952. (39 p.)

METHODISM IN THE INNER CITY OF ATLANTA, RRC, 1962. (36 p.)

METHODISM IN THE PADUCAH DISTRICT OF THE MEMPHIS CONFERENCE, 1955. (56 p.)

METHODISM IN THE TAMPA DISTRICT OF THE FLORIDA CONFERENCE, RRC, 1961. (79 p.)

METHODISM IN YADKIN COUNTY, NORTH CAROLINA, 1954. (40 p.)

MISSION IN THE SEVENTIES: A BACKGROUND PAPER ON SOME TRENDS AND ISSUES, National Council of Churches, New York, 1969. (69 p.)

"Our Small Country Churches: Must They Die?" *Together,* (September, 1967), p. 16-19.

PRELIMINARY REPORTS AND WORKING PAPERS OF THE METHODIST PARISH PROJECT, PLAINS CIRCUIT, RRC, 1963. (62 p.)

PRELIMINARY STUDIES OF METHODISM IN MEMPHIS, TENNESSEE, 1954. (26 p.)

PROTESTANT PARISH (with Theodore H. Runyan, Jr., et al), Communicative Arts Press, Atlanta, 1967. (129 p.)

"Reflections On Reports And Renewal," found in *Southeastern Jurisdictional United Methodist* (newspaper), Vol. 4, No. 3, May-June, 1981, p. 6-7.

"Relation of the Episcopacy to Pastoral Charges and Special Appointments," in THE STUDY OF THE GENERAL SUPERINTENDENCY OF THE METHODIST CHURCH—A REPORT TO THE GENERAL CONFERENCE OF 1964, Coordinating Council, Evanston, 1964, p. 88-102.

"Religion and Atlanta International," in Carole F. Hill and Robert E. Garren's (eds.), ATLANTA INTERNATIONAL: PROBLEMS AND PROSPECTS, 1976, p. 73-89.

"Religion and the Churches," in THE SOUTHERN APPLACHIAN REGION, Thomas Ford, ed., Univ. of Kentucky Press, Lexington, 1962, p. 201-219.

"Religion In Georgia," in William H. Schabacker, et al (eds.), FOCUS ON THE FUTURE OF GEORGIA, 1970-1986, Georgia Department of Education, Atlanta, 1970, p. 281-302.

"Religion in Relation to Southern Growth," in OPTIMIZING INSTITUTIONS FOR ECONOMIC GROWTH, Agricultural Policy Institute, North Carolina State and the

Southern Land Economics Research Committee, Raleigh, 1964, p. 168-181.

"Religious Research Center," *The Candler Advocate,* Vol. IV, No. 4, (April, 1965), p. 1-3.

REPORT OF TASK FORCE ON LOCAL CHURCH CLUSTERS (Part II), Consultation on Church Union, Princeton, 1974, p. 3-11.

REPORT TO THE GENERAL CONFERENCE CONCERNING METHODIST MEMBERSHIP, Board of Evangelism of The Methodist Church, Nashville, 1963. (47 p.)

RESEARCH AND PLANNING FOR CHRISTIAN MISSION, UNITED METHODIST CHURCHES, KNOXVILLE, TENNESSEE, RRC, 1968. (152 p.)

"Research Documents in the H. Paul Douglas Collection," (with Douglas W. Johnson), REVIEW OF RELIGIOUS RESEARCH, 13 (Winter, 1972), p. 107-111.

"Sect and Churches in Methodism," *Social Forces,* Vol. 30, No. 4, (May, 1952), p. 400-408.

"Sect and Church In Methodism," COLLECTIVE BEHAVIOR, Ralph H. Turner and Lewis M. Killiam, eds., Prentice-Hall, New York, 1957, p. 482-491.

"Seminary as Community," *The Iliff Review,* Vol. XXI, No. 1 (Winter, 1964), p. 3-8.

"Some Suggestions about Future—Oriented Studies in Religion," *Review of Religious Research,* 13 (Fall, 1971), p. 13-17.

STUDIES IN NORTH GEORGIA METHODISM, 1955. (39 p.)

STUDIES IN WESTERN NORTH CAROLINA METHODISM, Piedmont Press, Greensboro, N.C., 1953. (51 p.)

THE CHURCH AT THE CROSSROADS, Abingdon-Cokesbury, Nashville, Tenn., 1947. (128 p.)

THE CHURCHES OF THE GASTONIA DISTRICT, THE WESTERN NORTH CAROLINA CONFERENCE OF THE METHODIST CHURCH, RRC, 1964. (38 p.)

THE FAMILY MINISTRY PROJECT: RESEARCH AND EVALUATION, RRC, 1969. (198).

THE MENTAL HEALTH COUNSELOR IN THE COMMUNITY, (with David S. Shapiro, et al), Charles C. Thomas, Publisher, Springfield, Ill., 1968. (207 p.)

THE METHODIST CHURCHES IN GEORGIA: GEORGIA CONFERENCE, RRC, 1961, Vols. I and II (101 p.)

THE METHODIST CHURCHES IN THE NORTH GA. CONFERENCE, 2v, by Earl Brewer and Marie Townsend, Atlanta, Religious Research Center, Candler School of Theology, Emory University, Atlanta, 1961. (v. 1: 74 p.); (v. 2: approx. 93 p.)

THE METHODIST CHURCHES IN THE SOUTH GEORGIA CONFERENCE, 2v., by Earl Brewer and Marie Townsend, Atlanta, Religious Research Center, Candler School of Theology, Emory University, Atlanta, 1961. (v. 1: 70 p.); (v. 2: 282 p.)

THE METHODIST MINISTRY IN 1956, (with Frederick A. Shippey), Section of Ministerial Education, Division of Educational Institutions, The Board of Education, Nashville, Tenn., 1956. (41 p.)

THE MINISTRY IN THE SOUTH GEORGIA CONFERENCE, RRC, 1965. (32 p.)

"The 1972 H. Paul Douglass Lecture: Social Indicators and Religious Indicators," *Review of Religious Research,* 14 (Winter, 1973), p. 77-90.

"The Religioning Process in Future Forms of Ministry in the Military," *Military Chaplains Review,* (Winter, 1978), p. 59-74.

"The South as a Community," *Church In Mission,* (June-August, 1967), p. 11-16.

"The Town and Country Methodist Parish of the Future," *Methodist Rural Fellowship Bulletin,* Vol. XVI, No. 4, (Fall, 1956), p. 1, 4-7.

"The Southern Region—A Laboratory for Ecumenical Christian Mission?" THE ST. LUKE'S JOURNAL OF THEOLOGY, XI (June, 1968), p. 50-66.

THE VOCATIONAL REHABILITATION STUDY OF PRISONERS, PROBATIONERS, AND PAROLEES, Department of Health, Education and Welfare, Washington, D.C., 1964. (135 p.)

"Theological Schools in the Modern World," *The Iliff Review,* XI (Spring, 1954), p. 39-49.

TRANSCENDENCE AND MYSTERY, (ed.), IDOC/NA, New York, 1976. (164 p.)

"Two Dimensions of Applachian Religiosity," (with Loyde H. Hartley), in John D. Photiadis (ed.), RELIGION IN APPLACHIA, West Virginia University, Morgantown, 1978, p. 229-254.

UP AHEAD FOR METHODISM, Department of Town and Country, Division of National Missions of The Methodist Church, Philadelphia, 1959. (31 p.)

"What's Ahead for Methodism in Town and Country?" *Together* (May, 1964), p. 18-19.

Brewer, Tommy, SKETCHES OF SHELTON'S CHAPEL, LUMBER CITY, GA. (62 p.)

Brewton, William W., "Inevitable Result of Tractarianism (m)," *The Methodist Review,* (H.M. DuBose, ed.), v. 65, Oct. 1916, p. 695-702.

Bridgers, Luther B., TRINITY METHODIST EPISCOPAL CHURCH, SOUTH, (Atlanta) 1854-1935, Private Publishing, 1935. (133 p.) Candler Library has following pamphlets on the same church: "Trinity Centennial Program, 1854-1954;" "The Working Church, Trinity MECS., 1879"

Britton, Charles, A., Jr., ed., OFFICIAL JOURNAL OF THE 1ST SESSION OF THE SOUTH GEORGIA CONFERENCE OF THE METHODIST CHURCH, HELD AT MACON, GA., Nov. 8-12, 1939, Lyon, Harris & Brooks, Printers, Macon, Ga. (128 p.) OFFICIAL JOURNAL OF THE 2ND SESSION OF THE SOUTH GEORGIA CONFERENCE OF THE METHODIST CHURCH, HELD AT SAVANNAH, GA., Nov. 6-11, 1940, Lyon, Harris & Brooks, Printers, Macon, Ga. (99 m.p.)

Brooks, William E., FROM SADDLEBAGS TO SATELITTES, A HISTORY OF FLORIDA METHODISM, Parthenon Press, Nashville, 1969. (268 p.) HISTORY HIGHLIGHTS OF FLORIDA METHODISM, Tropical Press, Ft. Lauderdale Fla., 1965. (48 p.)

Brotherton, Levi, (1832-1919), 126 items — Georgia. Deacon and elder, builder of first church in Dalton, Georgia. Sp Cl Woodruff

Brown, Bernard L., ed., JOURNAL OF THE 1967 SESSION OF THE SOUTH GEORGIA ANNUAL CONFERENCE OF THE METHODIST CHURCH, 101 SESSION, BEING THE

29TH SESSION OF UNITED METHODISM, First Methodist Church, Tifton, Ga. (354 p.)

JOURNAL OF THE 1968 SESSION OF THE SOUTH GEORGIA ANNUAL CONFERENCE OF THE UNITED METHODIST CHURCH, Mulberry St. Methodist Church, Macon, Ga. (414 p.)

JOURNAL OF THE 1969 SESSION OF THE SOUTH GEORGIA ANNUAL CONFERENCE OF THE UNITED METHODIST CHURCH, 1st United Methodist Church, Valdosta, Ga. (377 p.)

JOURNAL OF THE 1970 SESSION OF THE SOUTH GEORGIA ANNUAL CONFERENCE OF THE UMC, (Trinity UMC, Savannah, Ga.). (346 p.)

JOURNAL OF THE 1971 SESSION OF THE SOUTH GEORGIA ANNUAL CONFERENCE OF THE UMC, EPWORTH-BY-THE-SEA, ST. SIMONS ISLAND GA. (399 p.)

OFFICIAL JOURNAL AND YEARBOOK OF THE SOUTH GEORGIA ANNUAL CONFERENCE OF THE METHODIST CHURCH, 85TH SESSION, SAVANNAH, 1950. (151 p.)

OFFICIAL JOURNAL AND YEARBOOK OF THE SOUTH GEORGIA ANNUAL CONFERENCE OF THE METHODIST CHURCH, 86TH SESSION, MACON, 1951. (147 m.p.)

OFFICIAL JOURNAL AND YEARBOOK OF THE SOUTH GEORGIA ANNUAL CONFERENCE OF THE METHODIST CHURCH, 87TH SESSION, THOMASVILLE, 1952, Scanland's Inc., Printers, Tampa, Fla. (120 p.)

OFFICIAL JOURNAL AND YEARBOOK OF THE SOUTH GEORGIA ANNUAL CONFERENCE OF THE METHODIST CHURCH, 88TH SESSION, ALBANY, 1953, Scanland's Inc., Printers, Tampa. (136 p.)

OFFICIAL JOURNAL AND YEARBOOK OF THE SOUTH GEORGIA ANNUAL CONFERENCE OF THE METHODIST CHURCH, 89TH SESSION, ST. SIMONS ISLAND, 1954. (146 m.p.)

OFFICIAL JOURNAL AND YEARBOOK OF THE SOUTH GEORGIA ANNUAL CONFERENCE OF THE METHODIST CHURCH, 90TH SESSION, SAVANNAH, GA., 1955. (187 m.p.)

OFFICIAL JOURNAL AND YEARBOOK OF THE SOUTH GEORGIA ANNUAL CONFERENCE OF THE METHODIST CHURCH, 91ST SESSION, WAYCROSS, 1956. (152 m.p.)

OFFICIAL JOURNAL AND YEARBOOK OF THE SOUTH GEORGIA ANNUAL CONFERENCE OF THE METHODIST CHURCH, 92ND SESSION, COLUMBUS, 1957. (159 p.)

OFFICIAL JOURNAL AND YEARBOOK OF THE SOUTH GEORGIA ANNUAL CONFERENCE OF THE METHODIST CHURCH, 93RD SESSION, VALDOSTA, 1958. (176 p.)

OFFICIAL JOURNAL AND YEARBOOK OF THE SOUTH GEORGIA ANNUAL CONFERENCE OF THE METHODIST CHURCH, 94TH SESSION, WESLEYAN COLLEGE, MACON, 1959. (367 p.)

OFFICIAL JOURNAL AND YEARBOOK OF THE SOUTH GEORGIA ANNUAL CONFERENCE OF THE METHODIST CHURCH, 95TH SESSION, EPWORTH-BY-THE-SEA, ST. SIMONS ISLAND, GA., 1960. (329 p.)

OFFICIAL JOURNAL AND YEARBOOK OF THE SOUTH GEORGIA ANNUAL CONFERENCE OF THE METHODIST CHURCH, 96TH SESSION, ST. LUKE, COLUMBUS, 1961, The Lyons Progress, Lyons, Ga. (327 p.)

OFFICIAL JOURNAL AND YEARBOOK OF THE SOUTH GEORGIA ANNUAL CONFERENCE OF THE METHODIST CHURCH, 97TH SESSION, WESLEYAN COLLEGE, MACON, 1962, The Lyons Progress, Lyons, Ga. (331 p.)

OFFICIAL JOURNAL AND YEARBOOK OF THE SOUTH GEORGIA ANNUAL CONFERENCE OF THE METHODIST CHURCH, 98TH SESSION, MULBERRY ST., MACON, 1963, The

Lyons Progress, Lyons, Ga. (343 p.)
OFFICIAL JOURNAL AND YEARBOOK OF THE SOUTH GEORGIA ANNUAL CONFERENCE OF THE METHODIST CHURCH, 99TH SESSION, 1ST METHODIST, ALBANY, 1964, The Lyons Progress, Lyons, Ga. (411 p.)
OFFICIAL JOURNAL AND YEARBOOK OF THE SOUTH GEORGIA ANNUAL CONFERENCE OF THE METHODIST CHURCH, 100TH SESSION, WESLEY MONUMENTAL, SAVANNAH, 1965, The Lyons Progress, Lyons, Ga. (396 p.)
OFFICIAL JOURNAL AND YEARBOOK OF THE SOUTH GEORGIA ANNUAL CONFERENCE OF THE METHODIST CHURCH, 101ST SESSION, EPWORTH-BY-THE-SEA, ST. SIMONS ISLAND, GA., 1966, The Lyons Progress, Lyons, Ga. (386 p.)

Brown, Oswald E., & Brown, Anna Muse, LIFE AND LETTERS OF LAURA ASKEW HAYGOOD, MECS Publishing House, Nashville, Dallas, 1904. (522 p.)

Brownlow, William G., THE GREAT IRON WHEEL EXAMINED OR ITS FALSE SPOKES EXTRACTED, published for the author, Nashville, Tenn., 1856. (331 p.)

Bryan, J.S., "Heredity and Regeneration," *The Methodist Review,* (J.J. Tigert, ed.), Vol. 22, No. 3, July-August, p. 408-412.
"Murphy's Genesis and The Documentary Hypothesis," *Methodist Quarterly Review,* (W.P. Harrison, ed.), Vol. 11, No. 1, Oct. 1891, p. 95-103.
"The Bible and the Manuscripts," *The Methodist Review,* v. 66, April, 1917, p. 269-278.
"The Immutability of Law," *The Methodist Quarterly Review,* (J.J. Tigert, ed.), v. 51, Nov.-Dec., 1902, p. 890-896.

Bucke, Emory Stevens, THE HISTORY OF AMERICAN METHODISM, Abingdon Press, New York & Nashville, 1964. 3 Vols. Vol. 1 — (721 p.) (Ga. Indexed) Vol. 2 — (750 p.) (Ga. Indexed) Vol. 3 — (699 p.) (Ga. Indexed)

Buckingham, Clyde E., "Early American Orphanages: Ebenezer and Bethseda," *Social Forces,* 26, March, 1948, p. 311-321.

Buckley, James M., A HISTORY OF METHODISM IN THE UNITED STATES, Christian Literature Co., New York, 1897. 2 Vols. Vol. 1 — (472 p.) Ga. Ref. — 72, 75. Vol. 2 — (481 p.) Ga. Ref. — 12, 192.

Budd, W.H., "Antioch—The Ideal Church For All Christian Ages," *The Methodist Quarterly Review,* v. 78, April, 1928, p. 240-248.

Budd, Warren Candler, "A Christian Meditation," *The Emory Univ. Quarterly Review,* v13, n4, Dec. 1957, p. 193-195.

Bullock, Henry Morton, A HISTORY OF EMORY UNIVERSITY, Parthenon Press, Nashville, Tenn., 1936. (391 p.)

Burge Family, (1832-1895; 1923-1952) — 5 boxes — Ga. **Parks, William**

Justice (1866-1873) 20 letters — Ga. Meth. Minister—letters describe Meth. conferences and church affairs. **Gray, John Davis** (1876-1885) — 14 letters — Ga. Meth. minister—letters abt. church activities. Other correspondents in collection include: **Candler, Warren** (7 letters — 1874-1886) **Dowman, Charles Edward** (26 letters — 1874-1881) **Haygood, Atticus G.** (7 letters — 1875-1885) Sp Cl Woodruff

Burge, Louisiana, "Louisiana Burge: The Diary of A Confederate College Girl," *Georgia Historical Quarterly,* 36, June, 1952, p. 144-163. (abt. Wesleyan College).

Burke, James, MY FATHER IN CHINA, Farrar and Rinehart, Inc., New York, Toronto, 1942. (431 p.)

Burke, John W., AUTOBIOGRAPHY, J.W. Burke & Co., Macon, Ga., 1884. (215 p.)
CHAPTERS FROM THE LIFE OF A PREACHER, J.W. Burke & Co., Macon, Ga., 1884. (formerly entitled, AUTOBIOGRAPHY).
BURKE'S FIRST CATECHISM FOR LITTLE FOLKS, (Rev. Ed.), J.W. Burke & Co., Macon, Ga., 1900. (32 p.)
BURKE'S FIRST CATECHISM FOR LITTLE FOLKS, (Rev. Ed.), J.W. Burke & Co., Macon, 1916. (32 p.)
BURKE'S SECOND CATECHISM OR QUESTIONS ON THE SCRIPTURE, 24th ed.) J.W. Burke & Co., Macon, 1895. (64 p.)

Burke, William B., (1887-1964) — 1 box — Ga. — China. Burke was a Methodist minister and missionary to Sungkiang, China. Sp Cl Woodruff

Burruss, John. C., LETTERS OF REV. LOVICK PIERCE, DD, J.C. Burruss, Nostasulga, Ala., 1853. (179 p.)

Burton, Rush, "History of Poplar Springs Campground," Franklin Co., Ga. Pamphlet of the Centennial Celebration, 8-18-1935, The Lavonia Times, Lavonia, Ga., 1935. (19 p.) (An earlier brochure on Poplar Springs Campground containing most of the information in Burton's pamphlet is also in the Ga. Room). Ga Room

Byrne, Donald E., Jr. NO FOOT OF LAND: FOLKLORE OF METHODIST ITINERANTS. Scarecrow Press, Metuchen, N.J. & American Theological Association. 1975. (354 p.) (Ga. Ref. — p. 126).

Byron, Dora. BISHOP OF HEARD COUNTY, Atlanta, Church and Community Institute, 1955. (120 p.)

Cade, John Brother (CME), HOLSEY—THE INCOMPARABLE, Pageant Press, Inc., New York, no date. (221 p.)

Calhoun, E. Clayton, OF MEN WHO VENTURED MUCH AND FAR, The Institute Press, Atlanta, 1961. (154 p.)

Callaway, Morgan, "A Fortunate Flogging," *The Quarterly Review of the MECS,* (J.W. Hinton, ed.), Vol. 7, No. 2, April, 1885, p. 237-255.
"Art and Woman," *The Quarterly Review of the MECS,* Vol. 4, No. 4, Oct. 1882, p. 649-667. (J.W. Hinton, ed.).
"Every Seventh Soul," Jas. P. Harrison and Co., Atlanta, Ga., 1884. (12 p. pamphlet)—printed in *The Quarterly Review of the MECS,* (J.W. Hinton, ed.) Vol. 6, No. 3, July, 1884, p. 513-524.
"The Helpfulness of Learning In The Ministry of the World," *The Methodist Review,"* (J.J. Tigert, ed.), Vol. 22, No. 3, July-August, 1897, p. 361-377.

Calloway, Morgan, D.D., The Aesthetics of Literature," found in *The Quarterly Review of the MECS,* (J.W. Hinton, ed.), Vol. 1, 1879, p. 60-75.

Cameron, Richard Morgan, ed., THE RISE OF METHODISM: A SOURCE BOOK, Philosophical Library, New York, 1954. (397 p.)

Candler, Charles Howard, (1900-1950) — 2846 items — Ga. Glenn Memorial Methodist Church Buildings on the Emory Campus built in honor of his wife's father, Rev. Wilbur Fisk Glenn. Sp Cl Woodruff
"Asa Griggs Candler." Atlanta, Emory Univ. Press, 1950. (502 p.)
"Asa Griggs Candler—Coco-Cola and Emory College, 1888," The Library of Emory Univ., Atlanta, 1953. (20 p.)

Candler, Warran Akin, (1890-1938) — 30,000 pieces — Ga. Bishop—M.E. Church, S. Collection covers topics: Methodist missions in Cuba, the establishment of the Wesley Memorial Hospital, Vanderbilt controversy, Methodist unification, development of Emory University—correspondents include famous Methodists. Sp Cl Woodruff
(Collection of Sermons and Tracts and Pamphlets in Woodruff Library, Emory University, Atlanta, Ga.) Includes: "An Appeal To Promote Peace and End Strife"—(2 p.). "The Day of Opportunity," (1907)—(16 p.). "Enlist In College In Order to Render Your Country a Larger Service," (tract). "Fraternal Address," (May, 1921)—(7 p.). "A Duty To Ourselves and The Nation," (tract)—(4 p.). "Resolute and Revolutionary Rationalism" (tract)—(6 p.). "Our Leaders and Their Labors" (6-10-1902)—(24 p.). "Our Advancing and Vistorious Methodism,"—(8 p.). "A Peace Building To Serve The Prince of Peace" (tract). "Higher Education," 7-23-1889—(8 p.). "The Universities of the Church In the Life of Today"—(7 p.). "Some Stirring Facts and Startling Figures" (tract). "Who Misunderstands and Who Is Misled?" 8-15-1924—(16 p.). "Dangerous Donations and Degrading Doles"—(53 p.). "If You Don't Love the South, Don't Read This"—(12 p.). "Our National Blessings In 1895"—(8 p.).
(ed.), A MANUAL OF DISCIPLINE OF THE METHODIST EPISCOPAL CHURCH, SOUTH, (14th ed.), MECS Publishing House, Nashville, Tenn., 1911. (357 p.)

"Another Christian College In The South," (Agnes-Scott, Decatur, Ga., 11-12-1891), Constitution Job Office, Atlanta, Ga., 1891. (7 p.)

"Atheism," MECS Publishing House, Nashville, Tenn. (11 p.)

"Bishop Candler's 70th Birthday" brochure published by his friends, no date. (approx. 20 p.) Ga Room

BISHOP CHARLES BETTS GALLOWAY, Cokesbury Press, Nashville, Tenn., 1927. (307 p.)

"Bishop George F. Pierce As A Preacher," *The Methodist Review Quarterly*, v. 58, July, 1909, p. 464-474.

"Can One Be a Christian and an Evolutionist?" —Reprint from *Richmond Christian Advocate*, 7-26-1923, by Harvey C. Brown, Richmond, Va. (8 p.)

"Christian Colleges Necessary To The Process of Our Church," Annual Report to the Board of Education, MECS, 1896. (2 p.)

CHRISTUS AUCTOR, MECS Publishing House, Nashville, Tenn. & Dallas, Texas. 1900. (255 p.)

CHRISTUS AUCTOR, MECS Publishing House, Nashville, Tenn. & Dallas, Tex., 1909. (255 p.)

"Correspondence Between W.A. Candler and Judge T.M. Norwood, 1903," Savannah Morning News Print, Savannah, Ga., 1903. (20 p.)

CURRENT COMMENTS ON TIMELY TOPICS, Cokesbury Press, Nashville, Tenn., 1926. (280 p.)

EASTER MEDITATIONS, Cokesbury Press, Nashville, Tenn., 1930. (116 p.)

"Educational Essays,"—Bulletin of Emory University, Vol. 4, No. 2, Feb. 1918. (31 p.)

"Evolution," (tract), MECS Publishing House, Nashville, Tenn., 1929. (16 p.)

"Georgian Who Foretold Wonder of Electricity," *The Atlanta Journal*, 12-15-1935, p. 6. (Alexander Means).

GEORGIA'S EDUCATIONAL WORK, The Foote & Davies Co., Atlanta, Ga. (123 p.)

GREAT REVIVALS AND THE GREAT REPUBLIC, MECS Publishing House, Nashville, Tenn. & Dallas, Tex., 1904. (344 p.)

GREAT REVIVALS AND THE GREAT REPUBLIC, MECS Publishing House, Nashville, Dallas, Richmond, San Francisco, 1924. (344 p.)

HIGH LIVING AND HIGH LIVES, Foote & Davies Co., Atlanta, Ga., 1901. (239 p.)

HIGH LIVING AND HIGH LIVES, MECS Publishing House, Nashville, Tenn., 1902. (239 p.)

HIGH LIVING & HIGH LIVES, ME Church, S. Publishing House, Nashville, 1912. (239 p.)

"If You Don't Love The South, Don't Read This," 1921. (12 p.)

"Is the South's Greatest Industry Threatened?" *The Methodist Quarterly Review*, (J.J. Tigert, ed.), v. 53, Oct. 1904, p. 743-751.

LIFE OF THOMAS COKE, M.E. Church, South Publishing House, Nashville, 1923. (408 p.) (Ga. Ref. — 108, 111, 130, 131, 133, 134, 137).

"Make Your Liberty Bonds Do Double Service," (tract), Foote & Davies, Atlanta, Ga.

ed., MINUTES OF THE NORTH GEORGIA CONFERENCE, HELD IN TRINITY CHURCH, ATLANTA, GA., 1884. (43 p.)

ed., MINUTES OF THE NORTH GEORGIA CONFERENCE, HELD IN NEWNAN, GA.,

1885. (37 p.)

MISCELLANEOUS PAMPHLETS. (2 bound vols. in Candler Library).

ed., NORTH GEORGIA CONFERENCE, MINUTES OF THE 20TH SESSION, HELD IN AUGUSTA, GA., ST. JOHN's CHURCH, DEC. 1-7, 1886, Southern Methodist Publishing House, Nashville, Tenn., 1887. (57 p.)

"Not Less Education But More Of The Right Sort," Barbee & Smith, Nashville, Tenn., 1897. (32 p.)

"Our Common Schools and Our Common People," *The Methodist Quarterly Review*, (J.J. Tigert, ed.), v. 52, Jan., 1903, p. 3-10.

PRACTICAL STUDIES IN THE 4TH GOSPEL, 2 Vol., MECS Publishing House, Nashville, Dallas, Richmond, 1922. (Vol. 1 — 298 p.; Vol. 2 — 376 p.)

"T.H. Yun of Korea and The School at Songdo," MECS Board of Missions, Nashville, Tenn. (32 p.)

THE CHRIST AND THE CREED, The Jarrell Lectures for 1927, Cokesbury Press, Nashville, Tenn., 1927. (134 p.)

THE CHRIST AND THE CREED, Pentecostal Publishing Company, Louisville, 1927. (134 p.)

"The Church, The Fullness of Christ, and the Hope of the Universe," (sermon), 1st MEC, Baltimore, Md., 12-28-1916. (34 p.)

THE FEAST OF THE FAMILY ON THE BIRTHDAY OF THE KING, The Cokesbury Press, Nashville, 1923. (68 p.)

THE HISTORY OF SUNDAY SCHOOLS, Phillips & Hunt, New York, 1880. (149 p.)

THE HISTORY OF SUNDAY SCHOOLS, (2nd ed.), J.W. Burke & Co., Macon, 1881. (149 p.)

D.D., LL.D., THE KINGDOM OF GOD's DEAR SON, (The Quillian Lectures for 1921), MECS Publishing House, Nashville, Dallas, Richmond, 1922. (183 p.)

"The Ministerial Orders of Episcopal Methodism," *The Methodist Quarterly Review*, v. 71, April, 1922, p. 187-200.

"The Origin, Mission, and Destiny of the Church," *The Methodist Review*, v. 69, Jan. 1920, p. 3-12.

"The Phenomenal Philanthropy of 1916," Foote & Davies, Atlanta, Ga. (8 p.)

"The Place of Our Universities In the Educational System of Our Church," Foote & Davies Co., Atlanta, Ga. (tract).

"The Resurrection of Christ," printed by Harvey C. Brown, Richmond, Va., 1924. (20 p.)

"The Universities of The Church In The Life of Today,' np, 192__. (7 p.) Candler

"Theater'Going and Dancing Incompatible With Church Membership," MECS Publishing House, Nahsville, Tenn., 1890. (32 p.)

WESLEY AND HIS WORK ON METHODISM AND MISSIONS, MECS Publishing House, Nashville and Dallas, 1912. (223 p.)

YOUNG J. ALLEN, Cokesbury Press, Nashville, 1931. (245 p.)

Cannon, James, III, HISTORY OF SOUTHERN METHODIST MISSIONS, Cokesbury Press, Nashville, Tenn., 1926. (356 p.)

Cannon, William Ragsdale, (ca. 1960-1977) 1 box — Ga. Papers are mainly clippings re this Methodist bishop and of his column in the Advocate. Also included is a broadside of the prayer he delivered at President Carter's inauguration. (see Catalog of Broadsides). Sp Cl Woodruff

A FAITH FOR THESE TIMES, Univ. of Ga. Press, Athens, Ga., 1944. (93 p.)

"Address to the World Methodist Conference," (delivered in Honolulu, Ha. 7-27-1981), *Wesleyan Christian Advocate*, v. 146, n. 7, 8-19-81, p. 4.

"An Abhorrent, but Necessary, Evil," *Engage/Social Action*, 8, Jan. 1980, p. 16-19.

"And Thou, Bethlehem," *The Emory Univ. Quarterly Review*, v9, n4, Dec. 1953, p. 193-198.

EVANGELISM IN A CONTEMPORARY CONTEXT, Tidings, Nashville, 1974. (110 p.)

HISTORY OF CHRISTIANITY IN THE MIDDLE AGES, Abingdon Press, Nashville, 1960. (352 p.)

JESUS THE SERVANT, The Upper Room, Nashville, Tenn., 1978. (128 p.)

"John Wesley's Doctrine of Sanctification and Perfection," *Mennonite Quarterly Review*, 35, April 1961, p. 91-95.

"John Wesley's Years In Georgia," *Methodist History*, v1, n4, July, 1963, p. 1-7.

"John Wyclif and John Hus," *The Emory Univ. Quarterly Review*, v15, n2, June, 1959, p. 80-87.

JOURNEYS AFTER ST. PAUL, MacMillian, New York, 1963. (276 p.)

"Meaning of the Ministry in Methodism," *Methodist History*, 8, Oct. 1969, p. 3-19.

"Methodism In a Philosophy of History," *Methodist History*, 12, July, 1974, p. 27-43.

"New and Old Israel," *The Emory University Quarterly Review*, v9, n1, March, 1953, p. 9-17.

OUR PROTESTANT FAITH, Tidings, Nashville, Tenn., 1949. (63 p.)

"Palmyra, Queen of the Desert," *The Emory Univ. Quarterly Review*, v17, n1, Spring, 1961, p. 35-41.

"Perfection," *London Quarterly and Holborn Review*, 184, July, 1959, p. 213-17.

"Pierces: Father and Son," *Methodist History*, 17, Oct. 1978, p. 3-15.

"Salvation In The Theology of John Wesley," *Methodist History*, 9, Oct. 1970, p. 3-12.

THE CHRISTIAN CHURCH, Abingdon-Cokesbury, New York, Nashville, Tenn., 1955. (104 p.)

(review of) The Doctrine of the Church, Dow Kirkpatrick, ed., *The Wesleyan Quarterly Review*, Vol. 1, No. 3, Aug. 1964, p. 183.

"The Nature and Significance of Dogma in Early Christianity," *The Emory Univ. Quarterly Review*, v2, n3, Oct. 1946, p. 153-160.

THE REDEEMER: THE WORK AND PERSON OF JESUS CHRIST, Nashville, Tenn., Abingdon-Cokesbury Press, 1951. (224 p.)

THE THEOLOGY OF JOHN WESLEY, Abingdon-Cokesbury Press, New York & Nashville, 1946. (284 p.) (Ga. Ref. — 60, 62, 69-74, 187).

"The Work of Christ: A Clue to the Understanding of His Person," *The Emory Univ. Quarterly Review*, v6, n4, Dec. 1950, p. 236-245.

"Theological Stance of Methodism In The Ecumenical Movement," *Methodist History*, 6, October, 1967, p. 3-13.

Cantrell, Mrs. Warren C., ed., 26TH ANNUAL REPORT OF THE WOMAN'S MISSIONARY SOCIETY OF THE N. GA. CONFERENCE, 1935, (Dalton, Ga.). (84 p.)
27TH ANNUAL REPORT OF THE WOMAN'S MISSIONARY SOCIETY OF THE N. GA. CONFERENCE, 1936, (Griffin, Ga.), Adamson Printing Co., Atlanta, Ga. (80 p.)
28TH ANNUAL REPORT OF THE WOMAN'S MISSIONARY SOCIETY OF THE N. GA., CONFERENCE, 1937, (Carrollton, Ga.), Adamson Printing Co., Atlanta, Ga. (91 p.)
29TH ANNUAL REPORT OF THE WOMAN'S MISSIONARY SOCIETY OF THE NORTH GA. CONFERENCE, 1938, (St. James MECS, Augusta, Ga.), Adamson Printing Co., Atlanta, Ga. (92 p.)
13TH ANNUAL REPORT OF THE WOMAN'S MISSIONARY SOCIETY OF THE NORTH GEORGIA CONFERENCE, 1939, Adamson Printing Co., Atlanta, (110 p.)

Capers, William, EXPOSITION OF THE CAUSES AND—CHARACTER OF THE DIFFICULTIES IN THE CHURCH IN CHARLESTON, 1833, (bound series of pamphlets, some of which were printed by J.S. Burges, Charleston, 1835).
"Letter from Milledgeville," dated 1-23-1824, concerning the mission at Asbury, found in *The Methodist Magazine,* (Soule & Mason, eds.), Vol. 7, 1824, p. 119.
Letter to J.O. Andrew, recorded in *Quarterly Review of the MECS,* April, 1860, p. 312-313. (D.S. Doggett, ed.).
"Letter Written from Savannah, Ga.," 9-17-1819, found in *The Methodist Magazine* (Soule & Mason eds.), Vol. 2, 1819, (bound), p. 476-477.

Carlton, Wilbur Allen, IN MEMORY OF OLD EMORY, Emory Univ., Atlanta, 1962. (65 p.)
THE OXFORD CHURCH, (N. Ga. Conf.), 1973. (25 p.) (softbound)

Carmichael, Marion Walter, (1895-1935) 1 box — Ga. Ga. minister's collection includes various journals and reports of the S. Ga. Conference of the ME Church South and the Annual Conferences of the ME Church, South. Sp Cl Woodruff

Carr, James McLeod, GLORIOUS RIDE, Atlanta, Church & Community Press, 1958. (156 p.)

Carroll, Grady L.E., FRANCIS ASBURY IN NORTH CAROLINA, Parthenon Press, Nashville, 1966. (300 p.) (Ga. Ref. — 30, 93, 98, 121, 159, 177, 237).

Carroll, Rev. J. E., AN AUTOBIOGRAPHY, The Shenango Printing Co., Greenville, Pa., 1899. (157 p.)
"Mexico As A Mission Field," *Methodist Quarterly Review,* (W.P. Harrison, ed.), Vol. 9, No. 2, Jan., 1891, p. 319-335.

Cary, Clement, C., CENTENNIAL ANNIVERSARY OF MT. PLEASANT METHODIST CHURCH, OGLETHORPE CO., GA., Foote & Davies Co., Atlanta, Ga., 1920. (93 p.)

Doctrinal Pamphlets, No. 1-7 in Ga. Room. Remainder listed in advertisements. 1. The Doctrine of Election, Atlanta, Ga. (16 p.) 2. Infant Baptism, (30 p.) 3. Jesus Christ's Doctrine of Hell, Walton News Print, Monroe, Ga. (19 p.) 4. What Is A Methodist, Atlanta. (16 p.) 5. The Witness of the Spirit, News & Messenger Print, Monroe, Ga. (13 p.) 6. Regeneration—Is It Necessary?, Walton News Print, Monroe, Ga. (13 p.) 7. The Mode of Baptism, (32 p.) News & Messenger Pt., Monroe. 8. Apostasy or Falling From Grace 9. Scriptural Views of Election 10. May Christians Dance 11. The 7th Chapter of Romans 12. The Divine Rule of Giving 13. Close Communion, Press of Augusta Chronicle (13 p.) 14. Inherited Depravity, (30 p.) 15. Family Prayer 16. The Atonement 17. The Sacrament 18. Perfect Love 19. Objections to Holiness Considered 20. The Second Coming of Christ, (137 p.) Dr. Blosser Co. 1902. 21. Scripture View of Election 22. Regeneration—The Character of the New Birth. Ga Room

Chesnut, Roberta C., Book Reviews found in the following Journals and Periodicals: *Anglican Theological Review*
"The Two Prosopa in Nestorius' BAZAAR OF HERACLEIDES," *Journal of Theological Studies*, n.s. xxix, 1978, p. 392-409.
THREE MONOPHYSITE CHRISTOLOGIES: SEVERUS OF ANTIOCH, PHILOXENUS OF MABBUG AND JACOB OF SARUG, Oxford University Press, London and New York, 1976.

Chreitzberg, A.M., "Beverly Allen: The First Apostate Presbyter of American Methodism," *The Methodist Review,* (J.J. Tigert, ed.), Vol. 19, No. 3, Jan-Feb, 1896, p. 368-375.
EARLY METHODISM IN THE CAROLINAS. M.E. Church S. Publishing House, 1897. Reprint by Reprint Co., Spartanburg, S.C., 1972. (364 p.)
"James Jenkins: A Pioneer of Southern Methodism," *Methodist Quarterly Review,* (W.P. Harrison, ed.), Vol. 15, No. 2, Jan. 1894, p. 314-326.

Clarendon, Lizzie, "Bishop Capers," *The Home Circle,* v.1., MECS Publishing House, Nashville, Tenn., 1855, p. 208-209. (Huston, L.D., ed.).

Clark, Elmer T., ARTHUR JAMES MOORE, WORLD EVANGELIST, Editorial Dept., Board of Missions of the Methodist Church, 1960. (45 p.)
ed., THE JOURNAL AND LETTERS OF FRANCIS ASBURY — 3 volumes, Epworth Press, London & Abingdon Press, Nashville, 1958. (Vol. 1 — 778 p.) Ga. Ref. — 35, 593, 627, 667, 669, 707-9, 743-46, 752, 778. (Vol. 2 — 871 p.) Ga. Ref. — 35, 76, 80, 83, 90, 91, 189, 213, 217, 254, 265, 267, 271, 280, 304, 311, 312, 317, 318, 365, 415-421, 484, 521-25, 558-59, 560, 573, 582, 585-89, 617, 622, 652, 745, 764, 765-67. (Vol. 3 — 603 p.) Ga. Ref. — 30, 33, 48, 84, 96, 108, 143, 159, 160, 164, 171, 192, 193, 199, 222, 229, 247, 251, 252, 253, 255, 261, 262, 273, 276, 306, 310, 314, 337, 343, 354, 369, 376, 379, 402, 407, 408, 432, 449, 477, 503, 504, 507, 513, 538, 563, 570, 575, 272, 289, 194, 195, 198, 238.

Clark, James Osgood Andrew, (1850-1900) — 9 boxes — Ga. Ga. Methodist leader responsible for building the Wesley Monumental Church in Savannah—collection includes correspondence with prominent Methodists and sermons. Sp Cl Woodruff

A Sketch of the Late Alfred T. Mann, D.D., J.W. Burke & Co., Macon, Ga., 1889. (89 p.)

"American Methodism" (sermon) Centennial Sermon before the S. Ga. Conference, Savannah, 12-20-1884. J.W. Burke & Co., Macon, 1885. (32 p.) Ga Room

Elijah Vindicated, Southern Methodist Publishing House, Nashville, Tenn., 1886. (399 p.)

"Methodism—Modern Sunday Schools," *The Quarterly Review of the MECS,* (J.W. Hinton, ed.), Vol. 6, No. 4, Oct. 1884, p. 619-634.

"The Baptism of the Spirit," found in *The Quarterly Review of the MECS,* (J.W. Hinton, ed.), Vol. 1, 1879, p. 493-524.

The Wesley Memorial Volume, Phillips & Hunt, New York, 1881. (743 p.) Ga. Ref. — 5f, 285f, 606f, 700f.

Clark, Myrtice N., Pioneering For Christ, The Naylor Co., San Antonia, Texas, 1963. (Biography of Rev. C.A. Clark, son of Rev. J.O.A. Clark) (307 p.)

Clary, George Esmond, Jr., Our Methodist Heritage in South Georgia. Collected papers of the S. Ga. Methodist Historical Society, 1956-1960, Savannah, Ga., published by the S. Ga. Conf. Historical Society, 1960. (65 p.)

"Southern Methodism's Unique Adventure in Race Relations—Paine College, 1882-1903," *Methodist History,* v9, n2, Jan. 1971, p. 22-23.

The Beginnings of the South Georgiaa Conference, (Some Notes on Georgia Methodist History), published by the S. Ga. Conf. Historical Society, 1966-67. (21 p.)

Clifford's Temple CME Church, "An Imparative Need," (An appeal to White Christians in Thomasville, Ga. and Thomas County), Fletcherville, Ga., 1926. (4 p.) Ga Room

Coan, Josephus R., The Expansion of Missions of the African Methodist Episcopal Church In South Africa, 1896-1908, (thesis), Hartford, Conn. May, 1961. (509 p.) (typed copy in Ga. Room).

Cochran, A. H., Jr., "History of St. John's Methodist Church For 50 Years, 1877-1927," (Fulton Co., Ga.), (typescript). Ga. Archives

Cochran, Leonard H., Man at His Best, Abingdon Press, Nashville, 1957. (174 p.)

Coke, Thomas, A Series of Letters Addressed to the Methodist Connection, London, A. Paris, printer, 1810. (382 p.)

"The Grace of God Manifested," *The Methodist Magazine,* Vol. 1 (1818); Vol. 2 (1819), MECS Publishing—J. Soule & T. Mason, New York. v1 — ?-474; v2 —

63-66; 106-110; 139-144.
"The Substance of a Sermon on The Godhead of Christ," preached at Baltimore, Dec. 26, 1784 before the General Conference of the Methodist Episcopal Church, D. Hitt and T. Ware, J.C. Totten, printer, New York, 1815. (24 p.)

Cokesbury—"Reminiscences of Cokesbury, S.C., Manual-Labor School," *The Home Circle*, 1860, p. 105-112, MECS Publishing House, Nashville, Tenn. (Huston, L.D., ed.).

Cokesbury Press, Fifteen Years and An Idea, Cokesbury Press, Nashville, Tenn., 1938. (87 p.)

Colclough, J.C., The Spirit of John Wesley Gilbert, Cokesbury Press, Nashville, Tenn., 1925. (108 p.)

Coldwell, Rev. John G. (Ga. Conf. of Meth. Prot. Ch.) The Sacrament of Baptism, W.H. Scott, Atlanta, 1887. (123 p.)

Commission on Archives & History of the S. Ga. Conference of the United Methodist Church, "Historical Highlights," semi-annual. Vol. 1, No. 1 — June, 1971 — per.

Concord Methodist Church (Putnam Co., Ga.), "Sesquicentennial, 1810-1960" booklet. Pvt. Pt., 6-12-1960. (9 p.)

Conway, Marion H., The Country Parson, 1964, Pvt. Pt. (83 p.)

Conyers Methodist Church, "The Methodist Episcopal Church South, 1852-1939; The Methodist Church, 1939-1952, Conyers, Ga." (88 p.)

Cook, Ellison R., ed., Year Book and Minutes of the 25th Session of the North Georgia Conference, MECS, Held in Cartersville, Ga., Dec. 9-15, 1891, J.W. Burke & Co., Printers and Stationers, Macon, Ga., 1891. (76 p.) Year Book and Minutes of the 26th Session of the North Georgia Conference, MECS, Held In Methodist Church, Madison, Ga., Nov. 30-Dec. 6, 1892, The Christian Giver Co., Sparta, Ga.; Constitution Job Office, Atlanta, 1892. (92 p.)

Cook, Ellison R., and Daves, Joel T., Jr., eds., Year Book and Minutes of the 27th Session of the North Georgia Conference, MECS, Held in the County Courthouse, Gainesville, Ga., Nov. 29-Dec. 5, 1893, The Christian Giver Co., Pub., Atlanta; Press of The Foote & Davies Co., Atlanta, Ga., 1893. (72 p.)

Cook, Ed. F., ed., Minutes of the 32nd Session of the South Georgia Conference of the MECS, Held in Hawkinsville, Ga., Dec. 7-12, 1898,

Thos. Gilbert, printer & manufacturing stationer, Columbus, Ga., 1899. (48 m.p.)

Cook, E. F., and Smith, J.A., eds., YEAR-BOOK AND MINUTES OF THE SOUTH GEORGIA CONFERENCE OF THE METHODIST EPISCOPAL CHURCH SOUTH, 33RD SESSION, HELD IN DUBLIN, GA., DEC. 6-10, 1899, Thos. Gilbert, Printer & Manufacturing Stationer, 1899. (87 m.p.)

Cook, Edmund F., METHODISM AND WORLD SERVICE, Cokesbury Press, Nashville, Tenn., 1928. (172 p.)
THE MISSIONARY MESSAGE OF THE BIBLE, MECS Publishing House, Nashville, Tenn., Dallas, Texas, Richmond, Va., and San Francisco, California, 1925. (138 p.)

Cook, Jacquelyn, A TABERNACLE OF LIVING WATER, Dooly Campground Trustees, Vienna, Ga. (146 p.)

Cooper, Ezekia, "THE SUBSTANCE OF A FUNERAL DISCOURSE," (on the death of Francis Asbury), Jonathan Pounder, Philadelphia, 1819. (230 p.)

Cotter, William Jasper, MY AUTOBIOGRAPHY, M.E. Church South Publishing House, Nashville, 1917. (190 p.)
"The Methodist Publishing House War Claim," (pamphlet). (15 p.)

Crogman, Dr. W. H., "He Became The Golden Clasp," (A Memorial Tribute to Bishop Atticus G. Haygood, delivered in Atlanta, 2-23-1896), The Advisory Council of Clark College, 1953. (11 p.) Ga. Room

Crumley, H. L., ed., MINUTES OF THE 24TH SESSION, NORTH GEORGIA CONFERENCE, MECS, HELD IN METHODIST CHURCH, WASHINGTON, GA., DEC. 3-8, 1890, Constitution Publishing Co., Atlanta, Ga. 1890. (58 p.)
NORTH GEORGIA CONFERENCE, MINUTES OF THE 21ST SESSION, HELD IN MARIETTA, GA., COURTHOUSE, DEC. 7-12, 1887. (45 p.)
NORTH GEORGIA CONFERENCE, MECS, MINUTES OF THE 22ND SESSION, HELD IN METHODIST CHURCH, MILLEDGEVILLE, GA., DEC. 5-11, 1888, Constitution Publishing Co., Print, Atlanta. (45 p.)
NORTH GEORGIA CONFERENCE, MECS, MINUTES OF THE 23RD SESSION, HELD IN METHODIST CHURCH CEDARTOWN, GA., NOV. 27-DEC. 3, 1889, Constitution Publishing Co., Print, Atlanta, Ga. (56 p.)

Crumly, William W., THE SOLDIER'S BIBLE, Raleigh, N.C., 186__, (15 p.) also published by Soldier's Tract Association, MECS, 186__. (12 p.) (Univ. of Ga. has copy) (Crumly was chaplain of Ga. hospitals in Richmond, Va.) CSA Biblio Willingham

Crumpler, Rev. P. H. & Robertson, Rev. Wm. J., CATECHISM & HISTORICAL CHAIN OF THE BIBLE FOR THE LITTLE PEOPLE OF ALL EVANGELICAL CHURCHES,

J.W. Burke & Co., Macon, 1885. (104 p.)

Culpepper, John B., Dick Davis and The Devil—and Other Sermons, Pentecostal Publishing Co., Louisville, Ky. (167 p.)
Backsliders, (uv).
Just For Children, (uv).
Malice, (uv).
Men Only, (uv).
Some Women I Have Known, Pickett Publishing Co., Louisville, Ky., 1902. (198 p.)
The Black Horses, (uv).
The Divine Atlas, Pentecostal Publishing Co., Louisville, Ky., 1921. (124 p.)
The Wandering Lover or Christ Enthroned, (uv).

Culver, Dwight W., Negro Segregation In The Methodist Church, Yale Univ. Press, New Haven, 1953. (218 p.) Ga. Ref. — p. 26, 38, 49, 116, 125, 152, 155, 157, 72, 129, 131, 140, 60.

Cummings, A. W., The Early Schools of Methodism, Phillips & Hunt, New York; Cranston & Stowe, Cincinnati, 1886. (Contains information on Wesley & Whitefield School, Georgia).

Cummings, Arthur D., A Portrait In Pottery, The Epworth Press, London, 1962. (48 p.)

Curnock, Nehemiah (ed.), The Journal of John Wesley, The Epworth Press, London, 1938, 8 vols. Vol. 1 — (404 p.); Vol. 2 — (536 p.); Vol. 3 — (540 p.) Vol. 4 — (542 p.); Vol. 5 — (526 p.); Vol. 6 — (526 p.) Vol. 7 — (528 p.); Vol. 8 — (476 p.) (Ga. Ref. — Vol. 1).

Curry, Daniel, Platform Papers, Hitchcock and Walden, Cincinnati, Ohio, (1879-80). (389 p.)
"Winter Birds of Georgia," Southern Ladies' Book, Vol. 1, Benj. F. Griffin, printer, Macon, Ga., 1840, p. 100-102. (Pierce, G.F., ed.).

Curry, J. H., "The Way to 'Get' and Keep The Experience of Holiness," J.W. Burke & Co., Macon, Ga. (23 p.)

Dallimore, Arnold, George Whitefield, The Banner of Truth Trust, London, 1970. (598 p.)

Daniel, J. W., "The Need of Conversion," *The Methodist Review,* v. 70, Jan. 1921, p. 55-75.

Daniels, Rev. W. H., The Illustrated History of Methodism, Hunt & Eaton, New York. (884 p.)
The Illustrated History of Methodism In Great Britain and America,

Phillips & Hunt, New York, 1879. (784 p.)

Darley, Prof. J., A.M., "Review of Prof. Sasnett's 'Theory of Female Education,'" found in *Quarterly Review*, (H.B. Bascomb, Ed.), July, 1853, p. 340-362.

Davenport, Fred P., JOHN ANDREW, PATRIOT, 1969, (father of Bishop J.O. Andrew) (14 p.)

Daves, Joel T., Jr., "A New Light In Non-Conformity," *The Methodist Quarterly Review*, (J.J. Tigert, ed.), v. 53, April, 1904, p. 289-299.
"The Three English Versions of the Scriptures," *The Methodist Quarterly Review*, (J.J. Tigert, ed.), v. 55, Jan. 1906, p. 64-83.
"The Two Episcopal Methodisms In The South," *The Methodist Review*, Vol. 21, No. 3, Jan.-Feb., 1897, p.404-418. (J.J. Tigert, ed.).
ed., YEAR BOOK AND MINUTES OF THE NORTH GEORGIA CONFERENCE, MECS, 28TH SESSION, HELD AT ROME, GA., Nov. 22-28, 1894, The Foote & Davies Co., Atlanta, Ga., 1894. (97 m.p.)

Davidson, William H., WEST POINT METHODISM, 1830-1962, (West Point, Ga.) (9 p.) (pamphlet).

Davis, Mrs. Blair Wilson, THE FIRST ONE HUNDRED YEARS, CENTENNIAL CELEBRATION. (Wesley Monumental Methodist Church, Savannah, Ga.). (29 p.) (softbound)

Davis, J.A. (AME Church), "What Constitutes The Accomplished Christian Pastor," Thos. Gilbert, printer, Columbus, Ga., 1886. (10 p.) Ga. Room

Deems, Charles F., (ed.), THE SOUTHERN METHODIST PULPIT, Vol. 3, 1850, Richmond Christian Advocate Printing. Contains following sermon: Gassaway, William, "The Apostleship and Apostacy of Judas Iscariot." (p. 281)

Dempsey, Elam Franklin, (1855-1952, 23 boxes — Ga. Methodist minister, dean of the theology school at Oxford College, editor and business manager of the Wesleyan Christian Advocate, biographer of 3 bishops who served as presidents of Emory. Collection includes his sermons, correspondence, clippings, and notes on the biographies. Sp Cl Woodruff
ATTICUS GREEY HAYGOOD, Centennial Edition, 1839-1939, Parthenon Press, Methodist Publishing House, Nashville, 1940. (720 p.)
"Francis Asbury The Theologian," *The Methodist Review*, (H.M. DuBose, ed.), v. 65, April, 1916, p. 334-340.
"James Edward Dickey: A Memorial Tribute," *The Methodist Quarterly Review*, v. 77, July 1928, p. 406-426.
LIFE OF BISHOP DICKEY—Bishop of the Methodist Episcopal Church, South, Published by M.E. Church, S. Publishing House, Nashville, 1937, Parthenon Press. (304 p.)

WHO'S WHO IN PAN-METHODISM, Vol. 1, 1940-41., (Souvenir of the First Gen. Conf. of the Methodist Church), Parthenon Press, 1940, Nashville, Tenn. (295 p.)
ed., WIT & WISDOM OF WARREN AKIN CANDLER, Cokesbury Press, Nashville, 1922. (285 p.)

Dewey, Maybelle Jones, "The Early History of Emory University Hospital," THE JOURNAL OF THE MEDICAL ASSOCIATION OF GEORGIA, 41, June, 1952, p. 462-465.

Dick, E. G., A CENTURY OF SPLENDOR—Gaithers UMC (Covington, Ga.), (43 p.) (softbound).

Dickey, James Edward, (1903-1913) — 10 folders — Ga. Methodist bishop in Ga. and president of Emory College. Collection includes sermon notes. Sp Cl Woodruff

Dickson, Lester C., "History of Fayetteville Methodist Church, South." (4 pages, typescript). Ga. Archives

Dillard, Walter, ed., YEAR BOOK AND MINUTES OF THE 43RD SESSION OF THE NORTH GEORGIA CONFERENCE, MECS, HELD AT ST. PAUL CHURCH, ATLANTA, GA., Nov. 17-22, 1909. (128 p.)
YEAR BOOK AND MINUTES OF THE 44TH SESSION OF THE NORTH GEORGIA CONFERENCE, MECS, HELD IN 1ST METHODIST CHURCH, ATHENS, GA., Nov. 16-21, 1910. (86 m.p.)
YEAR BOOK AND MINUTES OF THE 45TH SESSION OF THE NORTH GEORGIA CONFERENCE, MECS, HELD IN ST. JAMES CHURCH, AUGUSTA, GA., Nov. 15-20, 1911, Rome, Ga. (91 m.p.)

Dimond, Sydney G., THE PSYCHOLOGY OF METHODISM, The Epworth Press, London, 1932. (154 p.) (Ga. Ref. — 22, 32, 42-3)
THE PSYCHOLOGY OF THE METHODIST REVIVAL, Oxford University Press, London, 1926. (296 p.) (Ga. Ref. — p. 22, 23, 45, 52, 56, 57, 72, 86, 226.)

Dixon, James, METHODISM IN AMERICA, John Mason, London, 1859. (498 p.)

Dodd, Hubert, THE WEEPING GOD, New York, Vantage Press, 1956. (70 p.)

Doggett, D.S., (ed.), *Quarterly Review of the Methodist Episcopal Church, South,* E. Stevenson & F.A. Owen, Nashville, Tenn., 1857. (periodical). (formerly, Richmond, Va.)

Douglas, Miss Lucretia J., GRACE FOR EVERY TRIAL, K.H. Walker, Dublin, Ga., 1893. (258 p.)

Dow, Lorenzo, A CHAIN, WITH ITS CONCOMITANTS; OR POLEMICAL

REFLECTIONS, John C. Totten, New York, 1807. (81 p.)
HISTORY OF COSMOPOLITE, 8th ed., Applegate & Co., Cincinnati, 1855. (720 p.) (similar ed. printed in 1857).
HISTORY OF COSMOPOLITE, Applegate & Co., Cincinnati, 1857. (270 p.) (Ga. Ref. — Chapters 8 & 10)
THE LIFE, TRAVELS, LABOR, AND WRITINGS OF LORENZO DOW, John E. Potter & Co., Philadelphia, no date. (508 p.)

Dow, Lorenzo & Dow, Peggy, COMPLETE WORKS OF LORENZO AND PEGGY Dow, Applegate & Co., Cincinnati, 1859. (350 p.) (Ga. Ref. — p. 81f and 59f).

Drake, C.B., "The Rise of Methodism is Georgia." (Thesis, 1922, Emory Univ.) (47 p.)

Drew, Samuel, THE LIFE OF THE REV. THOMAS COKE, LL.D., M.E. Church Publishing House, New York, 1818. Reprint 1837. (391 p.)
THE LIFE OF THE REV. THOMAS COKE, Lane and Tippett, New York, 1847. (Joseph Longking, printer). (381 p.)

Drinkard, Eugene T., "A Christmas Meditation," *The Emory Univ. Quarterly Review,* v15, n4, Dec. 1959, p. 193-196.

Drinkhouse, Edward J., HISTORY OF THE METHODIST REFORM with (History of the Methodist Protestant Church), 2 vols., Norwood Press, Norwood, Mass., 1899. Vol. 1 — (1703-1820) — (610 p.) Vol. 2 — (1820-1898) — (715 p.)

DuBose, Horace M., A HISTORY OF METHODISM, M.E. Church, S. Publishing House, Nashville, 1916. Vol. 2 — (592 p.) Ga. Ref. — 31, 35. Supplement to "A History of Methodism" by Holland N. McTyeire.
"A Universe of Consciousness," *The Methodist Review,* v. 67, July, 1918, p. 387-397.
FRANCIS ASBURY, MECS Publishing House, Nashville, Tenn. & Dallas, Tex., 1909. (245 p.)
"Have We A Constitution?" *The Methodist Review,* v 66, Oct. 1917, p. 588-600.
LIFE OF JOSHUA SOULE, MECS Publishing House, Nashville, Tenn. & Dallas, Tex., 1911. (285 p.)
"Our Church Name: A Question For The Annual Conference," *The Methodist Review Quarterly,* (Gross Alexander, ed.), v. 62, April, 1913, p. 291-308.
"Points Overlooked By Radical Criticism," *The Methodist Quarterly Review,* v. 76, April, 1927, p. 179-192.
ed., THE AFTERMATH SERIES, MECS Publishing House, Nashville, Tenn., 1923-24. (271 p.) Containing the following by DuBose: "The Blood Atonelment of Jesus Christ," p. 447-500. "The Bodily Resurrection of Jesus Christ," p. 503-533. "The Crisis of Criticism," p. 3-43. "The Law and The Prophets," p. 385-427.
"The Atonement: Its Rationale," *The Methodist Quarterly Review,* v. 72, Oct. 1923, p. 601-610.

THE BIBLE AND THE AGES, Fleming H. Revell Co., New York, Chicago, 1930. (255 p.)
THE CONSCIOUSNESS OF JESUS, Methodist Book Concern, New York, 1917. (144 p.)
"The Consciousness of Jesus," *The Methodist Review*, v. 66, Jan. 1917, p. 35-46.
"The Epistle To The Colossians," *The Methodist Review*, v. 66, Jan. 1917, p. 69-78.
"The Epistle To The Galatians," *The Methodist Review*, v. 65, July, 1916, p. 419-432.
"The Epistle To The Ephesians," *The Methodist Review*, v. 66, April, 1917, p. 241-247.
"The Failure of Higher Criticism," *The Methodist Review*, v. 66, July, 1917, p. 395-406.
THE GANG OF SIX, MECS Publishing House, Nashville, Tenn. & Dallas, Tex., 1906. (147 p.)
"The Lion Gospel," *The Methodist Review*, v. 65, April, 1916, p. 269-281.
ed., *The Methodist Review*, v. 65-57, MECS Publishing House, Nashville, Tenn., Jan. 1916-July, 1918. (Previously called, *The Methodist Quarterly Review* and *The Methodist Review Quarterly*.)
"The Open Cabinet," *The Methodist Quarterly Review*, v. 79, April, 1930, p. 195-200.
"The Pastoral Epistles," *The Methodist Review*, v. 65, Oct. 1916, p. 654-669.
"The Star of the Bab," *The Methodist Review*, v. 65, April, 1916, p. 211-221.
THE SYMBOL OF METHODISM, MECS Publishing House, Nashville & Dallas, 1907. (249 p.)
"The Values of Mysticism," *The Methodist Quarterly Review*, v. 77, April, 1928, p. 193-204.
"Theology and Experience," *The Methodist Quarterly Review*, v. 78, April, 1929, p. 192-199.

Dudley, F.J., 100 YEARS HISTORY OF ST. LUKE M.E. CHURCH, SOUTH (Columbus, Ga.), Columbus Office Supply Company, 1929. (150 p.)

Dunlap, Rev. W. C., LIFE OF S. MILLER WILLIS, Constitution Publishing Co., 1892. (293 p.) (Includes writings of Rev. R. W. Bigham, Rev. C. C. Carey, Rev. M.D. Smith, Rev. T.B. Willis of Fla. Conf., Rev. John Ivey, etc.)

Dunwoody, Rev. James, REMINISCENCES AND SERMONS, J.W. Burke & Co., printers and binders, Macon, Ga., 1872. (123 p.)

Duren, William Larkin, (c.1930) — 3 items — Ga. Typescripts of 3 books by Duren, Methodist minister of the North Ga. Conference, on Francis Asbury, Methodism, etc. Sp Cl Woodruff
CHARLES BETTS GALLOWAY, Emory University, Atlanta, Ga. (Banner Press), 1932. (331 p.)
FRANCIS ASBURY, The Macmillian Co., New York, 1928. (264 p.)
THE TOP SERGEANT OF THE PIONEERS, Emory Univ., Ga., Banner Press, 1930.

(Jesse Lee biog.) (191 p.)
THE TRAIL OF THE CIRCUIT RIDER, Chalmers Printing House, New Orleans, 1936. (425 p.) (Ga. Ref. — 18f, 44, 173).

Durham, Plato Tracy, (1898-1919) — 8 pieces — Ga. Methodist minister who served as dean of Emory University's Candler School of Theology. Sp Cl Woodruff
"Address," found in the "Spelman Messenger" published by Spelman College, Atlanta, Ga., (qtrly), April, 1930. (p. 93).
"Lee The American," *The Emory Univ. Quarterly Review,* v9, n4, Dec. 1953, p. 241-249.

Durrence, George T., HISTORY OF CLAXTON 1ST UNITED METHODIST CHURCH, 1884-1976. (112 p.)

Eakes, R.F., ed., YEAR-BOOK AND MINUTES OF THE 46TH SESSION OF THE NORTH GEORGIA CONFERENCE, MECS, HELD IN 1ST CHURCH, CARROLLTON, GA., NOV. 20-25, 1912, Atlanta, Ga. (87 m.p.)
YEAR-BOOK AND MINUTES OF THE 47TH SESSION OF THE NORTH GEORGIA CONFERENCE, MECS, HELD IN 1ST CHURCH, ELBERTON, GA., NOV. 20-24, 1913, Atlanta, Ga. (82 m.p.)
YEAR-BOOK AND MINUTES OF THE 48TH SESSION OF THE NORTH GEORGIA CONFERENCE, MECS, HELD IN MARIETTA, GA., NOV. 18-23, 1914, Atlanta, Ga. (94 m.p.).
YEAR-BOOK AND MINUTES OF THE 49TH SESSION OF THE NORTH GEORGIA CONFERENCE, MECS, HELD IN ROME, GA., NOV. 10-15, 1915, Atlanta, Ga. (96 m.p.).
YEAR-BOOK AND MINUTES OF THE 50TH SESSION OF THE NORTH GEORGIA CONFERENCE, MECS, HELD AT GRIFFIN, GA., NOV. 22-27, 1916. (97 m.p.).
YEAR-BOOK AND MINUTES OF THE 51ST SESSION OF THE NORTH GEORGIA CONFERENCE, MECS, HELD AT LAGRANGE, GA., NOV. 7-12, 1917, Atlanta, Ga. (99 m.p.).
YEAR-BOOK AND MINUTES OF THE 52ND SESSION OF THE NORTH GEORGIA CONFERENCE, MECS, HELD AT WESLEY MEMORIAL CHURCH, ATLANTA, GA., NOV. 13-18, 1918, Atlanta, Ga. (90 m.p.).

Edwards, Kate F., "A College Girl in Wartime," *Georgia Review,* 1, Summer, 1947, p. 198-206. (abt. Wesleyan College).

Edwards, Lawrence, "Augustus Baldwin Longstreet: A Study In Contrasts, The Turn Out, Inaugural Address," *The Wesleyan Quarterly Review,* Vol. 1, No. 2, May, 1964. p. 75-92.

Edward, Maldwyn, SON OF SAMUEL, Epworth Press, London, 1961. (Biography of Charles Wesley) (134 p.) (Ga. Ref. — 24, 35, 38, 49, 53, 54, 62).

Edwards, R. L., Letter dated 10-15-1820, found in *The Methodist Magazine,*

(Soule & Mason, eds.), Vol. 4, 1821, p. 36-37.

Elliot, Rev. Charles, HISTORY OF THE GREAT SECESSION FROM THE M.E. CHURCH IN THE YEAR 1845, Swormstedt & Poe, Cincinnati, 1855. (1143 p.) (Ga. Ref. — 190, 191, 75, 224, 226, 420, 954, 955, 956).

Ellison, W. H., EVIDENCES OF THE AUTHENTICITY OF THE HOLY SCRIPTURES, Sorin & Ball, Philadelphia, Pa., 1848. (108 p.)

(Emory) "Emory Portraits II: Four Figures of the College Campus," THE EMORY UNIVERSITY QUARTERLY, 4, March, 1948, p. 40-54. (re Ignatius Few, Wm. Sassnett, A.B. Longstreet).

Emory, H. C., ed., YEAR BOOK AND MINUTES OF THE NORTH GEORGIA CONFERENCE, MECS, HELD AT WESLEY MEMORIAL CHURCH, ATLANTA, GA., Nov. 10-15, 1920, Emory University, Ga. (152 p.)
YEAR BOOK AND MINUTES OF THE 55TH SESSION OF THE NORTH GEORGIA CONFERENCE, MECS, HELD AT ST. JOHN CHURCH, AUGUSTA, GA., Nov. 9-14, 1921, Emory University, Ga. (148 p.)
YEAR BOOK AND MINUTES OF THE 56TH SESSION OF THE NORTH GEORGIA CONFERENCE, MECS, WESLEY MEMORIAL CHURCH, ATLANTA, GA., Nov. 8-13, 1922, P.O. Box 327, Atlanta, Ga. (157 p.)
YEAR BOOK AND MINUTES OF THE 57TH SESSION OF THE NORTH GEORGIA CONFERENCE, MECS, WESLEY MEMORIAL CHURCH, ATLANTA, GA., Nov. 21-26, 1923, The A.J. Showalter Co., Dalton, Ga. (143 p.)
YEAR BOOK AND MINUTES OF THE 58TH SESSION OF THE NORTH GEORGIA CONFERENCE, MECS, WESLEY MEMORIAL CHURCH, ATLANTA, Nov. 19-24, 1924. (150 p.)
YEAR BOOK AND MINUTES OF THE 59TH SESSION OF THE NORTH GEORGIA CONFERENCE, MECS, 1ST CHURCH, GRIFFIN, GA., Nov. 18-23, 1925, Lyon-Young Printing Co., Atlanta, Ga. (152 p.)
YEAR BOOK AND MINUTES OF THE 60TH SESSION OF THE NORTH GEORGIA CONFERENCE, MECS, WESLEY MEMORIAL CHURCH, ATLANTA, GA., Nov. 10-15, 1926. (156 p.)

Emory, J. and Waugh, B. (eds)., THE METHODIST MAGAZINE & QUARTERLY REVIEW, (New Series) (old Vol. 12 is new Vol. 1), J. Collord, New York, 1830 (periodical).

Emory University, Atlanta. Library — 1784 — open — Ga. Ga. Methodist Church records collections. Includes recording steward's book for the quarterly conference meeting of Newton Circuit, with minutes for Oxford, Conyers, West Newton, and Yellow River Circuits for various dates, 1855, 1878. Also includes recording steward's book for the quarterly conference meetings of Oxford Circuit, 1866-1878; the first few pages include the minutes of the East Newton Circuit. Sp Cl Woodruff

English, Thomas H., EMORY UNIVERSITY 1915-1965, Emory Univ., Atlanta, Ga., 1966. (269 p.)

Estes, David E., "Emory's Nat G. Long Collection, 1900-1981," *Wesleyan Christian Advocate,* Vol. 46, No. 3, July 22, 1981, p. 9.

Estes, Lud H., (ed.), JOURNAL OF THE UNITING CONFERENCES OF THE METHODIST EPISCOPAL CHURCH, METHODIST EPISCOPAL CHURCH, SOUTH AND THE METHODIST PROTESTANT CHURCH, 1939, The Methodist Publishing Houses, Whitmore & Smith, Nashville, 1939. (980 p.) Ga. Ref. — 44, 171, 178.

Etheridge, J. W., THE LIFE OF THE REV. THOMAS COKE, D.C.L., London, John Mason, 1860. (446 p.)

Ethridge, Willie Snow. STRANGE FIRES. Vanguard Press, Inc., New York. 1971. (254 p.)

Evans, J. E., "A Short Method With High Churchmen," Southern Methodist Publishing House, Nashville, Tenn., 1870. (88 p.)
DD., "The Impeccability of Jesus Christ," found in *The Quarterly Review of the MECS,* (J.W. Hinton, ed.), Vol. 1, 1879, p. 613-623.

Evans, Rev. Josiah, "State of Religion In East Florida," (letter from Tallahassee, 4-4-1825) found in *The Methodist Magazine,* (Soule & Mason, eds.), Vol. 8, 1825, p. 286-287. A second letter, dated 4-8-1826, on similar subject found in same publication, Vol. 9, 1826, p. 272-273. A third letter, written 10-18-1826 concerning the Tallahassee Mission, found in same publication, Vol. 10, 1827, p. 36-37. A fourth letter on the same subject, dated 11-28-1827, found in same publication, Vol. 11, 1828, p. 78.

Evans, Rev. R. F., CHRISTIANITY: THE SECOND BLESSING, J.W. Burke & Co., Book and Job Printers, Macon, Ga., 1891. (67 p.)

Fair, H. L., SOUTHERN METHODISTS ON EDUCATION & RACE, 1900-1920, University Microfilms, Ann Arbor, Mich., 1972 (532 p.) (thesis)

Farish, Hunter Dickinson, THE CIRCUIT RIDER DISMOUNTS (A Social History of Southern Methodism 1865-1900), The Deitz Press, Richmond, 1938. (400 p.)

Felton, William Harrell. (1823-1909). Doctor, Methodist minister (1874-1880), member of Ga. Legislature (1884-90). Resident of Cartersville, Ga. Volumnious documents on wife, Rebecca Latimer Felton (1835-1930), 1st U.S. woman Senator, 1922, writer, speaker, educator, pioneer in Temperance movements, advocate of Women's Suffrage, penal reform, important figure in Ga. politics. Collection includes letters, sermons, speeches, etc. See: Talmage, John E., REBECCA LATIMER FORTSON: NINE STORMY DECADES, Athens, Univ. of Ga. Press, 1960. Sp. Cl. Univ. Ga.

Few, Ignatius Alphonso, "Reminiscences of the Olden Time," *Methodist Quarterly Review,* (W.P. Harrison, ed.), Vol. 8, No. 1, April, 1890, p. 3-24.

First AME Church, "The Heritage of the Past Is The Seed that Brings Forth The Harvest of the Future, 1874-1969" (pamphlet). (7 p.) Ga. Room

First Methodist Church, Athens, Ga. (Materials in the Ga. Room, Univ. of Ga.) Leader's Report, 1962-63, (25 p.) Directory, 1953, publ by Men's Club, (118 p.) Directory, 1955, Speering Printing Co., Athens, (87 p.) Directory, 1968, Pictoral Directory of America, St. Louis. Statement of Financial Condition, 7-1-1900. Ga. Room

First Methodist Church, Brunswick, Ga., "Church Directory," 1916. (24 p.) Ga. Room

Firth, Raymond H., THE LIFE OF ANDREW SLEDD, (thesis) Emory Univ., Atlanta, Ga., 1940. (44 p.)

Fitchett, Rev. W. H., WESLEY AND HIS CENTURY, Abingdon Press, New York and Cincinnati, 1917. (521 p.) (Ga. Ref. — 70, 74, 82, 85, 92-117, 127, 161, 163, 165, 171, 186, 321, 442, 444, 452.)

Fitzgerald, Oscar Penn, "A Good Book, But Obsolete," *Methodist Quarterly Review,* (W.P. Harridon, ed.), Vol. 13, No. 1, Oct. 1892, p. 62-77.
"Bishop Atticus Greene Haygood, DD, LL.D," *The Methodist Review,* (J.J. Tigert, ed.), Vol. 20, No. 2, May-June, 1896, p. 163-174.
"Bishop Hubbard Hinde Kavanaugh," *The Methodist Review,* (J.J. Tigert, ed.), Vol. 18, No. 2, May-June, 1895, p. 179-192.
"Bishop Pierce In California," *Methodist Quarterly Review,* (W.P. Harrison, ed.), Vol. 6, No. 1, April, 1889, p. 108-117.
"California Life Sketches," *The Home Circle,* v.3., MECS Publishing House, Nashville, Tenn., p. 201-203; 281-283; 321-323. (Huston, L.D., ed.). 1857.
CALIFORNIA SKETCHES, MECS Publishing House, Nashville, Tenn., (1st ed.), 1879. (336 p.)
CALIFORNIA SKETCHES, Southern Methodist Publishing House, Nashville, Tenn., 1881. (288 p.)
CALIFORNIA SKETCHES, MECS Publishing House, Nashville, Tenn., 1894. (336 p.)
CALIFORNIA SKETCHES, MECS Publishing House, Nashville, Tenn., 1903. (336 p.)
CENTENARY CAMEOS, 1784-1884, Southern Methodist Publishing House, Nashville, 1885. (Biographical sketches) (352 p.)
CHRISTIAN GROWTH, MECS Publishing House, Nashville, Tenn., 1882. (120 p.)
DR. T. O. SUMMERS—A LIFE STUDY, Southern Methodist Publishing House, Nashville, Tenn., 1884. (350 p.)
DR. SUMMERS: A LIFE STUDY, Southern Methodist Publishing House, Nashville, Tenn., 1885. (352 p.)

D.D., Dr. Summers: A Life Study, Southern Methodist Publishing House, Nashville, Tenn., 1886. (378 p.)

Fifty Years: Observations, Opinions, Experiences, Publishing House of the MECS, Nashville & Dallas, 1908. (253 p.)

General Conference Daily Advocate, Southern Methodist Publishing House, Nashville, Tenn., 1882.

Glimpses of Truth, Southern Methodist Publishing House, Nashville, Tenn., 1883. (288 p.)

John B. McFerrin, MECS Publishing House, Nashville, Tenn., 1888. (448 p.)

John B. McFerrin, MECS Publishing House, Nashville, Tenn., 1889. (448 p.)

"Joshua Soule," *The Methodist Quarterly Review*, (J.J. Tigert, ed.), v. 54, July 1905, p. 525-528.

Judge Longstreet, MECS Publishing House, Nashville, Tenn., 1891. (318 p.)

"McTyeire As An Editor," *The Methodist Quarterly Review*, (J.J. Tigert, ed.), v. 53, July, 1904, p. 419-424.

"Spanish California," *The Methodist Review*, (J.J. Tigert, ed.), Vol. 25, No. 3, May-June, 1899, p. 389-392.

Sunset Views, MECS Publishing House, Nashville & Dallas, 1900. (343 p.)

The Class Meeting, Southern Methodist Publishing House, Nashville, Tenn., 1880. (104 p.)

"The Credentials of the Preacher," *The Methodist Review Quarterly*, (Gross Alexander, ed.), v. 60, July, 1911, p. 431-436.

"The Educated Woman of Today," *The Methodist Review*, (J.J. Tigert, ed.), Vol. 21, No. 2, Nov.-Dec. 1896, p. 191-203.

The Epworth Book, Southwestern Pub-House, Nashville, Tenn., 1893. (318 p.)

"Tributes From Other Colleagues of Bishop Keener," *The Methodist Quarterly Review*, (J.J. Tigert, ed.), v. 55, April, 1906, p. 233-244.

Upper Room Meditations, MECS Publishing House, Nashville & Dallas, 1902. (317 p.)

"William McKendree," *The Methodist Quarterly Review*, (J.J. Tigert, ed.), v. 54, April, 1905, p. 328-331.

Fitzgerald, O. P., and Galloway, C.B., Eminent Methodists, MECS Publishing House, Nashville, Tenn., 1897. (375 p.)

Eminent Methodists, M.E. Church, South Publishing House, Nashville, 1898. (Biographical sketches) (375 p.)

Flanders, Bertram Holland, Early Georgia Magazines, The Univ. of Ga. Press, Athens, 1944. (289 p.)

Flanigan, J. C., Gwinnett Churches, pvt. pt., 1911. (388 p.) Ga. Room

Fleming, Neal Bond, "The North Georgia Conference Young People's Assembly—A Study of Trends from 1929-1936." (Thesis, 1936, Emory Univ.) (173 p.)

Flint, Charles Wesley, CHARLES WESLEY & HIS COLLEAGUES, Public Affairs Press, Washington, D.C., 1957. (221 p.) (Ga. Ref. — 28, 31, 42)

Flood, Theodore L. & Hamilton, John W., LIVES OF METHODIST BISHOPS, Phillips & Hunt, New York, 1882. (789 p.)

Flournoy, Rev. Robert, "State of Religion on the Savannah District," (letter dated 9-7-1825), found in *The Methodist Magazine,* (Soule & Mason, eds.), Vol. 8, 1825, p. 443.

Floyd, Arva Corbert, (c.1930-1970) — 11 boxes — Ga. — Japan. Methodist missionary to Japan for 4 years, in 1934 becoming professor of Christian Missions and world religions at the Candler School of Theology at Emory. He edited "The Diary of Young J. Allen." Sp Cl Woodruff
"China and The Open Door Policy," *The Emory Univ. Quarterly Review,* v5, n4, Dec. 1949, p. 240-249.
THE HISTORY OF CHRISTIANITY IN JAPAN, (thesis), Emory Univ., Atlanta, Ga., 1924. (45 p.)
THE RISE OF THE YOUNGER CHURCHES OVERSEAS: GOAL OF THE MISSIONARY PROCESS, unpublished.
WHITE MAN—YELLOW MAN, Abingdon Press, 1946, Nashville, Tenn. (207 p.)
"Will Japan Crack," *Atlanta Journal Sunday Magazine,* (Sept. 26, 1943).

Fowler, James W., "Agenda Toward a New Coalition," *Engage/Social Action,* Vol. 1, No. 5, June, 1973, p. 45-63.
"Alienation as a Human Experience," in FROM ALIENATION TO AT-ONENESS, Francis Eigo, O.S.A., ed., Proceedings of the 1975 Theological Institute, Villanova Univ., Villanova Univ. Press, 1977, p. 1-18.
Book Reviews found in the following Journals and Periodicals: *Religion in Life, Methodist History, Catalyst, Christian Century, Religious Media Today.*
FAITH AND HUMAN DEVELOPMENT, Harper & Row, New York, 1980.
"Faith and the Structuring of Meaning," in TOWARD MORAL AND RELIGIOUS MATURITY, Fowler, Vergote, et al., Silver Burdett Co., Morristown, N.J., 1980.
"Faith Development Theory and the Aims of Religious Socialization," in EMERGING ISSUES IN RELIGIOUS EDUCATION, G. Durka and A. Smith, eds., Paulist Press, New York, 1976, p. 187-211.
FAITH, LIBERATION AND HUMAN DEVELOPMENT, being the Thirkield Jones Lectures, Gammon Theological Seminary, Published in *Foundations,* Vol. LXXIX, Spring, 1974.
"Forward" to Carlyle Marney, THE RECOVERY OF THE PERSON, (2nd ed.), Abingdon Press, Nashville, Tenn., 1979.
"Future Christians and Church Education," in HOPE FOR THE CHURCH, J. Moltmann, et al., Abingdon Press, Nashville, Tenn., 1979, p. 93-111.
"H. Richard Niebuhr as Philosopher," *The Journal of Religion,* Vol. 57, No. 3, July, 1977, p. 307-313.
LIFE MAPS: CONVERSATIONS ON THE JOURNEY OF FAITH, (with Sam Keen), Word Books, Waco, Texas, 1978.

"Moral Stages and the Development of Faith," in KOHLBERG AND MORAL EDUCATION: BASIC ISSUES IN PHILOSOPHY, PSYCHOLOGY, RELIGION, AND EDUCATION, Brenda Munsell, ed., Religious Education Press, Notre Dame, Indiana, 1980.

"Perspectives on the Family From the Standpoint of Faith Development Theory," *Perkins Journal,* Vol. XXXIII, Fall, 1979, p. 1-19.

"Psychological Perspectives on the Faith Development of Children," in M. Sawicki and B. Marthaler, eds., CATHCHESIS: REALITIES AND VISIONS, United States Catholic Conference, Washington, D.C., 1977, p. 72-82.

"Stage Six and the Kingdom of God," in *Religious Education,* Vol. 75, No. 3, May-June, 1980, p. 231-248.

"Stages in Faith: The Structural Development Approach," in VALUES AND MORAL EDUCATION, Thomas Hennessey, ed., Paulist Press, New York, 1976, p. 173-211.

To SEE THE KINGDOM: THE THEOLOGICAL VISION OF H. RICHARD NIEBUHR, Abingdon Press, Nashville, Tenn., 1974.

"Toward a Developmental Perspective on Faith," *Religious Education,* Vol. LXIX, March-April, 1974, p. 207-219.

TOWARD MORAL AND RELIGIOUS MATURITY, (Sr. Author and Editor), Silver Burdett, Morristown, N.J., 1980.

TRAJECTORIES IN FAITH: FIVE LIFE-STUDIES, (with Robin Lovin and others), Abingdon Press, Nashville, Tenn., 1979.

Fox, Mary Walker, THE SESQUICENTENNIAL CELEBRATION, 1973, (First UMC, Decatur, Ga.). (88 p.) (softbound).

Free Methodist Church of North America, YEARBOOKS, by Free Methodist Publishing House, Winona Lake, Ind. (Candler has following yearbooks: 1958, 1960, 1961, 1963, 1964, 1965, 1966-69, 1970-73.)

Freeman, G. Ross, ed., "Meet the Circuits for 1952," Commission on Town and Country Work, South Georgia Conference, published by the Commission on Town & Country, 1952. (38 p.)

"Meet the Circuits for 1953," published by the South Georgia Town and Country Commission, 1953. (47 p.)

Fries, Adelaide L., THE MORAVIANS IN GEORGIA, 1735-1740, Edwards & Broughton, Raleigh, N.C., 1905. (252 p.)

THE MORAVIANS IN GEORGIA, 1735-1740, Genealogical Publishing Company, Baltimore, Md., 1967. (Reprint of the 1905 ed.). (252 p.)

Fruit, Charles W., ed., YEARBOOK AND MINUTES OF THE 7TH SESSION OF THE NORTH GEORGIA CONFERENCE, METHODIST CHURCH, WESLEY MEMORIAL METHODIST CHURCH, ATLANTA, GA., Nov. 20-23, 1945, Whitmore and Stone, Methodist Publishing House, Nashville, Tenn. (147 p.)

YEARBOOK AND MINUTES OF THE 8TH SESSION OF THE NORTH GEORGIA CONFERENCE, METHODIST CHURCH, WESLEY MEMORIAL METHODIST CHURCH,

ATLANTA, GA., NOV. 20-24, 1946, Stone and Pierce, Methodist Publishing House, Nashville, Tenn. (175 p.)

YEARBOOK AND MINUTES OF THE 9TH SESSION OF THE NORTH GEORGIA CONFERENCE, METHODIST CHURCH, WESLEY MEMORIAL CHURCH, ATLANTA, GA., JULY 9-13, 1947, Stone and Pierce, Methodist Publishing House, Nashville, Tenn. (185 p.)

YEARBOOK AND MINUTES OF THE 10TH SESSION OF THE NORTH GEORGIA CONFERENCE, METHODIST CHURCH, WESLEY MEMORIAL METHODIST CHURCH, ATLANTA, GA., JULY 14-18, 1948, Parthenon Press, Nashville, Tenn. (181 p.)

YEARBOOK AND MINUTES OF THE 11TH SESSION OF THE NORTH GEORGIA CONFERENCE, METHODIST CHURCH, WESLEY MEMORIAL METHODIST CHURCH, ATLANTA, GA., JUNE 21-24, 1949, Parthenon Press, Nashville, Tenn. (179 p.)

YEARBOOK AND MINUTES OF THE 12TH SESSION OF THE NORTH GEORGIA CONFERENCE, METHODIST CHURCH, WESLEY MEMORIAL METHODIST CHURCH, ATLANTA, GA., JUNE 20-23, 1950, Parthenon Press, Nashville, Tenn. (171 p.)

YEARBOOK AND MINUTES OF THE 13TH SESSION OF THE NORTH GEORGIA CONFERENCE, METHODIST CHURCH, WESLEY MEMORIAL METHODIST CHURCH, ATLANTA, GA., JUNE 26-30, 1951, Scanland's Inc., Printers, Tampa, Fla. (132 p.)

Ft. Valley Methodist Church, MINUTES, 1847-1885, (xerox of the original) (509 p.) Ga. Archives

Fulton, John, LETTERS ON CHRISTIAN UNITY, ADDRESSED TO A METHODIST MINISTER, Pott & Amery, Cooper Union, New York, 1869. (American Church Press Co., printers) (95 p.) (*Minister is Rev. J.E. Evans).

Funston, John Wesley, THE WESLEYS IN PICTURE AND STORY, Kable Bros. Co., Mt. Morris, Ill., 1939. (137 p.)

Gaines, Wesley J., AFRICAN METHODISM IN THE SOUTH, Franklin Publishing House, Atlanta, Ga., 1890. (305 p.)
AFRICAN METHODISM IN THE SOUTH, Afro-American Press, Chicago, 1969. (305 p.)

Galloway, Charles Betts, (1879-1910) — 3 folders — Ga. — Tenn. — La. — Miss. Prominent Methodist Bishop (MECS) from Miss. who was closely associated with Bishop Warren Candler who wrote his biography. Papers are mainly correspondence. Sp Cl Woodruff

Gamble, Thomas, Bethesda, AN HISTORICAL SKETCH OF WHITEFIELD'S HOUSE OF MERCY IN GEORGIA AND OF THE UNION SOCIETY, HIS ASSOCIATE AND SUCCESSOR IN PHILANTROPHY, Morning News Print, Savannah, Ga., 1902. (150 p.)

Gamble, Thomas, THE LOVE STORIES OF JOHN AND CHARLES WESLEY, Review Publishing & Printing Co., Savannah, Ga., 1927. (68 p.)

Garber, Paul Neff, THE METHODISTS ARE ONE PEOPLE, Cokesbury Press, Nashville, 1939. (144 p.) Ga. Ref. — 44, 62.

Garbutt, Mrs. J. William, REV. W.A. DODGE AS WE KNEW HIM, Franklin Printing Co., Atlanta, 1906. (165 p.)

Gardner, E. Clinton, "A Critique of Christocentric Models of Ethical Analysis," *Religion in Life*, XXXIX:2 (Summer, 1970), p. 205-220.
"Abortion From the Perspective of Responsibility," *Perkins Journal*, XXX:3 (Spring, 1977), p. 10-28.
"Altruism in Classical Hinduism and Christianity," *The Journal of Bible and Religion*, XXII:3 (July, 1945), p. 172-177. (In Same Publication): "Reply to Professor Piper," p. 184.
BIBLICAL FAITH AND SOCIAL ETHICS, Harper & Row, 1960. Portuguese Ed. printed by the Association of Evangelical Theological Seminaries, Sao Paulo, 1965.
"Christian Bases of Brotherhood," *Christian Action*, XVIII:1 (January, 1963), p. 12-35.
Contributions made to the following books: DICTIONARY OF CHRISTIAN ETHICS, 1967; STORM OVER ETHICS, 1967; SOCIAL ETHICS: ISSUES IN ETHICS AND SOCIETY, 1968; APPALACHIA IN TRANSITION, 1970; CONTEMPORARY RELIGIOUS TRENDS, 1972; THE POPULAR CRISIS AND MORAL RESPONSIBILITY, 1973; ENCYCLOPEDIA OF WORLD METHODISM, 1974; THE AMERICAN SOCIETY OF CHRISTIAN ETHICS: SELECTED PAPERS, SIXTEENTH ANNUAL MEETING, 1975
"Ethical Issues in the Testing of New Drugs," *Journal of Drug Issues*, 7:3, (Summer, 1977), p. 275-286.
"Foreword," in DEATH BY DECISION, by Jerry Wilson, Westminster Press, 1975, p. 9-12.
"Horace Bushnell's Concept of Response," *Religion In Life*, XXVII:1 (Winter, 1957-58), p. 119-131.
"Horace Bushnell's Doctrine of Depravity," *Theology Today*, XII:1 (April, 1955), p. 10-26.
"Interprofessional Seminar on the Role of the Professions—A Report," *Theological Education*, VIII:1 (Autumn, 1971), p. 35-45.
"Love and Justice," *Theology Today*, XIV:2 (July, 1957) p. 212-222.
"Man's Responsibility for God's Creation," *Adult Student*, XXII:2 (February, 1963), p. 24-34.
"Narcotics and Other Addicting Drugs," *Concern*, IV:11 (June 1, 1962), p. 9-12.
"Paying the Price for Peace," *Christian Action*, XVIII:1 (January, 1963), p. 29-44.
"Religion and the Political Order, 1960," YEARBOOK OF THE AMERICAN SOCIETY OF CHRISTIAN SOCIAL ETHICS, 1960-61, p. 22-24.
"Religious Pluralism and the Churches," *Interpretation*, XIX:4, October, 1965, p. 428-434.
"Responsibility and Moral Direction in the Ethics of H. Richard Niebuhr," *Encounter*, 40:2, (Spring, 1979), p. 143-168.
"Rethinking the Protestant Doctrine of Vocation," *Religion In Life*, XXV:3

(Summer, 1956), p. 366-377.

"Sexuality and Marriage," *Junction*, 8:3 (Spring, 1973), p. 16-20.

THE CHURCH AS A PROPHETIC COMMUNITY, The Westminster Press, Philadelphia, 1967. (254 p.)

"The Role of Law and Moral Principles in Christians Ethics," *Religion in Life*, XVIII:2 (Spring, 1959), p. 236-247.

"The Sacredness of All Human Life," *engage/social action*, 2:2 (February, 1974), p. 15-28.

Garrison, Webb Black (c 1958-1975) — 10 boxes — Ga. — N.C. — Ill. Materials relating to his writing as a Methodist minister and author. Collection includes manuscript and correspondence for his book STRANGELY WARM. Sp Cl Woodruff

A GUIDE TO READING THE ENTIRE BIBLE IN ONE YEAR, Bobbs-Merrill, Indianapolis, 1963. (320 p.)

"Art of Public Bible Reading," *Christianity Today*, 10, Jan. 21, 1966, p. 11-12.

"Bible Lessons For Youth" *The Teacher's Quarterly*, 1950-55, Methodist Publishing House, Cincinnati, Ohio. Published Quarterly: Sunday School Material. (Garrison was writer of materials). Ga. Room

CODFISH, CATS AND CIVILIZATION (uv).

CREATIVE IMAGINATION IN PREACHING, Abingdon Press, New York, Nashville, 1960. (175 p.)

"Georgia In Wesley's Aldersgate Experience," *Wesleyan Christian Advocate*, Vol. 145, No. 49, June 17, 1981, p. 3.

GIVING WINGS TO A WARM HEART, (Com. on Promotion & Cultivation of the Methodist Church), Evanston, Ill., 1968. (118 p.)

GUIDE FOR YOUTH BIBLICAL STUDIES, Graded Press, Nashville, Tenn., 1972. (31 p.)

HOW IT STARTED, Abington, Nashville, Tenn., 1972. (237 p.)

IMPROVE YOUR CHURCH BULLETINS, Fleming H. Revell, Westwood, N.J., 1957. (127 p.)

"Indomitable Baron Yun: An Emory Immortal," *The Emory Univ. Quarterly Review*, v8, n4, Dec. 1952, p. 208-216.

"Joy of Memorizing Scripture," *Christianity Today*, 11, Nov. 25, 1966, p. 12-13.

JOURNEY INTO LIGHT, (uv).

LAUGHTER IN THE BIBLE, Bethany Press, St. Louis, 1960. (160 p.)

"Romans For Three Cents," *Christianity Today*, 9, Sept. 24, 1965, p. 8-9.

SERMON SEEDS FROM THE GOSPELS, Fleming H. Revell, Westwood, N.J., 1958. (126 p.)

STRANGE FACTS ABOUT DEATH, Abingdon, Nashville, Tenn., 1978. (158 p.)

STRANGE FACTS ABOUT THE BIBLE, Abingdon Press, Nashville, Tenn., 1968. (304 p.)

STRANGELY WARM, (Text for Youth) Graded Press, 1971, Nashville, Tenn. (96 p.)

TEN PATHS TO PEACE AND POWER, Abingdon Press, Nashville, New York, 1967. (174 p.)

THE IGNORANCE BOOK, William Morrow & Co., Inc., New York, 1971. (250 p.)

The Man Who Found Out Why, (uv)
The Preacher and His Audience, Fleming H. Revell Company, Westwood, N.J., 1954. (285 p.)
The Sacramental Forms of the Methodist Church, (thesis), Emory Univ., Atlanta, Ga., 1949. (135 p.)
What's In A Word, Abingdon Press, New York, 1965. (351 p.)
Why You Say It, Abingdon Press, New York, Nashville, 1955. (448 p.)
Women In The Life Of Jesus, Bobbs-Merrill Co., Indianapolis, 1962. (192 p.)
Wonders of Earth, (uv).
Wonders of Man, (uv).
Wonders of Science, Sheed and Ward, 1956. (135 p.)

Gassaway, William, "Letter regarding St. Augustine and Alachua Mission," (East Florida), dated, 6-17-1828, found in *The Methodist Magazine,* (Soule & Mason, eds.), Vol. 11, 1828, p. 353.

Gay, Mary A. H., The Pastor's Story, and Other Pieces, 10th ed., Southern Methodist Publishing House, Nashville, Tenn. (1879 or 1880). (263 p.)

George, Enoch, "Address to the Managers of the Missionary Society of the Methodist Episcopal Church," found in *The Methodist Magazine,* Vol. 4, 1821, p. 276-278. (Soule & Mason, eds.).
"Memoir of Late Bishop George," (compiled from original manuscript left by himself and never before published), found in *The Methodist Magazine and Quarterly Review,* (Emory & Waugh, eds.), Vol. 1, 1830, pp. 5-16; 128-142; 248-259; 412-435.
"2 Letters to Rev. Daniel Hitt," dated 5-26-1803 and 5-30-1803, found in *Quarterly Review of the MECS,* D.S. Doggett, ed., July, 1860, p. 475. Additional (3) letters from George to Hitt are found in the same publication, Jan. 1861, p. 156-57; and Jan. 1861, p. 160. Letter dates are 12-16-1803; 12-19-1804; and 2-25-1805.

Georgia Conference, Athens Dist., Covington Circuit. Minutes of qtr. meetings, 1836-52. Entry varies: Minutes for 1838-42 are Newton Circuit. Minutes sometimes include Monroe or Oxford Charges. Minutes of Newton Circuit sometimes include Walton or Monroe Charges. Sp. Cl. Candler
Athens Dist., Suwanne Circuit Minutes of the qtr. meeting, 1831-33. Sp Cl Candler
(MECS), Augusta District, Louisville Circuit. Minutes 1836-64; Misc. papers. (19 items) Sp Cl Candler
Augusta District, Louisville Cir. Qtr. Conf. Minutes, 1836-64. Entry varies: Lacking minutes for 3rd qtr. 1851 & 2nd qtr. 1852. 1855—Louisville & Richmond Cir. Min. for 1861-64 sometimes include Jefferson Mission and/or Concord Mission. Misc. papers. (19 items) Sp Cl Candler
Board of Finance. Steward's Report 1849-57. Sp Cl Candler
Centenary Subscription Record Book, 1841?; Misc. Correspondence. (23 items) Sp Cl Candler

Cherokee District, Gainesville Cir. Minutes of qtr. conf. 1834-35. (bound with this is qtr. conf. meetings of the Lawrenceville Cir., 1836-53). Sp Cl Candler
Cherokee Dist, Lawrenceville Cir. Minutes of qtr. meeting, 1836-53. Entry varies: 1836—1st qtr. report is for Gwinnett Cir. bound with Gainesville Cir. Min. 1834-35. Sp Cl Candler
Minutes of Annual Conference 1831-45. (Conf. met in Jan. & Dec. of 1836 and did not meet in 1840). Sp Cl Candler
(MECS)—Minutes of the Annual Conference 1846-66. (Annual Conf. met in Jan. & Dec. of 1846, 1851. Did not meet in 1848). Sp Cl Candler
(MECS), MINUTES OF THE GEORGIA ANNUAL CONFERENCE OF THE MECS, HELD AT ATLANTA, GA., DEC. 13-20, 1854, Printed by Benjamin F. Griffin, Macon, Ga., 1855. (38 p.)
(MECS), MINUTES OF THE GEORGIA ANNUAL CONFERENCE OF THE MECS HELD AT LAGRANGE, GA., DEC. 12-19, 1855, B.F. Griffin, printer, Macon, Ga. (40 p.)
(MECS), MINUTES OF THE GEORGIA ANNUAL CONFERENCE OF THE MECS HELD AT AMERICUS, GA., DEC. 3-12, 1856, G.P. Eddy & Co., Atlanta, Ga., 1857. 39 p.)
(MECS) MINUTES OF THE GEORGIA ANNUAL CONFERENCE OF THE MECS, HELD AT WASHINGTON, GA., DEC. 9-18, 1857, Lewis H. Andrews, Book and Job Printer, Macon, Ga., 1858. (35 p.)
(MECS), MINUTES OF THE GEORGIA ANNUAL CONFERENCE OF THE MECS, HELD AT COLUMBUS, GA., DEC. 15-23, 1858, Southern Christian Advocate Power Press, Charleston, S.C., 1859. (43 p.)
(MECS), MINUTES OF THE GEORGIA ANNUAL CONFERENCE OF THE MECS, HELD AT ROME, GA., DEC. 12-24, 1859, Lewis H. Andrews, Book and Job Printer, Macon, Ga., 1860. (40 p.)
(MECS), MINUTES OF THE GEORGIA ANNUAL CONFERENCE, HELD IN AUGUSTA, 11-28-1860 - 12-6-1860, Macon, Telegraph Steam Power Press, 1861. (31 p.)
(MECS), MINUTES OF THE GEORGIA ANNUAL CONFERENCE, HELD IN ATLANTA, GA., NOV. 27-DEC. 3, 1861; AND AT MACON, GA., NOV. 26-DEC. 4, 1862, Macon, 1963. (39 p.) CSA Bib. Willingham
(MECS), MINUTES OF THE GEORGIA ANNUAL CCNFERENCE HELD IN COLUMBUS, GA., NOV. 25-DEC. 3, 1863, Burke, Boykin & Co., Steam Book & Job Printers, Macon, Ga., 1864. (30 p.)
(MECS), MINUTES OF THE 1864 CONFERENCE HELD AT ATHENS, GA., JAN. 5-10M 1865, Macon, 1865. (24 p.) CSA Bib. Willingham
MINUTES OF THE GEORGIA CONFERENCE FOR THE YEAR 1835, Printed by State Rights' Sentinel Office, Augusta, Ga., 1835. (24 p.)
Minutes of the Georgia Conference, Central Jurisdiction. (Formerly the Atlanta & Savannah Conferences). Candler Library has 1935-55; 1957-63.
Minutes of the Georgia Conference, 1968-70. (Formerly of the Central Jurisdiction; became N. Ga. Conference in 1971).
Minutes of the Georgia Conference, Methodist Protestant Churhch, 1830-1939. Candler Library has 1872-73; 1875-77; 1890-93; 1897-1905.
(MECS)—Missionary Society Minutes, 1830-1866 (7 items). Sp Cl Candler
Missionary Society. Minutes of the Annual Meeting & Minutes of the Board of Managers 1830-36. (S. C. Conf. in 1830) (Met in Jan. & Dec. of 1836)

(Monticello Cir. Report—1 item) Sp Cl Candler
Missionary Society. Minutes of Annual Meeting & Meetings of the Board of
Managers, 1836-66. (Met twice in 1936, 1846, 1851, 1865) (1830 was S.C.
Conf.) (No minutes for 1840, 1848, 1864-4) Misc. Items. (7 items) Sp Cl
Candler
Missionary Society. Treasurer's Book 1831-35; 1840-50 (2 v) Sp Cl Candler
Steward's Report 1832-35; 1838; 1841; 1843; 1846. Sp Cl Candler
Sunday School Society. Recrds 1852-61, 1865-66. (Constitution, Minutes of
Anniversary meetings & meetings of Bd. of Managers, treasurer's report for
1868) (Also 6 misc. pieces) Sp Cl Candler
(MECS) Sunday School Society Records 1852-61; 1865-66. (7 items) Sp Cl
Candler
(MECS) Sunday School Society. Treasurer's Account Book, 1852-61. Sp Cl
Candler

Ga. Methodism, 5 Pamphlets of Camp Meetings, including the History of
Salem Campground and History of Taylor's Creek Campground. (Candler
Library)

Georgia State Sunday School Association. Correspondence (80 items). Sp Cl
Candler
Minutes of The Annual Convention of the Ga. State SS Assoc. & Executive
Committee meetings, 1874 or 1875. (Library has 1st to 24th, 1897) (80 items) Sp
Cl Candler

Georgia Woman's Christian Temperance Union, Oxford Branch. Minutes—
1883-92. Sp Cl Candler

Gerkin, Charles V., "A Religious Story Test: Some Findings with Delinquent
Boys," *Journal of Pastoral Care,* Vol. 8, No. 2.
"A Theologian's View of Cardian Resuscitation," in Hurst, Willis M., ed.,
Cardiac Resuscitation, Charles Thomas, 1960.
"Changing Dilemmas of a Maturing Pastor," *The Christian Advocate,* October 2,
1969.
"Clinical Pastral Education and Social Change," *The Journal of Pastoral Care,*
September, 1971.
CRISIS EXPERIENCE IN MODERN LIFE, Parthenon Press, Abingdon, Nashville,
Tenn., 1979. (352 p.)
"Four Steps Toward Ministerial Burn-Out," *Ministry & Mission,* Vol. 6, No. 2,
(Spring, 1981), p. 1, 8.
"Helping Parents Whose Children are 'In Trouble,' " *The Christian Advocate,*
Oct. 7, 1954.
"Interprofessional Healing and Pastoral Identity," *The St. Luke's Journal of
Theology,* The School of Theology, University of the South, Vol. XI, No. 1,
October, 1967.
"Is Pastoral Counseling a Credible Alternative in the Ministry?", *The Journal of
Pastoral Care,* Dec., 1972.

"Objectives of Clinical Pastoral Education," *Trends In Clinical Pastoral Education*, Proceedings of Seventh National Conference on Clinical Pastoral Education, 1960.

"On Becoming a Pastor," *Pastoral Psychology*, Vol. 16, No. 151, February, 1965.

"On the Boundary: The Minister as Catalyst," *Bulletin*, Columbia Theological Seminary, Vol. LIX, No. 4, December, 1966.

"On the Renewal of Ministry as Pastoral Guidance," *The Candler Review*, January, 1974.

"Pastoral Ministry Between The Times," *Journal of Pastoral Care*, Fall, 1976.

"Power and Powerlessness in Clinical Pastoral Education," *Journal of Pastoral Care*, Summer, 1980.

"Scapegoat," (Review Article), *Pastoral Psychology*, Summer, 1976.

"The Identity of the Pastoral Supervisor," THE PASTORAL SUPERVISOR AND HIS IDENTITY, Proceedings of National Conference on Clinical Pastoral Education, 1966.

"The Pastor and Parents of Delinquent Children," *Pastoral Psychology*, Vol. 6, No. 57, Oct., 1955.

"The Religious Story Test as a Tool for Evaluating Religious Growth," *Journal of Pastoral Care*, Vol. 9, No. 1.

Gilbert, Creighton, "Emory Portraits I: The 1820's and 1930's," *The Emory University Quarterly*, 3, Oct. 1947, p. 165-175. (Wm. Capers, C.F. Pierce).

Giles, Samuel H., "Three Studies on the Negro Church," *Summaries of Research Projects,* Atlanta Univ. Center, 1953, (Tillman, Nathaniel, ed.), p. 54-55.

Gill, Frederick C., CHARLES WESLEY: THE FIRST METHODIST, Abingdon Press, N.Y. & Nashville, 1964. (239 p.)
IN THE STEPS OF JOHN WESLEY, Abingdon, New York & Nashville, 1963. (240 p.) (Ga. Ref. — 91, 101, 223, 224).
ed., SELECTED LETTERS OF JOHN WESLEY, The Epworth Press, London, 1956. (244 p.) Ga. Ref. — 29, 32-39, 43-44, 148, 151, 173, 209.

Gillies, John, MEMOIRS OF THE LIFE OF THE REV. GEORGE WHITEFIELD, M.A., E and C Dilly, London, 1772. (357 p.) (Wesleyan College)

Glenn, Mr., "Letter on the Mission at St. Augustine," dated 12-29-1823, found in *The Methodist Magazine,* (Soule & Mason, eds.), Vol. 7, 1824, p. 119.

Glenn, James E., "An Effort To Make All Things According To The Pattern Shewed In The Mount," Camak & Ragland, Milledgeville, 1827. (55 p.) (Glenn was a local pastor of S.C. Conf., Abbeville Dist.) Ga. Room
"An Effort To Make All Things According To The Pattern Shewed In The Mount," Ga. Courier Office, Augusta, Ga., 1827. (46 p.)
"Moral Truth Fairly Stated," Hobby & Bunce, Augusta, Ga., 1815. (84 p.)

Glenn, Prof. J.W., "Modern Theology," found in *The Quarterly Review of the*

MECS, (J. W. Hinton, ed.), Vol. 1, 1879, p. 416-425.

"The Atomic Theory," found in *The Quarterly Review of the MECS,* (J.W. Hinton, ed.), Vol. 1, 1879, p. 45-59.

Glenn, Wilber Fisk, "A Brief Account of the Division of the M.E. Church In 1844 and the Inter Church Transactions Following that Division," Atlanta, Ga., 3-24-1920. (16 p.)

A LIFE SKETCH OF REV. AND MRS. WILBUR FISK GLENN, D.D., Foote & Davies Co., Atlanta, 1913. (116 p.)

"Who Should Educate?", *The Methodist Review,* (J.J. Tigert, ed.), May-June, 1898, p. 256-260.

Godley, Margaret, THE CENTENNIAL STORY OF TRINITY METHODIST CHURCH, MOTHER CHURCH OF SAVANNAH METHODISM, 1848-1948, Kennickell Printing Co., Savannah, Ga., 1948. (51 p.)

Gorrie, Rev. P. Douglas, THE LIVES OF EMINENT METHODIST MINISTERS, Auburn: Derby and Miller; Buffalo: Derby, Orton & Mulligan, 1853. (408 p.)

THE LIVES OF EMINENT METHODIST MINISTERS, R. Worthington, New York, 1881. (Biographical sketches) (408 p.)

Gramling, Roger M., A MINISTRY OF HOPE—A Portrait of Arthur J. Moore, The Upper Room, Nashville, Tenn., 1979. (108 p.)

Gravely, William B., GILBERT HAVEN, METHODIST ABOLITIONIST., Abingdon Press, Nashville & New York, 1973. (272 p.) Ga. Ref. — 106, 110, 169, 171, 172, 187, 188, 205, 209-210, 214, 216, 219, 221-222, 224-225, and 187, 197, 199, 208-9, 210, 219, 231-34, 237, 246.

Graves, J. R., THE GREAT IRON WHEEL: OR REPUBLICANISM BACKWARDS AND CHRISTIANITY REVERSED, Graves, Marks & Rutland, Nashville; Sheldon, Lamport & Co., New York, 1855. 7th ed. (570 p.)

THE LITTLE IRON WHEEL, South-Western Publishing House, Graves, Marks & Co., Nashville, Tenn., 1857. (321 p.)

Green, V.H.H., THE YOUNG MR. WESLEY, St. Martin's Press, New York, 1961. (342 p.) Ga. Ref. — 47, 52, 59, 100, 140, 143, 188, 190, 194, 200, 233, 235, 240, 245, 246, 247, 248, 249, 250, 251, 252, 253, 254, 256, 58, 261, 264, 265, 267, 270, 278-279, 284, 322, 323.

Greene, Reynolds W., Jr., BETWEEN AN ATOM AND A STAR, Wm. B. Erdmans Pub. Co., Grand Rapids, Mich., 1963. (89 p.)

CRUCIAL QUESTIONS WITH CHRISTIAN ANSWERS, Advocate Press, Franklin Springs, Ga., 1976. (98 p.)

LISTEN! GOD IS SPEAKING, (uv).

Greene, Walter Kirkland, MULBERRY STREET METHODIST SUNDAY SCHOOL,

J.W. Burke Co., Macon, Ga., 1925. (86 p.)

Griffin, Mrs. Sarah Lawrence, ed., *The Family Companion and Ladies' Mirror,* Vol. 1, 1841, Benjamin F. Griffin, Macon, Ga. (v 1 & 2 in Wesleyan College).

Griffin, Richard W., "The Methodist Educational Ministry, 1829-1844," *The Wesleyan Quarterly Review,* Vol. 1, No. 4, Nov. 1964, p. 187-189.
ed., *The Wesleyan Quarterly Review,* A Methodist Historical Quarterly, published at Wesleyan College, Macon, Ga., Vol. 1, No. 1, Feb. 1964—Vol. 4, Nov. 1967. (periodical).

Gunter, Doyce Walton, "Hinton Rural Life Center: A Supportive Ministry To Aid the Rural Church," (thesis), Emory Univ., Atlanta, Ga., 1976. (169 p.)

Haddal, Ingvar, JOHN WESLEY, Abingdon Press, New York & Nashville, 1961. (175 p.) (Ga. Ref. — 47, 53f, 86f.)

Haden, Thomas Henry, (1896-1946) — 37 boxes — BV's — Hapan. Missionary to Japan for the MEC,S. Collection consists of his personal diaries from 1896-1946. Sp Cl Woodruff

Hagood, Rev. L.M., THE COLORED MAN IN THE METHODIST EPISCOPAL CHURCH, Negro Universities Press, Westport, Conn. Reprint 1970 of the 1890 ed. published by Cranston & Stowe, Cincinnati. (327 p.)

Haley, Curtis B., ed., MECS, COMBINED GENERAL MINUTES & YEARBOOK FOR 1923-1924, MECS Publishing House, Nashville, Richmond, Dallas, San Francisco. (432 p.) N. Ga. — p. 248-258; S. Ga. — p. 240-248.
MECS, COMBINED GENERAL MINUTES & YEARBOOK FOR 1924-1925, MECS Publishing House, Nashville, Richmond, Dallas, San Francisco. (463 p.). N. Ga. — p. 149-162; S. Ga. — p. 260-271.
MECS, COMBINED GENERAL MINUTES & YEARBOOK FOR 1925-1926, MECS Publishing House, Nashville, Richmond, Dallas, San Francisco. (496 p.) N. Ga. — p. 242-254; S. Ga. — p. 207-218.
MECS, COMBINED GENERAL MINUTES & YEARBOOK FOR 1926-1927, MECS Publishing House, Nashville, Dallas, Richmond, San Francisco. (496 p.) N. Ga. — p. 111-126; S. Ga. — p. 228-235.
GENERAL MINUTES AND YEARBOOK FOR 1927-28, MECS Publishing House, Nashville, Richmond, Dallas, San Francisco. (528 p.) N. Ga. — p. 226-236; S. Ga. — p. 246-256.
GENERAL MINUTES AND YEARBOOK FOR 1928-29, MECS Publishing House, Nashville, Richmond, Dallas, San Francisco. (528 p.) N. Ga. — p. 142-157; S. Ga. — p. 261-271.
GENERAL MINUTES AND YEARBOOK FOR 1929-1930, MECS Publishing House, Nashville, Richmond, Dallas, San Francisco. (560 p.) N. Ga. — p. 188-197; S. Ga. — p. 248-256.
GENERAL MINUTES AND YEARBOOK FOR 1930-31, MECS Publishing House,

Nashville, Richmond, Dallas, San Francisco. (447 p.) N. Ga. — p. 154-165; S. Ga. — p. 222-230.

General Minutes and Yearbook For 1931-32, MECS Publishing House, Nashville, Richmond, Dallas, San Francisco. (439 p.) N. Ga. — p. 147-158; S. Ga. — p. 206-214.

General Minutes and Yearbook For 1932-33, MECS Publishing House, Nashville, Richmond, Dallas, San Francisco. (439 p.) N. Ga. — p. 152-161; S. Ga. — p. 213-220.

General Minutes and Yearbook For 1933-34, MECS Publishing House, Nashville, Richmond, Dallas, San Francisco. (415 p.) N. Ga. — p. 140-150; S. Ga. — p. 198-205.

General Minutes and Yearbook For 1934-35, MECS Publishing House, Nashville, Dallas, Richmond. (407 p.) N. Ga. — p. 135-146; S. Ga. — 192-199.

General Minutes and Yearbook For 1935-36, MECS Publishing House, Nashville, Dallas, Richmond. (431 p.) N. Ga. — p. 143-152; S. Ga. — p. 202-209.

General Minutes and Yearbook For 1936-37, MECS Publishing House, Nashville, Dallas, Richmond. (423 p.) N. Ga. — p. 142-151; S. Ga. — p. 201-209.

General Minutes and Yearbook For 1937-38, MECS Publishing House, Nashville, Dallas, Richmond. (431 p.) N. Ga. — p. 137-147; S. Ga. — p. 195-203.

General Minutes and Yearbook For 1938-39, MECS Publishing House, Nashville, Dallas, Richmond. (455 p.) N. Ga. — p. 143-154; S. Ga. — p. 203-210.

General Minutes and Yearbook For 1939-40, MECS Publishing House, Nashville, Dallas, Richmond. (431 p.) N. Ga. — p. 135-147; S. Ga. — p. 199-206.

Journal of the 20th General Conference of the MECS Held In Memphis, Tenn., May 5-20, 1926, MECS Publishing House, Nashville, Dallas, Richmond, San Francisco, 1926. (500 p.)

Journal of the 21st General Conference of the MECS, Held at Dallas, Texas, May 7-24, 1930, MECS Publishing House, Nashville, Dallas, Richmond, San Francisco. (570 p.)

Journal of the 22nd General Conference of the MECS Held At Jackson, Miss., April 26-May 8, 1934, MECS Publishing House, Nashville, Dallas, Richmond. (518 p.)

Journal of the 23rd General Conference of the MECS, Held At Birmingham, Ala., April 28-May 5, 1938, MECS Publishing House, Nashville, Dallas, Richmond. (419 p.)

Minutes of the Annual Conferences of the MECS, 1921, MECS Publishing House, Nashville, Dallas, Richmond. (330 p.) N. Ga. — p. 196-206; S. Ga. — p. 228-235.

Minutes of the Annual Conferences of the MECS, 1922, MECS Publishing House, Nashville, Dallas, Richmond. (351 p.) N. Ga. — p. 228-239; S. Ga. — p. 241-248.

Hamby, Jesse Barton, Jr., "Definition of the Episcopal Office In American Methodism: The Doctrinal Division of 1844," *The Wesleyan Quarterly Review,* Vol. 2, No. 2, May 1965, p. 101-112.

Hamill, Rev. Andrew, "Letter on the Asbury Mission," dated 10-12-1827, found in *The Methodist Magazine,* (Soule & Mason, eds.), Vol. 11, 1828, p. 37. A second letter, dated 7-7-1828, found in same vol., p. 355.

Hamilton, J. W., MEMORIAL OF JESSE LEE AND THE OLD ELM, James P. MaGee, Boston, 1875. (55 p.)

Hammond, Edmund Jordan, SONGS OF A PILGRIM, Atlanta, Pvt. Printing, 1968. (87 p.) (poetry volume)
THE METHODIST EPISCOPAL CHURCH IN GEORGIA, being a brief history of the two Georgia Conferences of the Methodist Episcopal Church, together with a summary of the causes of major Methodist divisions in the U.S. and of the problems confronting Methodist Union. Atlanta, Ga., 1935. (232 p.)

Hammond, Mrs. J. D., "The Building of Homes," *The Methodist Review Quarterly,* (Gross Alexander, ed.), v. 64, April, 1915, p. 315-321.

Hand, Quentin L., "AAPC Constitution Revision: A Challenge to Integrate Function and Form," *Journal of Pastoral Care,* Vol. XXX, No. 4, Dec., 1976.
"Abstinence and Responsibility," (with Jack T. Sanders), *Christian Advocate,* Vol. X, No. 18, Sept. 22, 1966.
Book Reviews found in the following Journals and Periodicals: *Journal of Pastoral Care, Contemporary Psychology.*
"*Dangerous Shortcuts in Pastoral Care,*" *Christian Advocate,* Vol. XI, No. 9, May 4, 1967.
"Pastoral Counseling as Theological Practice," *Journal of Pastoral Care,* Vol. XXXII, No. 2, June, 1978.
"Personality Changes in Groups," in THE CREATIVE ROLE OF INTERPERSONAL GROUPS IN THE CHURCH TODAY, John L. Casteel, ed., 1962.
"Programmed Instruction as an Aid to Marriage Counseling," (with Charles W. Stewart), *Journal of Pastoral Care,* Vol. XXVI, No. 3, Sept., 1972.
"Supervision and the Therapist's Marriage," (with Jane Hand and Rives Chalmers, M.D.), *Voices: the Arts and Science of Psychotherapy,* Vol. 7, No. 4, Winter, 1971-72.

Handy, James A., SCRAPS OF AFRICAN METHODIST EPISCOPAL HISTORY, AME Book Concern, Philadelphia, Pa. (authorized facsimilie) University Microfilms International, Ann Arbor, Michigan, 1979.

Harben, Tyre B., "A Lecture On Methodism In Connection With The Great Iron Wheel," Stevenson & Owen, Nashville, Tenn., 1856. (66 p.)
THE DOCTRINES OF THE BIBLE OR, A SYSTEMATIC AND CONCISE VIEW OF THE CARDINAL DOCTRINES OF CHRISTIANITY, published for the author in Nashville.

(397 p.) (reviewed in *Quarterly Review of the MECS,* D.S. Doggett, ed., July, 1860, p. 435.

Harden, William, ed., "Bethesda's Crisis in 1791: Disaster To Whitefield's House of Mercy Averted," *Georgia Historical Quarterly,* 1, June, 1917, p. 108-134.

Hardy, Charles, "Letter on the Pensacola Mission," (dated 9-11-1827), found in *The Methodist Magazine,* (Soule & Mason, eds.), Vol. 11, 1828, p. 36. A second letter found in same publication, same volume, page 159, dated 1-23-1828.

Harmon, J. A., "The Negro: Our Duty and Relation to Him," *The Methodist Quarterly Review,* v. 75, Jan. 1926, p. 56-66.

Harmon, Nolan B., "Creating Official Methodist Hymnals," *Methodist History,* v16, n4, July, 1978, p. 230-244.
"Incarnation: A Seasonal Meditation," *The Emory Univ. Quarterly Review,* v6, n4, Dec. 1950, p. 193-197.
Is It Right or Wrong, Cokesbury Press, Nashville, Tenn., 1938. (231 p.)
Ministerial Ethics and Etiquette, Rev. ed., Abingdon-Cokesbury, New York and Nashville, 1950. (215 p.)
"St. Augustine and The Problem of Evil," *The Methodist Quarterly Review,* v. 70, Oct. 1921, p. 614-622.
"The Apostles' Creed In Methodism," *The Methodist Quarterly Review,* v. 79, Jan. 1930, p. 19-34.
ed., The District Superintendent: His Office and Work in the Methodist Church, Methodist Publishing House, Nashville, Tenn., 1954. (128 p.)
ed., The Encyclopedia of World Methodism, The United Methodist Publishing House, Nashville, Tenn., 1974. (2 vols.).
The Organization of the Methodist Church; Historical Development & Present Working Structure, Abingdon-Cokesbury, Nashville, Tenn., 1948. (281 p.)
The Organization of The Methodist Church, The Methodist Publishing House, Nashville, Tenn., 1953. (288 p.)
The Organization of The Methodist Church, The Methodist Publishing House, Nashville, Tenn., 1962. (287 p.)
ed., The Pastor's Ideal Funeral Manual, Abingdon-Cokesbury Press, New York & Nashville, 1942. (224 p.)
The Rites & Ritual of Episcopal Methodism, with Particular Reference to the Rituals of the Methodist Episcopal Church and Methodist Episcopal Church, South. Nashville, Tenn., Dallas, Etc., Publishing House of M.E. Church, S., 1926. (417 p.)
Understanding The Methodist Church, (rev. ed.), Methodist Publishing House, Nashville, 1961. (1955 ed. pub. by Pierce & Washabaugh) (190 p.)
Understanding The Methodist Church, Abingdon Press, Nashville, Tenn., 1974. (176 p.)
Understanding The Methodist Church, Abingdon Press, Nashville, Tenn., 1977. (176 p.)

Harmon, Rebecca Lamar, SUSANNA, MOTHER OF THE WESLEYS, Hodder & Stoughton, 1968; Abingdon Press, 1968. (175 p.) Ga. Ref. — 143, 153-55.

Harper, Marvin H., GURUS, SWAMIS AND AVATARAS, SPIRITUAL MASTERS AND THEIR AMERICAN DISCIPLES, Westminster Press, Philadelphia, Pa., 1967. (271 p.)
THE METHODIST EPISCOPAL CHURCH IN INDIA, The Lucknow Publishing House, Lucknow, India, 1936. (222 p.)

Harrell, Costen Jordan, (1828-1970) — 5,981 items — Ga. — N.C. — S.C. — Tenn. — Ala. — Va. Harrell, consecrated bishop of the Methodist Church in 1944, served various churches throughout the South as pastor and taught at Methodist-related Emory and Duke. He served on various boards and commissions of the Church—Sec. to the Methodist Commission on World Service and Finance, chairman of the Methodist Advance Committee and of the Commission to write local church legislation. Most of his papers relate to his association with the Methodist church and include correspondence, clippings, sermons, meditations, and materials relating to the jurisdiction system of the Methodist Church, union of the Methodist and Evangelical Unital Brethren Churches, the Methodist Federation for Social Action, Methodist higher education, and studies of Methodist ritual and doctrine. Sp Cl Woodruff
"A Service of Installation" (Official Board), General Bd. of Lay Activities, The Methodist Church, Chicago, 1943. (4 p.)
A METHODIST CHILD'S MEMBERSHIP MANUAL, The Methodist Publishing House, 1940. (32 p.)
"Aids to the Devotional Life," (pamphlet) from the General Commission on Evangelism, Nashville, Tenn.
CHRISTIAN AFFIRMATIONS, Abingdon Press, New York, 1961. (126 p.)
FRIENDS OF GOD, Cokesbury Press, Nashville, Tenn., 1931. (177 p.)
I BELIEVE IN GOD, Abingdon Press, New York, 1958. (64 p.)
IN THE SCHOOL OF PRAYER, Cokesbury Press, Nashville, Tenn., 1929. (132 p.)
"Overcoming Sorrow," (pamphlet) from Tidings, Nashville, Tenn.
"Preaching and The Preacher of Tomorrow," THE MINISTRY (?).
STEWARDSHIP AND THE TITHE, Abingdon—Cokesbury Press, New York, Nashville, 1953. (61 p.)
THE BIBLE—ITS ORIGIN AND GROWTH, Cokesbury Press, Nashville, Tenn., 1926. (190 p.)
THE LOCAL CHURCH IN METHODISM, Abingdon Press, New York, 1961. (64 p.)
THE PROPHETS OF ISRAEL, Cokesbury Press, Nashville, Tenn., 1933. (235 p.)
THE RADIANT HEART, Cokesbury Press, Nashville, Tenn., 1936. (80 p.)
THE UNFOLDING GLORY, Bd. of Missions, The Methodist Church, Cincinnati, 1958. (120 p.)
THE WAY OF THE TRANSGRESSOR, Abingdon—Cokesbury Press, New York, Nashville, 1942. (178 p.)
THE WONDERS OF HIS GRACE, Abingdon Cokesbury, Nashville, Tenn., 1966. (126 p.)
THE WORD OF HIS GRACE, Abingdon—Cokesbury Press, New York, Nashville,

1943. (78 p.)
WALKING WITH GOD, Cokesbury Press, Nashville, Tenn., 1928. (190 p.)

Harris, Corra May (White), (1900-1934) — 120 items — Ga. Papers of this author/journalist, who was married to a Methodist circuit rider and whose novel, THE CIRCUIT RIDERS WIFE, describing this kind of experience, is her most famous. Much of the correspondence in the collection is between Mr. and Mrs. Harris and Warren Candler. Sp Cl Woodruff
A CIRCUIT RIDER'S WIDOW, Doubleday, Page & Co., Garden City, N.Y., 1916. (374 p.)
A CIRCUIT RIDER'S WIFE, Henry Altemus Co., Philadelphia, 1910. (Curtis Publishing Co.). (336 p.)
THE CIRCUIT RIDER'S WIFE, Houghton-Mifflin; Boston, New York; 1933. (335 p.)

Harris, Henry H., Methodist Curriculum Writings: —Closely Graded Church School Course (8) Intermediate Pupil's Text, (Parts 1-4), c 1929-30. —Pilgrim Graded Course—Intermediate Pupil's Text 1st and 2nd yr. (1-3; (1-2), c 1909-17.

Harris, Hugh H., LEADERS OF YOUTH, The Methodist Book Concern, New York, Cininnati, 1922. (240 p.)
THE MAKING OF A BETTER WORLD, MECH Publishing House, Nashville, Tenn. (Graded Course), (Course 8), 1929-30.
THE ORGANIZATION AND ADMINISTRATION OF THE INTERMEDIATE DEPARTMENT, MECS Publishing House, Nashville, Tenn., 1924. (190 p.)
"What Has The Psychology of Religion Attempted?" *The Methodist Review,* v. 69, Oct. 1919, p. 627-638.

Harris, Pierce, SPIRITUAL REVOLUTION, Doubleday & Co., Inc., Garden City, New York, 1952. (191 p.)

Harris, Thomas Alonzo, (sermon) "The Fatherless and Motherless Priest," Winterville, Ga., Aug. 1900, E.D. Stone, Athens. (8 p.) Ga. Room

Harrison, G. Elsie, Son of Susannah, Cokesbury Press, Nashville, 1938. (377 p.) Ga. Ref. — 107, 113, 123, 130, 133, 135, 139, 141, 145, 152, 162, 172, 174, 176, 177, 180-82, 212, 307.

Harrison, William Pope, "A Short Manual For The Centenary Year, 1884," Southern Methodist Publishing House, Nashville, Tenn., 1884. (48 p.)
"Dissent In Russia," *Southern Methodist Review,* (W.P. Harrison, ed.), Vol. 3, No. 3, Jan. 1888, p. 311-322.
ed., JOURNAL OF THE GENERAL CONFERENCE OF THE MECS, HELD IN NASHVILLE, TENN., 1882, Southern Methodist Publishing House, Nashville, Tenn., 1882. (260 p.)
ed., JOURNAL OF THE GENERAL CONFERENCE OF THE MECS HELD IN RICHMOND,

Va., May, 1886, Southern Methodist Publishing House, Nashville, Tenn., 1886. (260 p.)

ed., Journal of the General Conference of the MECS, Held in St. Louis, Mo., May, 1890, MECS Publishing House, Nashville, Tenn., 1890. (328 p.)

Methodist Union: Threatened In 1844 was Formally Dissolved in 1848, M.E. Church S, Publishing House, Nashville, 1892. (259 p.)

"Rise of the Monthly Magazine," *Southern Methodist Review,* (W.P. Harrison, ed.), Vol. 3, No. 3, Jan. 1888, p. 353-361.

ed., Sermons on the Acts of The Apostles by J. Cynddylan Jones, 1883.

ed., Sermons on The Gospel of Matthew, by J. Cynddylan Jones, Southern Methodist Publishing House, Nashville, Tenn. 1884. (330 p.)

ed., Studies In The Gospel According To John, by J. Cynddylan Jones, Southern Methodist Publishing House, Nashville, Tenn., 1885. (337 p.)

"The Codex Vaticanus," *Methodist Quarterly Review,* (W.P. Harrison, ed.), Vol. 15, No. 2, Jan. 1894, p. 343-371.

ed., The Doctrines and Discipline of the Methodist Episcopal Church South, MECS Publishing House, Nashville, Tenn., 1891. (442 p.)

ed., The Gospel Among The Slaves, MECS Publishing House, Nashville, Tenn., 1893. (394 p.)

The High-Churchman Disarmed: A Defense of Our Methodist Fathers, Southern Methodist Publishing House, Nashville, Tenn., 1886. (510 p.)

The Living Christ, Southern Methodist Publishing House, Nashville, Tenn., 1883. (297 p.)

The Living Christ, MECS Publishing House, Nashville, Tenn., 1889. (356 p.)

"The Russian Church and Russian Dissent," *Southern Methodist Review,* (W.P. Harrison, ed.), Vol. 3, No. 2, Nov. 1887, p. 205-214.

The Wesleyan Standards, (Sermons by John Wesley), 2 Volumes, Southern Methodist Publishing House, Nashville, Tenn., 1887. Vol. 1—(423 p.); Vol. 2—(418 p.)

Theophilius Walton: or The Majesty of Truth, Stevenson & Owen, Nashville, Tenn., 1858. (408 p.)

Theophilius Walton: or The Majesty of Truty, Stevenson & Owen, Nashville, Tenn., (Southern Methodist Publishing House), 1859. (408 p.)

Hart, Bessie Lester, Pastors of Mulberry, 1826-1964, (Mulberry St. UMC, Macon, Ga.). (231 p.)

Hart, H.D., The Missionary Life and Work of W.R. Lambuth, (thesis), Emory Univ., Atlanta, Ga., 1924. (37 p.)

Harvard, L. Clyde, I Stand Amazed, The Millen News, Millen, Ga. 1977. (73 p.)

Haskin, Sara Estelle, Women and Missions In the MECS, MECS Publishing House, Nashville—Dallas—Richmond, 1920. (255 p.)

Haven, Gilbert, (1873-1875) — 17 letters — Ga. — Mex. Letters of this bishop of the ME Church to the U.S. Consul in Mexico City concern the missionary efforts of the M.E. Church in Mexico. Sp Cl Woodruff

Haviland, Thomas P., "Of Franklin, Whitefield and the Orphans," *Georgia Historical Quarterly,* 29, December, 1945, p. 211-216.

Hawes, Mrs. Lilla M., "Miscellaneous Papers of James Jackson, 1781-1798," *Georgia Historical Quarterly,* 37, Mar-Jun, 1953, p. 54-80. (contains "Notes on Bethesda"—Whitefield's Orphan Home).

Hawkins, Rev. Henry G., "Life Sketch of Rev. Tobias Gibson, First Methodist Preacher in Mississippi," pamphlets of address given at memorial service held 5-6-1934 at his grave. (4 p.) (Candler Library)

Hayes, Zach C., "Bishop George Foster Pierce," *The Georgia Review,* 6, Summer, 1953, p. 156-162.

Haygood, Atticus Greene, (1861-1952) — 435 items — Ga. Papers of this Methodist minister, bishop to the Los Angeles Conference of the MECS and editor of the *Wesleyan Christian Advocate,* include mainly news clippings re Bishop Haygood, his manuscript sermons, and material concerning members of the Haygood family.
"A Campaign of Education," *Methodist Quarterly Review,* (W.P. Harrison, ed.), Vol. 14, No. 2, July, 1893, p. 316-332.
ABOVE RUBIES, MECS Publishing House, Nashville, Tenn., 1872. (296 p.)
BISHOP PIERCE'S SERMONS & ADDRESSES, Southern Methodist Publishing House, Nashville, Tenn., 1886. (394 p.)
ed., BISHOP PIERCE'S SERMONS AND ADDRESSES, (G.F. Pierce), Southern Methodist Publishing House, Nashville, Tenn., 1887. (394 p.)
"Close The Saloons" (A Plea For Prohibition pamphlet), J.W. Burke & Co., Macon, Ga., (39 p.)
EL HOMBRE DE GALILEA, Barbee, Nashville, Tenn., 1894. (195 p.)
"Growth In Grace," J.W. Burke & Co., Macon, Ga., 1885. (23 p.)
ed., HEROINES OF EARLY METHODISM, (by Miss and Mrs. Martin) MECS Publishing House, Nashville, Tenn., 1881. (224 p.)
"High Steeple and Its Official Staff," *Methodist Quarterly Review,* (W.P. Harrison, ed.), Vol. 14, No. 1, April, 1893, p. 57-75.
"Hugh Miller," *Scott's Monthly Magazine,* Vol. 1 & 2, Franklin Steam Print, Atlanta, Ga., 1866, p. 300-313. (Scott, W.J., ed.).
JACK-KNIFE AND BRAMBLES, MECS Publishing House, Nashville, 1893. (308 p.)
JACK-KNIFE AND BRAMBLES, MECS Publishing House, Nashville, Tenn., 1894. (308 p.)
JESUS THE CHRIST, J.W. Burke & Co., Macon, Ga., 1877. (86 p.)
JESUS THE CHRIST, Advocate Publishing House, St. Louis, 1878.
"Loaf and Bottle To Hagar," *The Methodist Review,* (J.J. Tigert, ed.), Vol. 18, No. 3, July-August, 1895, p. 301-315.
OUR BROTHER IN BLACK: HIS FREEDOM AND HIS FUTURE, Southern Methodist

Publishing House, Nashville, Tenn.; Phillips & Hunt, New York, 1881. (252 p.)

OUR BROTHER IN BLACK: HIS FREEDOM & FUTURE, Hunt & Eaton, New York, 1889. (315 p.)

OUR CHILDREN, New York, Nelson & Phillips; J.W. Burke, Macon and Atlanta, 1876. (354 p.)

OUR CHILDREN, Southern Methodist Publishing House, Nashville, Tenn., 1878. (354 p.)

OUR CHILDREN, MECS Publishing House, Nashville, 1894. (212 p.)

PLEAS FOR PROGRESS, MECS Publishing House, Nashville, Tenn., 1889. (320 p.)

PURE SONGS FOR SUNDAY SCHOOL, J.W. Burke Co., Macon, Ga., 1889.

"Save Our Homes," A Prohibition Sermon, J.W. Burke & Co., Printers and Binders, Macon, Ga., 1884. (36 p.)

SERMONS, VOL. 1, M.E. Church South Publishing House, Nashville, 1895. (363 p.) 7 other Haygood titles listed in this book.

SERMONS AND SPEECHES, Southern Methodist Publishing House, Nashville, Tenn., 1883. (400 + p.)

SERMONS AND SPEECHES, Southern Methodist Publishing House, Nashville, Tenn., 1885. (428 p.)

ed., THE AMARANTH, MECS Publishing House, Nashville, Tenn., 1871.

ed., THE AMARANTH, MECS Publishing House, Nashville, Tenn., 1877. (160 p.)

"The Chief Characteristic of Our Century," *Methodist Quarterly Review,* (W.P. Harrison, ed.), Vol. 15, No. 1, Oct. 1893, p. 49-57.

"The Christian Citizen," (sermon), Southern Methodist Publishing House, Nashville, 1881. (37 p.) Ga. Room

"The Church and the Education of The People," MECS Publishing House, Nashville, Tenn., 1874. (47 p.)

ed., THE GEM, (SS Songbook), Southern Methodist Publishing House, Nashville, Tenn., 1880. (160 p.)

THE MAN OF GALILEE, Hunt & Eaton, New York; Cranston & Stowe, Cincinnati, 1889. (156 p.)

THE MAN OF GALILEE, Hunt & Eaton, New York; Cranston & Stowe, Cincinnati, 1890. (156 p.)

THE MONK AND THE PRINCE, MECS Publishing House, Nashville, Tenn., 1895. (371 p.)

"The Negro Problem: God Takes Time—Man Must," *The Methodist Review,* (J.J. Tigert, ed.), Vol. 19, No. 1, Sept.-Oct. 1895, p. 40-53.

"The New South," printed at Oxford, Ga., 1880. (In Wesleyan College).

"The New South: Gratitude, Amendment, Hope," (sermon, 11-25-1880), Oxford, Ga. (12 p.) Reprinted 1950, Emory Univ. Library, Atlanta.

"The State and Its Prisoners," (sermon), J.W. Burke & Co., Macon, 1886. (14 p.) Ga. Room

"The Sunday School," Atlanta Intelligencer Book and Job Office, Atlanta, Ga., 1868. (12 p.)

"Two Sermons: Prison Reform (11-8-1886) and The Good and the Bad (11-25-1886), preached at Atlanta and Oxford, J.W. Burke & Co., Macon, Ga.,

1887. (29 p.) Ga. Room

"Where Fools Rush In," *The Methodist Review,* (J.J. Tigert, ed.), Vol. 19, No. 3, Jan.-Feb., 1896, p. 307-314.

"Where Is Our Money?" J.W. Burke & Co., Macon, Ga., 1876.

Haygood, Atticus G., and McIntosh, R. M. (eds.), Prayer & Praise, (hymnal), J.W. Burke & Co., Macon, 1883. (284 p.)

Prayer and Praise, J.W. Burke & Co., Macon, Ga., 1888. (314 p.)

Prayer & Praise, (revised and enlarged, scores added), J.W. Burke & Co., Macon, 1890. (320 p.)

Pure Songs For Sunday Schools, J.W. Burke & Co., Macon, Ga., 1890. (180 p.)

Haynes, Claud M., I Remember, Biographical Sketch, 1969, (53 p.) (softbound)

Heard, William H., From Slavery to the Bishopric IN the African Methodist Episcopal Church, Arno Press & The N.Y. Times, New York, 1969. (104 p.)

Hearn, Anthony, comp., I Heard The Call To Preach, 1947. (55 p.)

Heidt, John W., ed., Year-Book and Minutes of the 33rd Session, North Georgia Conference, MECS, Held At LaGrange, Ga., Nov. 30-Dec. 4, 1899, E.D. Stone, Printer, Athens, Ga., 1899. (88 m.p.)

Year-Book and Minutes of the 34th Session of the North Georgia Conference, MECS, Held At Trinity Church, Atlanta, Ga., Nov. 21-26, 1900, Fletcher Smith, Printer, Rome, Ga. (87 m.p.)

Year Book and Minutes, 35th Session, North Georgia Conference, MECS, Held At 1st Church, Rome, Ga., Nov. 20-26, 1901, Blosser Printing Co., Atlanta, Ga. (61 m.p.)

Year Book and Minutes of the 36th Session of the North Georgia Conference, MECS, Held At 1st Church, Atlanta, Ga., Nov. 19-25, 1902, Doctor Blosser Co., Atlanta, Ga., 1902. (54 m.p.)

Year Book and Minutes of the 37th Session of the North Georgia Conference, MECS, Held At 1st Church, Griffin, Nov. 18-23, 1903, Doctor Blosser Co., Atlanta, Ga., 1903. (48 m.p.)

Year Book and Minutes, 38th Session, North Georgia Conference, MECS, Held At Marietta, Ga., Nov. 23-28, 1904, The Blosser Co., Atlanta, Ga., 1904. (70 m.p.)

Year Book and Minutes of the 39th Session of the North Georgia Conference, MECS, Held At Newnan, Ga., Nov. 22-27, 1905, The Blosser Co., Atlanta, Ga., 1906. (66 m.p.)

Year Book and Minites of the 40th Session of the North Georgia Conference, MECS, Held At Milledgeville, Ga., Nov. 22-27, 1906, The Blosser Co., Atlanta, Ga., 1907. (65 m.p.)

Year Book and Minutes, 41st Session, North Georgia Conference, MECS,

HELD AT CARTERSVILLE, GA., Nov. 20-25, 1907, Converse and Wing Pub. Co., Atlanta, Ga. (61 m.p.)
YEAR BOOK AND MINUTES OF THE 42ND SESSION OF THE NORTH GEORGIA CONFERENCE, MECS, HELD AT GAINESVILLE, GA., Nov. 18-23, 1908, Converse and Wing Pub. Co., Atlanta, Ga. (63 m.p.)

Heidt, John W., and Cook, Ellison R., eds., YEAR-BOOK AND MINUTES OF THE NORTH GEORGIA CONFERENCE, MECS 29TH SESSION, HELD AT ELBERTON, GA., Nov. 20-25, 1895, Methodist Book and Publishing Co., Publishers; Press of The Foote & Davies Co., Atlanta, Ga., 1895. (54 m.p.)
YEAR-BOOK AND MINUTES OF THE NORTH GEORGIA CONFERENCE, MECS, 30TH SESSION, HELD AT DALTON, GA., Nov. 25-30, 1896, Press of American Publishing and Engraving Co., Atlanta, Ga., 1896. (66 m.p.)
YEAR-BOOK AND MINUTES OF THE NORTH GEORGIA CONFERENCE, MECS, HELD AT ATHENS, GA., Nov. 24-30, 1897, Fletcher Smith, printer, Rome, Ga., 1897. (73 p.)
YEAR-BOOK AND MINUTES OF THE 32ND SESSION, NORTH GEORGIA CONFERENCE, MECS, HELD AT AUGUSTA, GA., Nov. 23-29, 1898, Fletcher Smith, Printer, Rome, Ga. (84 p.)

Hendrix, E.R., "Jonathan Edwards and John Wesley," *Methodist Quarterly Review*, 62, Jan. 1913, p. 28-38.

Henry, Mary Davis, ONE MILE FROM TRINITY, The Strode Publishers, Athens, Ala., 1955 & 1958. (246 p.)

Henry, Stuart C., GEORGE WHITEFIELD'S WAYFARING WITNESS, Abingdon Press, New York, Nashville, 1957. (224 p.)

Henry, Waights G., NEEDFUL KNOWLEDGE FOR WONDERFUL LIVING, Birmingham Printing Co., Ala., n.d. (151 p.)
THE ORGANIZATIONOF PERSONALITY, Birmingham Printing Co., Ala., 1922. (90 p.)
"Commencement Address: A Brief History of LaGrange College," (Sesqui-centennial 1831-1981). (8 p.)
"Methodism In Georgia," *Wesleyan Christian Advocate*, Vol. 46, No. 3, July 22, 1981, p. 3, 5, 7.

Herndon, J. Emmett, "A Christmas Meditation," *The Emory Univ. Quarterly Review*, v16, n4, Winter, 1960, p. 193-196.

Hill, Mrs. Albert M., comp., 11TH ANNUAL REPORT OF THE WOMAN'S MISSIONARY SOCIETY OF THE N. GA. CONFERENCE, 1921, GAINESVILLE, GA., FEB. 14-18, 1921. (96 p.)

Hilliard, Rev. Henry W., "On Preparation To Meet God," (sermon) found in *The Methodist Magazine and Quarterly Review*, (Emory & Waugh, eds.), Vol. 6,

1835, p. 394-401.

(of Ala.), "Sermon on 1 Cor. 1:22-24" delivered 6-24-1860 at Washington St., Columbia, S.C., published by Barrett, Wimbish & Co., Montgomery, mentioned in *Quarterly Review of the MECS* (D.S. Doggett, ed.), April, 1861, p. 301.

SPEECHES AND ADDRESSES, Harper & Brothers, Publishers, New York, 1855. (497 p.)

"The Life and Genius of Milton," *Methodist Quarterly Review,* Vol. 7, No. 1, Oct. 1889, p. 107-126.

"The Pulpit," *Scott's Monthly,* v. 4, n. 1, July, 1867, p. 670-672. (Hilliard also published material in *The Augusta Mirror.*)

Hinesville UMC, MILESTONES OF METHODISM, HINESVILLE, LIBERTY CO., GA., 1837-1972. (79 p.)

Hinton, J.C., "Macaulay's Essays," *The Quarterly Review of the MECS,* (J.W. Hinton, ed.), Vol. 4, No. 4, Oct. 1882, p. 668-681.

Hinton, J.W., "A National Convention Needed," *The Quarterly Review of the MECS,* (J.W. Hinton, ed.), Vol. 7, No. 4, Oct. 1885, p. 529-544.

"Attitudes of Atheism," *The Quarterly Review of the MECS,* (J.W. Hinton, ed.), Vol. 4, No. 4, Oct. 1882, p. 577-597.

"Bishop George Pierce," *The Quarterly Review of the MECS,* (J.W. Hinton, ed.), Vol. 6, No. 4, Oct., 1884, p. 577-592.

"Drummond's Discussions," *The Quarterly Review of the MECS,* (J.W. Hinton, ed.), Vol. 7, No. 3, July, 1885, p. 353-368.

"Educational Problems In The South," *The Quarterly Review of the MECS,* (J.W. Hiton, ed.), Vol. 5, No. 4, Oct. 1883, p. 688-708.

"Gladstone's Categories of Religious Thought," *The Methodist Review,* (J.J. Tigert, ed.), Vol. 26, No. 4, July-August, 1900, p. 544-547.

"Lodge's Life of Hamilton," *The Methodist Quarterly Review,* (J.J. Tigert, ed.), Jan.-Feb. 1901, v. 50, p. 87-96.

"Mountain Observatories," *The Quarterly Review of the MECS,* (J.W. Hinton, ed.), Vol 7, No. 2, April 1885, p. 186-192.

"Paradox," *The Quarterly Review of the MECS,* (J.W. Hinton, ed.), Vol. 6, No. 3, July, 1884, p. 494-503.

"Preachers and Preaching," *The Methodist Review,* (J.J. Tigert, ed.), Vol. 18, No. 2, May-June, 1895, p. 230-239.

"Restrictive Articles of Methodism," *The Quarterly Review of the MECS,* (J.W. Hinton, ed.), Vol. 8, No. 2, April, 1886, p. 177-192.

(review of) American Statesmen: Alexander Hamilton by Henry Cabot Lodge, *The Quarterly Review of the MECS,* (J.W. Hinton, ed.), Vol. 4, No. 4, Oct. 1882, p. 719-730.

(review of...) Theory of Morals by Paul Janet, C. Schribner's Sons, New York, *The Quarterly Review of the MECS,* Vol. 6, No. 2, April, 1884, (J.W. Hinton, ed.), p. 332-343.

ed., *The Quarterly Review of the Methodist Episcopal Church, South,* Vol. 1, Southern

Methodist Publishing House, Nashville, 1879. (periodical)
"The Methodist Revolution," *Methodist Quarterly Review,* (W.P. Harrison, ed.), Vol. 6, No. 1, April, 1889, p. 118-127.
"The Tongue and the Pen," found in *The Quarterly Review of the MECS,* (J.W. Hinton, ed.), Vol. 1, 1879, p. 1-13.
"The Ultimate and Universal in Philosophy," found in *The Quarterly Review of the MECS,* (J.W. Hinton, ed.), Vol. 1, 1879, p. 76-92.
"Valedictory," *The Southern Methodist Review,* (W.P. Harrison, ed.), Vol. 1, No. 1, Sept. 1886, p. 107-110.

Hinton, J. C., "Washington Irving," *The Quarterly Review of the MECS,* (J.W. Hinton, ed.), Vol. 8, No. 1, Jan. 1886, p. 1-16.

Hoffmann, Manfred E., Book Reviews found in the following Journals and Periodicals: *Union Seminary Quarterly Review, Christian Advocate, The Review of Books and Religion, Renaissance and Reformation, The Candler Review, Religious Studies Review, International Review of Scientific Literature.*
"Beobachtungen zum II. Vatikanischen Konzil," *Der Mitarbeiter,* 4, Jahrgang, No. 1, January, 1966, p. 21-26.
"Can You Not Watch With Me," *Ministry and Mission,* Vol. 2, No. 3, Sept. 1977, p. 2.
"Christian Ethics and the Political Order," *The Candler Review,* Vol. 1, No. 1, January, 1974, p. 19-27.
"Church and History in the Dogmatic Constitution 'De Ecclesia,' " *Theological Studies* Vol. 29, No. 2, June, 1968, p. 191-214.
"Denn Du bist bei mir," *Lied, Weisheit und Gebet im Alten Bund,* Frankfurt, 1956, p. 31-37. (In Same Publication): "Aber ich bin ja bei dir," p. 49-56.
DER DIALOG BEI DEN CHRISTLICHEN SCHRIFTSTELLERN DER ERSTEN VIER JAHRHUNDERTE, Akademie der Wissenschaften Berlin, Texte und Untersuchungen vol. 96, Berlin, 1966.
"Die Gabe des Lebenswassers," *Wir sahen seine Herrlichkeit,* Frankfurt, 1956, p. 25-36. (In Same Publication): "Das Brot des Lebens," p. 36-41.
ERKENNTNIS UND VERWIRKLICHUNG DER WAHREN THEOLOGIE NACH ERAMUS VON ROTTERDAM, Beltrage zur Historischen Theologie vol 44, J.C.B. Nohr (Paul Siebeck), Tubingen, 1972.
"Kerygma and History," *The Journal of Bible and Religion,* Vol. XXXIII, January, 1965, No. 1, p. 24-33.
"Lebendige Hoffnung," *Was der Apostel Schreibt (III),* Frankfurt, 1957, p. 10-15. (In Same Publication): "Der Christ im Leiden," p. 22-29.
"Luther, the Protestant Tradition and the Death of God," *Journal of the American Academy of Religion,* Vol. XL, No. 2, June, 1972, p. 164-175.
"Luther und die Bauern," *Das Zeitalter der Reformation auf dem Festlande,* Frankfurt, 1958, p. 29-36. (In Same Publication): "Martin Butzer," p. 37-44.
"Methodism's Double Answer," *Ministry and Mission,* Vol. 3, No. 7, March, 1978, p. 7.
"Praxisbezogene theologische Ausbildung," *emk aktuell,* No. 11, Nov., 1976, p. 6-10.

"The Protestant Tradition and the Death of God," *Religion in Contemporary Thought,* ed. George F. McLean, Albea House, 1973, p. 203-221.

ed., *Toleranz u. Reformation,* Texte zur Kirchen-u, Theologiegeschichte, Vol. 24, Gutersloh, 1979.

"Transcendence and Mystery in History," *Transcendence and Mystery,* ed. Earl D.C. Brewer, IDOC, North America, New York, 1975, p. 46-59.

(Translation) Colin W. Williams, DIE THEOLOGIE WESLEYS, Anker Verlag, Frankfurt am Main, 1967.

(Translation) Hans von Campenhausen, THE LATIN FATHERS OF THE CHURCH, A. and C. Black, London, 1964; American ed., MEN WHO SHAPED THE WESTERN CHURCH, Harper & Row, New York, 1965; 2nd ed. Stanford Univ. Press, 1969.

(Translation of intro. & ft. notes) J. Boozer, ed., RUDOLF OTTOS ETHISCHE SCHRIFTEN, C.H. Beck, Munchen.

"What is Theological Education?" CANDLER MEMO FROM EMORY'S COMMITTEE OF ONE HUNDRED, Vol. XII, No. 7, March, 1978, p. 2-3.

Hogue, Bishop Wilson T., HISTORY OF THE FREE METHODIST CHURCH OF NORTH AMERICA, 2 Vols., Free Methodist Publishing House, Chicago, 1918. Vol. 1 — (385 p.) Vol. 2 — (424 p.) (Ga. Ref. — Vol. 2 — p. 122)

Holcomb, Walt, ed., BEST LOVED SERMONS OF SAM JONES, Nashville, Tenn., Methodist Publishing House, 1951. (192 p.)

MODERN EVANGELISM AND ANCIENT ENVIRONMENT, Cokesbury, Nashville, Tenn., 1924. (138 p.)

"Protestant Outlook In Catholic Europe," *The Methodist Quarterly Review,* v. 72, Jan. 1923, p. 60-67.

SAM JONES—AN AMBASSADOR OF THE ALMIGHTY. Nashville, Tenn., Methodist Publishing House, 1951. (192 p.)

THE GOSPEL OF GRACE, Emory Univ., Ga., Town & Country Church Book Club, 1955. (144 p.)

Holden, Harrington William, JOHN WESLEY IN COMPANY WITH HIGH CHURCHMEN, Church Press Co., London, 1869. (158 p.)

Holifield, E. Brooks, Book Reviews found in the following Journals and Periodicals: *Religions Education, Theology Today, William and Mary Quarterly, The Candler Review, Church History, Reviews in American History, The Virginia Seminary Journal, The Journal of American History, The Catholic Historical Review, Historical Magazine of the Protestant Episcopal Church*

"Ethical Assumptions of Clinical Pastoral Education," *Theology Today,* 36 (April, 1979), p. 30-44. Reprinted in *The Journal of Pastoral Care,* 34 (March, 1980), p. 39-54.

"History and Selfhood: An Historian's View," *The Journal of Pastoral Care,* 28 (September, 1974), p. 147-151.

"How History Informs Selfhood," *The Christian Century,* 93, (February 4-11, 1976), p. 93-96.

"Mercersburg, Princeton, and the South: The Sacramental Controversy in the Nineteenth Century," *Journal of Presbyterian History,* 54 (Summer, 1976) p. 238-257.

"On Toleration in Massachusetts," *Church History,* 38 (June, 1969), p. 188-200.

THE COVENANT SEALED: THE DEVELOPMENT OF PURITAN SACRAMENTAL THEOLOGY IN OLD AND NEW ENGLAND, 1570-1720, Yale University Press, New Haven, 1974.

"The English Methodist Response to Darwin," *Methodist History,* (January, 1972), p. 14-22.

THE GENTLEMEN THEOLOGIANS: AMERICAN THEOLOGY IN SOUTHERN CULTURE, 1795-1860, Duke University Press, Durham, N.C., 1978.

"The Hero and the Minister in American Culture," *Theology Today,* 33 (January, 1977), p. 370-379.

"The Intellectual Sources of Stoddardeanism," *New England Quarterly,* 45 (September, 1972), p. 373-392.

"The Renaissance of Sacramental Piety in Colonial New England," *William and Mary Quarterly,* 3rd Series, 29 (January, 1972), p. 33-48.

"The Three Strands of Jimmy Carter's Religion," *The New Republic,* 174 (June 5, 1976), p. 15-17.

"Thomas Smyth: The Social Ideas of a Southern Evangelist," *Journal of Presbyterian History,* 51 (Spring, 1973), p. 24-39.

Holsey, Bishop L. H., AUTOBIOGRAPHY, SERMONS, ADDRESSES, Franklin Printing Co., Atlanta, Ga., 1899. (288 p.)

Holt, William M., "Cry, the Beloved City," *The Christian Connector,* Winter, 1980.

"HInton Rural Life Center: Concern for Small Congregations in Rural America," *Response,* March, 1977.

"Ministry to Youth in Crisis," *New World Outlook,* July-August 1976.

"New Life in North Georgia," *New World Outlook,* March, 1981.

"Now a Word from United Methodists (North American Protestant Churches and Their Theologies)," *Gospel Herald,* March 22, 1977.

"On the Roof of the World," *World Outlook,* January, 1951.

"The Role of a Church Secretary," *Pulpit Digest,* July-August, 1978.

Hood, J. W., THE NEGRO IN THE CHRISTIAN PULPIT, Edwards, Broughton & Co., Steam Power Printers and Binders, Raleigh, N. C., 1884. (363 p.)

Hoover, Dorothy E., A LAYMAN LOOKS WITH LOVE AT HER CHURCH, Dorrance & Co., Philadelphia, 1970. (African Methodism) (183 p.) (Ga. Ref. — p. 52).

Hopkins, I. S., "Is Science Worth Knowing," *The Quarterly Review of the MECS,* (J.W. Hinton, ed.), Vol. 7, No. 3, July, 1885, p. 432-446.

Hoskins, F. W., THE HISTORY OF METHODISM IN PENSACOLA, FLA., ME Church

South Pub. House, Nashville, 1928. (120 p.)

Howard, Mrs. C. B., PATHS THAT CROSSED (GLIMPSES INTO THE EARLY DAYS OF METHODISM AND OF GEORGIA), ME Church, South Publishing House, Sunday School Department, Nashville, 1885. (229 p.)

Howard, Henry Clay, (1891-1933) — 25 items — Ga. — Ala. Papers of this Methodist minister and professor in the School of Theology at Emory Univ. include a few items of correspondence with A.G. Haygood, W.A. Candler, E.D. Mouzon, an article on John Wesley, and sermons. Sp Cl Woodruff
"A Clinical Study of the Call to Preach," *The Methodist Quarterly Review,* v. 74, Jan. 1925, p. 43-65.
"John Know," *The Methodist Quarterly Review,* v. 72, Jan. 1923, p. 95-109.
PRINCES OF THE CHRISTIAN PULPIT AND PASTORATE, Cokesbury Press, Nashville, Tenn., 1928.
PROPHETIC AND PERSONAL ELEMENTS IN THE CHRISTIAN MINISTRY.
"What Is The Essence of The Christian Gospel," *The Methodist Quarterly Review,* v. 75, April, 1926, p. 212-230.
"William Booth and His Army," *The Methodist Review,* v. 66, July 1917, p. 415-429.
"William Tyndale: Father of the King James Version," *The Methodist Quarterly Review,* v. 74, April, 1925, p. 195-217.

Howard, J., "Revival of The Work of God in Savannah, Ga.," found in *The Methodist Magazine,* (Soule & Mason, eds.), Vol. 4, 1821, p. 391-392.

Huff, Archie Vernon, Jr., TRIAL BY FIRE (Washington Street UMC, Columbia, S.C.), R.L. Bryan Co., Columbia, S.C. 1975. (163 p.)

Hunnicutt, W.T., "Church Policy and Christian Democracy," *The Methodist Quarterly Review,* v. 79, Jan. 1930, p. 65-76.

Hunt, Rolfe, THE RIGHTEOUS IN REMEMBRANCE, Pvt. Printing, Jackson, Miss., 1946. (208 p.)

Hurst, John Fletcher, THE HISTORY OF METHODISM, Eaton & Mains, New York, 1902. 7 Vols. Vol. 1 — (1-504); Vol. 2 — (505-992); Vol. 3 — (993-1478). (Ga. Ref. — 74, 225, 228, 231, 234, 259, 272, 344, 751, 776, 827, 994, 1018.) Vol. 4 — (1-478); Vol. 5 — (479-464); Vol. 6 — (965-1428). (Ga. Ref. — 371, 456, 577). Vol. 7 — (615 p.)

Huston, L. D., ed., THE HOME CIRCLE, v.1, Methodist Episcopal Church South Publishing House, Nashville, Tenn., 1855. (572 p.)
THE HOME CIRCLE, V.3. MECS Publishing House, Nashville, Tenn., 1857.
THE HOME CIRCLE, v. 1860, MECS Publishing House, Nashville, Tenn., 1860. (Bound at Wesleyan College, Macon, Ga., numbered monthly).

Hutton, William Holden, John Wesley, MacMillan & Co., London, 1927. (181 p.) (Ga. Ref. — 45, 55, 60.)

Huxford, Folks, Early Methodism In Southern Georgia, 1947. (typescript). (182 p.) Ga. Archives

Hyde, A. B. (D.D.), The Story of Methodism, M.W. Hazen Co., New York, 1888. (469 p.) (Ga. Ref. — p. 83.)

Isle of Hope Methodist Church (Savannah, Ga.), ''History of Isle of Hope Methodist Church,'' (Centennial booklet, 1959). (24 p.)

Jackson, Crawford, ''Character As Related To Flesh And Spirit,'' *The Methodist Review,* (J.J. Tigert, ed.), Vol. 18, No. 3, July-August, 1895, p. 327-334.
''The Hermit Thrush'' (poem), *The Methodist Review,* v. 68, July, 1919, p. 519-521.
''The Three Dispensations In Christian Experience,'' *Methodist Quarterly Review,* (W.P. Harrison, ed.), Vol. 9, No. 1, Oct., 1890, p. 145-163.

Jackson, Douglas Ewing, Relationship of the Episcopacy to the District Superintendency, Council of The Methodist Church, Nashville, Tenn. 1963. Stumbling Block: A Study of Alcohol and Christian Responsibility, Bd. of Missions, The Methodist Church, New York, 1960. (128 p.)

Jackson, Thomas, The Life of the Rev. Charles Wesley, M.A., 2 Vols., John Mason, London, 1841. Vol. 1 — (392 p.) (Ga. Ref. — p. 39-73) Vol. 2 — (578 p.) (Ga. Ref. — p. 243)

Jarrell, A. J., ''Faint-Heartedness,'' (tract), Palmer & Hughes, New York. Sp Cl Woodruff
Writes on Ga. Holiness Association, no date. (4 p. tract). Ga. Room

Jarrell, Charles Crawford, (1826-1974) — 30 boxes — Ga. Papers of this Methodist minister, active in educational and hospital association, include correspondence, sermons, speeches, clippings and pamphlets. Sp Cl Woodruff
''Amos and His Modern Message,'' *The Methodist Quarterly Review,* (J.J. Tigert, ed.), May-June, 1902, v. 5, p. 400-409.
Go Thou and Do Likewise, Printed for the General Hospital Board, MECS Publishing House, Nashville, Tenn., 1929. (143 p.)
Methodism On The March, MECS Publishing House, Nashville, 1924. (307 p.)
Oxford Echoes, 1967, Pvt. Pt. (1st published as a series in The Wesleyan Christian Advocate). (104 p.)
''Some Educational Lessons From The War,'' *The Methodist Review,* v. 70, Jan. 1921, p. 21-30.
''The Social Creed For The Industrial Crisis,'' *The Methodist Quarterly Review,* v.

72, Jan. 1923, p. 31-46.
"Was Peter the First Pope," pamphet—6 p.
"Who Shall Educate In The South Today?" *The Methodist Review Quarterly,*
(Gross Alexander, ed.), v. 59, Oct. 1910, p. 697-705.
WITNESSES TO THE WORD, MECS Publishing House, Nashville, Dallas,
Richmond, 1916. (191 p.)

Jarrell, Mrs. C. C., ed., 22ND ANNUAL REPORT OF THE WOMAN'S MISSIONARY
SOCIETY OF THE N. GA. CONFERENCE, 1931, (Rome, Ga.), Brumby Press, Inc.,
Marietta, Ga. (97 p.)
23RD ANNUAL REPORT OF THE WOMAN'S MISSIONARY SOCIETY OF THE N. GA.
CONFERENCE, 1932, (Newnan, Ga.), Brumby Press, Inc., Marietta, Ga. (99 p.)
24TH ANNUAL REPORT OF THE WOMAN'S MISSIONARY SOCIETY OF THE N. GA.
CONFERENCE, 1933, (Elberton, Ga.) (100 p.)
25TH ANNUAL REPORT OF THE WOMAN'S MISSIONARY SOCIETY OF THE N. GA.
CONFERENCE, 1934, (Gainesville, Ga.). (100 p.)

Jenkins, Rev. James, EXPERIENCES, LABORS & SUFFERINGS OF REV. JAMES
JENKINS, 1842. Reprinted by State Commercial Printing Co., Columbia, S.C.,
1959. (232 p.)

Jenkins, John S., "A Historic Document," *The Methodist Review,* v. 69, Jan.
1920, p. 87-96.

Jenkins, Sara. THE BRAND NEW PARSON. New York, Crowell, 1951. (246 p.)
THE LOST LAMP. New York, Crowell, 1950. (244 p.)

Johnson, Charles A., THE FRONTIER CAMP MEETING, Southern University
Press, Dallas, 1955. (325 p.) (Ga. Ref. — p. 67, 83, 210, 217, 246).

Johnson, Elsa Ann, "The Church In The Pines," Tuckston Methodist Church,
Athens, Ga., 1960. (10 p.) Ga. Room

Johnson, Fred, "History of Dawnville Methodist Church" (Mt. Zion), private,
1980. (ca. 20 p.)

Johnson, Henry Morrison, THE METHODIST EPISCOPAL CHURCH AND THE
EDUCATION OF SOUTHERN NEGROES, 1862-1900. (thesis), Yale, 1939. (606 p.)

Johnson, Luke G., "Have Christ and The Gospel Failed?" *The Methodist
Review,* v. 67, July, 1918, p. 482-485.

Jones, Charles O., "Arrested Intellectual Development of the Preacher," *The
Methodist Review,* (H.M. DuBose, ed.), v. 65, April, 1916, p. 282-293.
"Lesson of the Snow," (sermon) preached St. Mark MECS, 1-31-1904, The
Blosser Press, Atlanta, 1904. Ga. Room
"Materials For Sermons," *The Methodist Review Quarterly,* (Gross Alexander,

ed.), v. 64, July, 1915, p. 548-559.

"Methodist Episcopacy," *The Methodist Quarterly Review*, v. 71, April, 1922, p. 201-216.

3 sermons in PRIMING FOR THE PUMP, Board of Church Extension of the M. E. Church, South, Louisville, Ky., no date. (171 p.)

"The Church, The Pulpit, and the State," *The Methodist Quarterly Review*, v. 79, April, 1930, p. 265-280.

Jones, H. H., "John B. Wardlaw, Jr., A.M." found in *Quarterly Review*, periodical listed under Bascomb, H.B. (ed.), January, 1882, p. 112-120.

Jones, Mrs. Sam, THE LIFE AND SAYINGS OF SAM P. JONES, The Franklin Turner Co., Atlanta, 1907. (464 p.)

Jones, Samuel Porter, (1859-1961) — 4 boxes, OBVs — Ga. Papers of this Methodist evangelist include correspondence, diaries, lecture and sermon notes and texts, clippings, scrapbooks, etc. Sp Cl Woodruff

ANECDOTES AND ILLUSTRATIONS, Rhodes & McClure Publishing Co., Chicago, Ill., 1888. (301 p.)

GOOD NEWS (Sermons by Sam Jones and Sam Small), J.S. Ogilvie & Co., New York, 1886. (189 p.)

HOT SHOTS OR SERMONS & SAYINGS, Southwestern Publishing House, Stanberry, Mo., 1897. (304 p.)

QUIT YOUR MEANNESS, Cranston & Stowe, Cincinnati; N.D. Thompson Publishing Co., St. Louis, 1886. (507 p.)

QUIT YOUR MEANNESS, Forshee & McMakin, Cincinnati, Ohio, 1888. (507 p.)

SAM JONES' OWN BOOK—A SERIES OF SERMONS, Cranston & Stowe, Cincinnati, Chicago & St. Louis, 1886. (539 p.)

SAM JONES' SERMONS, VOL. 1, Rhodes and McClure, Publishers, Chicago, 1891. (346 p.)

SAM JONES' SERMONS, VOL. 2, Rhodes & McClure, Publishers, Chicago, 1896. (p. 347-690).

SERMONS, Scammell & Co., Publishers, Philadelphia and St. Louis, 1886. (574 p.)

SERMONS, Scammell & Co., Publishers, Philadelphia and St. Louis, 1886. (569 p.)

SERMONS, Scammell and Co., Publishers, Philadelphia and St. Louis, 1887. (574 p.)

SERMONS AND SAYINGS, Southern Methodist Publishing House, Nashville, 1885. (284 p.) (reprinted, Cranston & Stowe, Cincinnati, 1886. 312 p.)

SERMONS AND SAYINGS, Cranston & Stowe, Cincinnati; Phillips and Hunt, New York, 1886. (319 p.)

"The Prodigal Son," (A Sermon To Men—and Others). (72 p.)

THUNDERBOLTS, Jones & Haynes, Nashville, Tenn., 1895. (584 p.)

THUNDERBOLTS, Jones and Haynes, Nashville, Tenn., 1896. (568 p.)

Jordan, Gerald Ray, ADVENTURES IN RADIANT LIVING, (uv).

BEYOND DESPAIR, New York, Macmillan, 1955. (166 p.)

CHRIST, COMMUNISM, AND THE CLOCK, Warner, Anderson, Ind., 1963. (128 p.)

CONSTITUTIONAL HISTORY OF THE METHODIST EPISCOPACY, (thesis), Emory Univ., Atlanta, Ga., 1920. (59 p.)

COURAGE THAT PROPELS, Cokesbury Press, Nashville, Tenn., 1933. (182 p.)

FAITH THAT PROPELS, Cokesbury Press, Nashville, Tenn., 1935. (208 p.)

"Faith With The Law," *The Methodist Quarterly Review,* v. 78, April, 1928, p. 280-286.

"If Marriage Is To Succeed," (pamphlet) from Tidings, Nashville, Tenn.

INTIMATE INTERESTS OF YOUTH, Cokesbury Press, Nashville, Tenn., 1931. (164 p.)

LIFE GIVING WORDS, Warner, Anderson, Ind., 1964. (112 p.)

LOOK AT THE STARS, Abingdon-Cokesbury Press, Nashville, Ten., 1942. (240 p.)

"LSD and Mystical Experiences," *Journal of Bible and Religion,* 31, April, 1963, p. 14-123.

"Mental Honesty and Seminary Recruitment," *Christianity Today,* 8, Sept. 24, 1964, p. 8-10.

PRAYER THAT PREVAILS, New York, Macmillan, 1958. (150 p.)

PREACHING DURING A REVOLUTION: PATTERNS OF PROCEDURE, Warner Press, Anderson, Ind., 1962. (192 p.)

RELIGION THAT IS ETERNAL, MacMillian, New York, 1960. (134 p.)

"St. Paul's Conception of Faith," *The Methodist Quarterly Review,* v. 77, April, 1928, p. 273-279.

"The Emerging Revival," *The Emory Univ. Quarterly Review,* v2, n2, June, 1946, p. 111-117.

THE EMERGING REVIVAL, Abingdon-Cokesbury, New York and Nashville, 1946. (186 p.)

THE HOUR HAS COME, Abingdon-Cokesbury Press, New York, 1948. (152 p.)

THE INTOLERANCE OF CHRISTIANITY, Fleming H. Revell, New York, 1931. (160 p.)

"The One and Only Authority in Religion," *The Methodist Quarterly Review,* v. 76, Jan. 1927, p. 172-176.

THE SUPREME POSSESSION, Abingdon-Cokesbury, New York and Nashville, 1945. (187 p.)

WE BELIEVE, Abingdon-Cokesbury Press, New York, Nashville, 1944. (135 p.)

WE FACE CALVARY AND LIFE, Cokesbury Press, Nashville, Tenn. (160 p.)

WHY THE CROSS?, Abingdon-Cokesbury Press, New York, Nashville, 1941. (138 p.)

YOU CAN PREACH, New York, Fleming H. Revell Co., 1951. (256 p.)

YOU CAN PREACH! BUILDING AND DELIVERING THE SERMON, Revell, Westwood, N.J., 1958. (256 p.)

Joy, James Richard, JOHN WESLEY'S AWAKENING, Commission On Archives & History, Tennessee Conf., 1937. (128 p.)

Keener, John Christian, "Job, A Prince of the East, And His Inspired Epic,"

The Methodist Review, (J.J. Tigert, ed.), Vol. 22, No. 3, July-August, 1897, p. 323-341.

POST OAK CIRCUIT, E. Stevenson & F.A. Owen, Nashville, Tenn., 1857. (275 p.)

POST OAK CIRCUIT, MECS Publishing House, Nashville, Tenn., 1893. (351 p.)

POST OAK CIRCUIT, MECS Publishing House, Nashville, Tenn., 1894. (351 p.)

POST OAK CIRCUIT, MECS Publishing House, Nashville & Dallas, 1904. (351 p.)

POST OAK CIRCUIT, MECS Publishing House, Nashville, Tenn., 1905. (351 p.)

ed., SERMONS AND LECTURES BY WILLIAM E. MUNSEY, MECS Publishing House, Nashville, Tenn., 1886.

ed., SERMONS AND LECTURES BY WILLIAM E. MUNSEY, MECS Publishing House, Nashville & Dallas, 1907. (406 p.)

STUDIES OF BIBLE TRUTHS, Barbee & Smith, Nashville, Tenn., 1899. (239 p.)

"The Apocalypse of Jesus Christ," *The Methodist Review,* (J.J. Tigert, ed.), Vol. 23, No. 3, Jan.-Feb., 1898, p. 363-380.

"The Creative Glory In Its Two Distinct Realms—The Natural and The Moral," *The Methodist Review,* (J.J. Tigert, ed.), Vol. 24, No. 2, May-June, 1898, p. 163-182.

THE GARDEN OF EDEN AND THE FLOOD, Barbee & Smith, Nashville & Dallas, 1901. (258 p.)

Kendall, Mrs. T. R., ed., ANNUAL REPORT OF THE WOMAN'S PARSONAGE AND HOME MISSION SOCIETY OF THE NORTH GEORGIA CONFERENCE, MECS, 1894, Franklin Printing and Publishing Company, Atlanta, Ga., 1894. (34 p.)

Key, Joseph Staunton (1829-1920) Sermons, one holograph book & 9 misc. items in folder including newspaper articles, correspondence and Conf. Journal portrait (1903-4). Sp Cl Candler

"Heart-Purity, and our Reasons for Urging it," sermon preached at Ga. Holiness Convention, Cartersville, Ga., 5-13-1887. J.W. Burke, Macon, 1887. (15 p.) Ga. Room

"Tributes From Other Colleagues of Bishop Keener," *The Methodist Quarterly Review,* (J.J. Tigert, ed.), v. 55, p. 233-244.

King, William, M.D., A SHORT SKETCH OF THE HISTORY AND TEACHINGS OF THE BIBLE, Foote & Davies Co., Atlanta, 1900. (89 p.) (for Merritts Ave. Church?).

A SURE POSSESSION & OTHER THOUGHTS OF A LAYMAN, A.B. Caldwell, Atlanta, 1909. (238 p.)

King, William Peter, "A Meditating Ministry," *The Methodist Quarterly Review,* v. 74, Jan. 1925, p. 66-72.

ADVENTISM: THE SECOND COMING OF CHRIST, ABINGDON-COKESBURY, NEW YORK, NASHVILLE, 1941. (134 P.)

ED., AFTER PENTECOST, WHAT?, Cokesbury Press, Nashville, Tenn. 1930. (180 p.)

"Behaviorism—A Battle Line," *The Methodist Quarterly Review,* v. 79, Jan. 1930, p. 3-18.

ed., BEHAVIORISM: A BATTLE LINE, Cokesbury Press, Nashville, Tenn., 1930. (376 p.)

"Christian Faith and the New Apologetics," *The Methodist Review Quarterly,* (Gross Alexander, ed.), v. 62, April, 1913, p. 334-344.

"Cruelty In Nature," *The Methodist Quarterly Review,* v. 77, Oct. 1928, p. 531-540.

"Essential Verities of the Faith," *The Methodist Review Quarterly,* (Gross Alexander, ed.), Jan. 1908, v. 57, p. 132-136.

FAITH IN THE DIVINE FATHERHOOD, Cokesbury Press, Nashville, Tenn. 1928. (372 p.)

"Humanism and Moral Motive Power," *The Methodist Quarterly Review,* v. 79, Oct. 1930, p. 547-566.

ed., HUMANISM: ANOTHER BATTLE LINE, Cokesbury Press, Nashville, Tenn. 1931. (298 p.)

MOTIVES FOR CHRISTIAN LIVING, Harper & Brothers, New York and London, 1942. (188 p.)

RIGHT AND WRONG IN AN AGE OF CONFUSION, The Abingdon Press, New York, Cincinnati, 1938. (246 p.)

ed., SERMONS OF POWER, Cokesbury Press, Nashville, Tenn.

ed., SOCIAL PROGRESS AND CHRISTIAN IDEALS, Cokesbury Press, Nashville, Tenn., 1931. (360 p.)

"The Crisis of Translation," *The Methodist Review,* v. 67, Jan. 1918, p. 44-48.

"The Failure of the Rationalistic Radicalism," *The Methodist Quarterly Review,* v. 79, July, 1930, p. 371-390.

"The Fallacies of Ultraism," *The Methodist Review Quarterly,* (Gross Alexander, ed.), v. 59, July, 1910, p. 568-580.

"The Fundamental Faith," *The Methodist Quarterly Review,* v. 71, April, 1922, p. 282-297.

"The Futile Fight of Fundamentalism," *The Methodist Quarterly Review,* v. 72, July, 1923, p. 409-417.

"The Margin of Mysteries and Vital Certainties," *The Methodist Quarterly Review,* v. 78, Jan. 1929, p. 3-13.

ed., THE METHODIST QUARTERLY REVIEW, v. 77-79, MECS Publishing House, Nashville, Tenn. Oct. 1928-Oct. 1930.

THE PRACTICE OF THE PRINCIPLES OF JESUS, Cokesbury Press, Nashville, Tenn. 1926. (238 p.)

THE SEARCH FOR HAPPINESS, Abingdon-Cokesbury Press, Nashville, Tenn., 1946. (182 p.)

"The Ultimate Authority In Religion," *The Methodist Review Quarterly,* (Gross Alexander, ed.), v. 60, April 1911, p. 328-335.

Kirby, John L., ed., MINUTES OF THE ANNUAL CONFERENCES OF THE MECS, 1895, MECS Publishing House, Nashville, Tenn. (243 p.) N. Ga. — p. 131-140; S. Ga. — p. 165-172.

MINUTES OF THE ANNUAL CONFERENCES OF THE MECS, 1896, MECS Publishing

House, Nashville, Tenn. (248 p.) N. Ga. — p. 142-151; S. Ga. — p. 208-215.
MINUTES OF THE ANNUAL CONFERENCES OF THE MECS, 1897, MECS Publishing
House, Nashville, Tenn. (251 p.) N. Ga. — p. 131-143; S. Ga. — 170-176.
MINUTES OF THE ANNUAL CONFERENCES OF THE MECS, 1898, MECS Publishing
House, Nashville, Tenn. (248 p.) N. Ga. — p. 134-144; S. Ga. — p. 195-203.
MINUTES OF THE ANNUAL CONFERENCES OF THE MECS, 1899, MECS Publishing
House, Nashville, Tenn. (268 p.) N. Ga. — p. 160-177; S. Ga. — p. 188-198.
MINUTES OF THE ANNUAL CONFERENCES OF THE MECS, 1900, MECS Publishing
House, Nashville, Tenn. (255 p.) N. Ga. — p. 129-139; S. Ga. — p. 186-194.
MINUTES OF THE ANNUAL CONFERENCES OF THE MECS, 1901, MECS Publishing
House, Nashville, Tenn. (258 p.) N. Ga. — p. 130-140; S. Ga. — p. 179-187.
MINUTES OF THE ANNUAL CONFERENCES OF THE MECS, 1902, MECS Publishing
House, Nashville, Tenn. (292 p.) N. Ga. — p. 149-159; S. Ga. — p. 209-219.
MINUTES OF THE ANNUAL CONFERENCES OF THE MECS, 1903, MECS Publishing
House, Nashville, Tenn. (268 p.) N. Ga. — p. 143-150; S. Ga. — p. 178-184.
MINUTES OF THE ANNUAL CONFERENCES OF THE MECS, 1904, MECS Publishing
House, Nashville, Tenn. (279 p.) N. Ga. — p. 150-164; S. Ga. — p. 183-192.
MINUTES OF THE ANNUAL CONFERENCES OF THE MECS, 1905, MECS Publishing
House, Nashville, Tenn. (296 p.) N. Ga. — p. 148-160; S. Ga. — p. 183-191.
MINUTES OF THE ANNUAL CONFERENCES OF THE MECS, 1906, MECS Publishing
House, Nashville & Dallas. (304 p.) N. Ga. — p. 144-153; S. Ga. — p. 177-186.
MINUTES OF THE ANNUAL CONFERENCES OF THE MECS, 1907, MECS Publishing
House, Nashville & Dallas. (306 p.) N. Ga. — p. 177-189; S. Ga. — p. 222-232.
MINUTES OF THE ANNUAL CONFERENCES OF THE MECS, 1908, MECS Publishing
House, Nashville & Dallas. (300 p.) N. Ga. — p. 146-156; S. Ga. — p. 227-235.
MINUTES OF THE ANNUAL CONFERENCES OF THE MECS, 1909, MECS Publishing
House, Nashville & Dallas. (321 p.) N. Ga. — p. 162-175; S. Ga. — p. 221-230.
MINUTES OF THE ANNUAL CONFERENCES OF THE MECS, 1910, MECS Publishing
House, Nashville & Dallas. (354 p.) N. Ga. — p. 165-179; S. Ga. — p. 230-239.
MINUTES OF THE ANNUAL CONFERENCES OF THE MECS, 1911, MECS Publishing
House, Nashville and Dallas. N. Ga. — p. 172-187; S. Ga. — p. 237-246.
MINUTES OF THE ANNUAL CONFERENCES OF THE MECS, 1912, MECS Publishing
House, Nashville, Dallas, Richmond. (366 p.) N. Ga. — p. 169-189; S. Ga. —
p. 222-233.
MINUTES OF THE ANNUAL CONFERENCES OF THE MECS, 1913, MECS Publishing
House, Nashville, Dallas, Richmond. (357 p.) N. Ga. — p. 172-184; S. Ga. —
p. 203-215.
MINUTES OF THE ANNUAL CONFERENCES OF THE MECS, 1914, MECS Publishing
House, Nashville, Dallas, Richmond. (372 p.) N. Ga. — p. 179-199; S. Ga. —
p. 232-240.
MINUTES OF THE ANNUAL CONFERENCES OF THE MECS, 1915, MECS Publishing
House, Nashville, Dallas, Richmond. (392 p.) N. Ga. — 153-162; S. Ga. — p.
229-242.
MINUTES OF THE ANNUAL CONFERENCES OF THE MECS, 1916, MECS Publishing
House, Nashville, Dallas, Richmond. (388 p.) N. Ga. — p. 209-216; S. Ga. —
p. 238-249.
MINUTES OF THE ANNUAL CONFERENCES OF THE MECS, 1917, MECS Publishing

House, Nashville, Dallas, Richmond. (390 p.) N. Ga. — p. 139-151; S. Ga. — p. 176-189.

Kirk, John, THE MOTHER OF THE WESLEYS, Jennings and Graham, Cincinnati; Eaton and Mains, New York; ca. 1865. (398 p.)

Kirkland, William C., THE SCOTCH CONTRIBUTION TO THE S.C. CONFERENCE, pamphlet—historical address, (biographical sketches) (15 p.)

Kirkpatrick, Dow N., AN HISTORICAL STUDY OF THE TRANSCENDENTAL THEOLOGY AND ITS EFFECTS ON AMERICAN THEOLOGY ESPECIALLY SEEN IN REINHOLD NIEBUHR, (thesis) Emory Univ., Atlanta, Ga., 1940. (41 p.)
SIX DAYS AND SUNDAYS, Abingdon Press, Nashville and New York, 1968. (158 p.)
ed., THE DOCTRINE OF THE CHURCH, Abingdon, Nashville, 1964. (224 p.)
ed., THE FINALITY OF CHRIST, Abingdon Press, Nashville, New York, 1966. (207 p.)
ed., THE HOLY SPIRIT, Tidings, Nashville, Tenn., 1974. (242 p.)
ed., THE LIVING GOD, Abingdon Press, Nashville & New York, 1971. (206 p.)

Kirkpatrick, Dow N., and Weber, Theodore R., LIBERATION EVANGELISM (cassette tape), Emory Univ., Atlanta, Ga., 1977.

Knight, Lucien Lamar, "A Sketch of the Work of John Wesley In Georgia," The Tech High Press. (8 p.)

Knowles, Rev. Joshua ed., "Educational Repository & Family Monthly," Atlanta, Ga. (Reviewed in *Quarterly Review of the MECS,* D.S. Doggett, ed., April, 1860, p. 300.) (and also in issue, July, 1860, p. 464.)

Lacy, Walter N., A HUNDRED YEARS OF CHINA METHODISM, Abingdon-Cokesbury Press, N.Y. and Nashville, 1958. (336 p.) (Ga. Ref. — index — Rev. Y.J. Allen)

LaGorce, Agnes de, WESLEY, MAITRE D'UN PEUPLE (1703-1791), A. Michel, Paris, 1940. (366 p.)

Lambuth, Walter Russell, "Korea: Past and Present," *The Methodist Review,* (J.J.Tigert, ed.), Vol. 17, No. 2, Nov.-Dec. 1894, p. 204-210.
MEDICAL MISSIONS: THE TWO-FOLD TASK, MECS Board of Missions, Nashville, Tenn., 1920. (262 p.)
REV. CHARLES TAYLOR, MECS Board of Missions, Nashville, Tenn., 19____. (36 p.)
SIDELIGHTS ON THE ORIENT, MECS Publishing House, Nashville & Dallas, 1908. (169 p.)
"The Missionary Situation on the Congo," *The Methodist Review Quarterly,* (Gross Alexander, ed.), v. 63, July, 1914, p. 438-445.

Lane, Bishop Isaac, Autobiography With a Short History of the C.M.E. Church in America, M.E. Church, South Publishing House, Nashville, 1916. (192 p.)

Laney, James T., "Bonhoeffer's Ethical Contextualism," in Essays on Bonhoeffer, ed. by A.J. Kalssen, Eerdmans.
Character and the Moral Life, Louisiana State Univ. Press.
"Characterization and Moral Judgments," *The Journal of Religion,* Vol. 55, No. 4, Oct. 1975, p. 405-414.
"Conversion from Other Religions," in On Conversion, Four Views, John B. Cobb, et al. Methodist Board of Missions, New York, 1968.
"Ethics and Death," in Perspectives On Death, ed. by Liston O. Mills, Abingdon Press, Nashville, Ten., 1969; also published in Reflections, Yale Divinity School, March, 1969.
ed., Evangelism, Mandates For Action, Hawthorn Books, Inc., W. Clement Stone, Publisher, New York, 1975. (128 p.)
"Human Rights and the Meaning of Revolution," in Human Rights and World Perspective, St. Paul School of Theology, Kansas City, 1968.
"Norm—Context Debate in Christian Ethics—A Reconsideration," *Soundings,* Autumn, 1969.
"Prophetic and Consensual Morality," in Ethical Issues In American Life, Southern Educational Reporting Service, Nashville, Tenn., 1968.
"The Decline and Fall of Character," *The Candler Review,* Winter, 1974.
"The New Morality and the Churches," in The Annals, Journal of the American Academy of Political and Social Sciences, Jan. 1970.

Laney, James T., and Gustafson, James, On Being Responsible, Harper & Row, 1968.

Laney, Rev. Noah, "St. Augustine Mission," (letter written from Charleston, 1-20-1825) found in *The Methodist Magazine,* (Soule & Mason, eds.), Vol. 8, 1825, p. 112-113.

Larrabee, Prof. B. F., "Sasnett's 'Views of Female Education' Reviewed," found in *Quarterly Review,* (H.B. Bascomb, ed.), October, 1856, p. 508-526.

Larrabee, Rev. William C., Wesley and His Coadjutors, Vol. 2, Swormstedt & Poe, Cincinnati, 1853. (Biography of Charles Wesley) (280 p.) (Ga. Ref. — 110-116)

Lawrence, Harold A., ed., Records of the Tignall Charge (Wilkes Co., Ga.) The Tignall United Methodist Women, 1978. (708 p.)
"The Adventures of Roger Doger," (Children's Stories on cassette tapes—6 hours), Harold Lawrence, 1981.
ed., The 1850 Census of Abbeville District, South Carolina, The Boyd Publishing Co., Tignall, Ga., 1981.
ed., The Lavonia Charge Records (Franklin Co., Ga.), Harold Lawrence,

Lavonia, Ga., 1981. (1200 p.)
"Toward Clergy Peership," *The Circuit Rider,* v.4, n.1, Jan. 1980, p. 10-11.

Lawson, John, A THEOLOGICAL AND HISTORICAL INTRODUCTION TO THE APOSTOLIC FATHERS, MacMillan Co., New York, 1961. (334 p.)
AN EVANGELICAL FAITH FOR TODAY, Abingdon Press, Nashville, Tenn., 1972. (95 p.)
COMPREHENSIVE HANDBOOK OF CHRISTIAN DOCTRINE, Prentice-Hall, Englewood Cliffs, N.J., 1967. (287 p.)
GREEN AND PLEASANT LAND, SCM Press, London, 1955. (126 p.)
MAN AND HIS NEEDS, Edinburgh House Press, London, 1955. (136 p.)
METHODISM AND CATHOLICISM, SPCK, London, 1954. (51 p.)
NOTES ON WESLEY'S FOURTY FOUR SERMONS, Epworth Press, London, 1946. (291 p.) (reprint 1952).
SELECTIONS FROM JOHN WESLEY'S "NOTES ON THE NEW TESTAMENT," Alec R. Allenson, Chicago, 1955. (219 p.)
STUDY NOTES ON CHRISTIAN DOCTRINE, (with Alan T. Dale), Epworth Press, London, 1952. (88 p.)
THE BIBLICAL THEOLOGY OF SAINT IRENAEUS, Epworth Press, London, 1948. (307 p.)
THE BIG 2½ BY LICINIUS, St. Botolph Publishing Co., London, 1947. (99 p.)
THE CHRISTIAN YEAR WITH CHARLES WESLEY, Epworth Press, London, 1966. (121 p.)
"The Poetry of Charles Wesley," *The Emory University Quarterly Review,* v15, n1, March 1959, p. 31-47.
"Today I Go To Communion," Epworth Press, London, 1950. (14 p.)
VOTE LABOR? WHY? by Licinius, London, V. Gollancz, 1945. (77 p.)
WHAT DO WE BELIEVE, SPCK, London, 1951. (188 p.)
WHO JOINS THE GLORIOUS HOST?, Epworth Press, London, 1950. (64 p.)

Lednum, John, A HISTORY OF THE RISE OF METHODISM IN AMERICA, Philadelphia, 1859. (435 p.)

Lee, James W.; Luccock, Naphtali; & Dixon, James Main; eds., THE ILLUSTRATED HISTORY OF METHODISM, The Methodist Magazine Publishing Co., St. Louis & New York, 1900. (760 p.) (Pages pertaining to Ga. Methodism — 64, 67, 308, 309.)

Lee, Jesse, A SHORT HISTORY OF THE METHODISTS, Magill & Cline, Baltimore, 1810. (402 p.)
A SHORT HISTORY OF THE METHODISTS, ACADEMY BOOKS, RUTLAND, VT., 1974. (BEING A FACSIMILIE OF THE 1810 ED.) (385 P.)

Lee, John David, FROM BETHLEHEM TO OLIVET, Abingdon-Cokesbury Press, New York, Nashville, 1942. (120 p.)
"Glenn Memorial at Midnight," (poem), *The Emory Univ. Quarterly Review,* v4, n3, Oct. 1948, p. 183.

THE EMERGING REVIVAL: A RE-APPRAISAL, Seabury-Western, Evanston, Ill., 1951. (32 p.)
"V-J Day, Two Years After," *The Emory Univ. Quarterly Review,* v3, n3, Oct. 1947, p. 152-153.

Lee, Leroy M., THE LIFE AND TIMES OF REV. JESSE LEE, John Early, Louisville, Ky., 1848. (517 p.)
THE LIFE AND TIMES OF THE REV. JESSE LEE, E. Stevenson and J. Evans, Nashville, Tenn., 1856. (517 p.)
D.D., THE LIFE AND TIMES OF THE REV. JESSE LEE, Southern Methodist Publishing House, Nashville, Tenn., 1860. (517 p.)

Lee, Umphrey, THE LORD'S HORSEMAN, The Century Company, New York and London, 1928. (358 p.)
THE LORD'S HORSEMAN: JOHN WESLEY THE MAN, Abingdon, New York, Nashville, 1954. (220 p.) Ga. Ref. — 40-41, 46-47, 62-63, 70, 184.
JOHN WESLEY AND MODERN RELIGION, Cokesbury Press, Nashville, Tenn., 1936. (354 p.)
"John Wesley In Arcadia," *Southwest Review,* 13, July, 1928, p. 413-432.

Leete, Frederick DeLand, ADVENTURES OF A TRAVELING PREACHER: A MANIFOLD AUTOBIOGRAPHY, W.A. Wilde Co., Boston, 1952. (454 p.)
CHRISTIAN BROTHERHOOD, Jennings and Gordon, Cincinnati; Eaton and Mains, New York, 1912. (415 p.)
EVERYDAY EVANGELISM, (uv).
METHODIST BISHOPS: PERSONAL NOTES & BIBLIOGRAPHY, Parthenon Press, Nashville, 1948. (457 p.)

Letts, Mrs. W. E., ed., FOURTEENTH ANNUAL REPORT OF THE WSCS, N. GA. CONFERENCE, THE METHODIST CHURCH, DALTON, GA., APRIL 27-29, 1954, Adamson Printing Co., Atlanta, Ga. (182 p.)

LeVert, Mrs. E. H. Jr., "A History of Inman Park Methodist Church," Georgia Methodist Information, Atlanta, 1968. (Atlanta) (36 p.)

Lewis, James, FRANCIS ASBURY, Epworth Press, London, 1927. (227 p.)

Lewis, Walker, "George Foster Pierce," *The Methodist Review,* (J.J. Tigert, ed.), Vol. 26, No. 6, Nov.-Dec. 1900, p. 820-830.
"Jacob Unfolding His Son's Future," *The Methodist Quarterly Review,* (J.J. Tigert, ed.), v. 53, Jan. 1904, p. 124-132.
"Lovick Pierce, D.D.," *The Methodist Review,* (J.J. Tigert, ed.), Vol. 21, No. 3, Jan.-Feb. 1897, p. 323-331.
"The Conquest of Georgia by the Methodists and Baptists," *The Methodist Quarterly Review,* (J.J. Tigert, ed.), Nov.-Dec., 1901, v. 50, p. 816-826.
"William Pope Harrison, DD, LL.D," *The Methodist Review, (J.J. Tigert, ed.), Vol. 18, No. 3, July-August, 1895, p. 291-200.*

Lipscomb, Andrew A., "Christian Heroism," J.W. Burke & Co., Macon, Ga., 1880. (56 p.)

"Consecrated Heroism" (Memorial Discourse on the death of Bishop Pierce), *The Quarterly Review of the MECS,* (J.W. Hinton, ed.), Vol. 6, No. 4, Oct. 1884, p. 719-731.

"Letters From the Old World: Addressed to the Students of Senior Class, Georgia University," *Scott's Monthly,* v.8, n.2,3,4, Aug. 1869, Phillips & Crew, Atlanta, p. 619-626; 683-686; 793-794.

STUDIES IN THE FORTY DAYS BETWEEN CHRIST'S RESURRECTION AND ASCENSION, Southern Methodist Publishing House, Nashville, Tenn., 1884. (363 p.)

STUDIES IN THE FORTY DAYS BETWEEN CHRIST'S RESURRECTION AND ASCENSION, Southern Methodist Publishing House, Nashville, Tenn., 1885. (362 p.)

STUDIES SUPPLEMENTARY TO THE STUDIES IN THE FORTY DAYS BETWEEN OUR LORD'S RESURRECTION AND ASCENSION, Southern Methodist Publishing House, Nashville, Tenn., 1885. (300 p.)

"The Relations of the Anglo-Saxon Race To Christian Womanhood," Rose & Co., Book and Job Print, Macon, Ga., 1860. (26 p.)

Lipsky, Abram, JOHN WESLEY, A PORTRAIT, Simon & Schuster, New York, 1928. (305 p.) Ga. Ref. — p. 31.

Littell, Franklin H., A TRIBUTE TO MENNO SIMONS, Herald Press, Scottdale, Pa., 1971. (71 p.)

"Barmen; A 25th Anniversary Tribute," *Christianity and Crisis,* 19, May 25, 1959, p. 71-74.

"Basis of Religious Liberty In American History," *Journal of Church and State,* 6, Autumn, 1964, p. 314-332.

"Basis of Religious Liberty in Christian Belief," *Journal of Church and State,* 6 Spring, 1964, p. 132-146.

"C & C Deutsches Christentum and a "renegade jew," *Christinity and Crisis,* 32, May 1, 1972, p. 111.

"Christendom, Holocaust and Israel," *Journal of Ecumenical Studies,* 10, Summer, 1973, p. 483-497.

"Christian Primitivism," *Encounter,* 20, Summer, 1959, p. 292-296.

"Christian Style of Politics," *Review and Expositer,* 65, Summer, 1968, p. 287-297.

CHRISTIANITY AND FREEDOM, Payne Theological Seminary, Wilberforce, Ohio, 1966. (32 p.)

"Christians and Jews and Ecumenism," *Dialog,* 10, Autumn, 1971, p. 249-255.

"Christians and Jews In The Historical Process," *Judaism,* 22, Summer, 1973, p. 263-277.

"Christians In a Violent Age," *Dialog,* 8, Winter, 1969, p. 33-35.

"Common Language," *Journal of Ecumenical Studies,* Spring, 1966, p. 362-365.

"Church of the Brethren and the Metropolis," *Brethren Life and Thought,* 11, Sept., 1966, p. 11-18.

"Embarrassments of a Methodist Ecumenic," *Journal of Ecumenical Studies,* 2, Spring, 1965, p. 277-282.

"Ethics After Auschwitz," *Worldview,* 18, Sept. 1975, p. 22-26.

"Federal Common Law or National Idealogy?" *Journal of Church and State,* 14, Spring, 1972, p. 187-189.

"Foundations and Traditions of Religious Liberty," *Journal of Ecumenical Studies,* 14, Fall, 1977, p. 572-578.

FROM STATE CHURCH TO PLURALISM, Anchor Books, Garden City, New York, 1962. (174 p.)

"German Kirchentag, 1973," *Christian Century,* 90, August 29, 1973, p. 833.

"Have Jews and Christians A Common Future," *Journal of Church and State,* 13, Spring, 1971, p. 303-315.

"Historical Free Church Defined," *Brethren Life and Thought,* 9, Autumn, 1964, p. 78-90.

"Importance of Anabaptist Studies," *Archiv fur Reformations geschichte,* no. 1, 1967, p. 15-28.

"In Response To Hans Hillerbrand," *Mennonite Quarterly Review,* 45, Oct. 1971, p. 377-380.

"Is The University Done For," *Union Seminary Quarterly Review,* 20, Nov. 1964, p. 49-59.

"Israel, Christendom and Islam," *Engage/Social Action,* 2, Dec. 1974, p. 49-54.

"Kirchenkampf and holocaust," *Journal of Church and State,* 13, Spring, 1971, p. 209-226.

"Kirchentag Reborn; Frankfurt, 1975," *Christian Century,* 92, Sept. 17, 1975, p. 795-797.

Landgraf Phillipp und die Toleranz; ein christlicher Furst der linke Flugel der Reformation und der christ liche Primitiuismus, (thesis), Univ. of Marburg, 1957. (54 p.)

"Ministry of the Laity," *Pastoral Psychology,* 15, Dec. 1964, p. 6-12.

"Moment of Trust For Protestantism," *Journal of Ecumenical Studies,* 1, Spring, 1964, 315-317.

"New Shape of the Church-State Issue," *Mennonite Quarterly Review,* 40, July, 1966, p. 179-189.

"Nixon and American Isolationism," *Christian Century,* 90, March 14, 1973, p. 310-311.

"Pastoral Care Under Tolatitarianism, *Christianity and Crisis,* 13, No. 6, 1953, p. 42-46.

"Plea For Israel," *Christian Century,* 90, Nov. 7, 1973, p. 1094-1095.

"Politics, Theology and the Jews," *Journal of Ecumenical Studies,* 2, Fall, 1965, p. 475-477.

"Problem of Discipline In American Religious Life," *Journal of Ecumenical Studies,* 4, Fall, 1967, p. 726-729.

"Reflections on Religious Liberty," (thesis), *Theology Cassettes,* 7, No. 3, Mar. 1976.

REFORMATION STUDIES, John Knox Press, Richmond, Va., 1962. (285 p.)

"Religion In The American Experience," *Religious Education,* 71, May-June, 1976, p. 303-317.

"Religious Liberty," *Journal of Ecumenical Studies,* 1, Autumn, 1964, p. 508-514.

"Religious Liberty and Missions," *Journal of Church and State,* 7, Autumn, 1965,

p. 374-387.

"Religious Liberty In a Pluralistic Society," *Journal of Church and State*, 8, Autumn, 1966, p. 430-444.

ed., "Religious Liberty In The Crossfires of Creeds," *Journal of Ecumenical Studies*, 14, Fall, 1977, p. 572-736.

"Secularism, Secularization and Secularity, *Journal of Ecumenical Studies*, 4, Summer, 1967, p. 472-476.

"Selected Books on the Laity," *Journal of Bible and Religion*, 33, July, 1965, p. 260-261.

"Seminary Provides For Dialogue," *Theological Education*, 1, Winter, 1965, p. 83-89.

ed., SERMONS TO INTELLECTUALS FROM THREE CONTINENTS, Macmillan, New York, 1963. (160 p.)

"Shalom In Memoriam: Bernhard E. Olson," *Journal of Ecumenical Studies*, 12, Fall, 1975, p. 582-583.

"Significance of the Declaration on Religious Liberty," *Journal of Ecumenical Studies*, 5, Spring, 1968, p. 326-337.

"Spiritualizers, Anabaptists and the Church," *Mennonite Quarterly Review*, 29, Jan. 1955, p. 34-43.

"Strober Report," *Journal of Ecumenical Studies*, 9, Fall, 1972, p. 860-862.

THE ANABAPTIST VIEW OF THE CHURCH, American Society of Church History, Hartford, 1952. (148 p.)

THE ANABAPTIST VIEW OF THE CHURCH, Starr King Press, Boston, 1958. (229 p.)

THE CHURCH AND THE BODY POLITIC, Seabury Press, New York, 1969. (175 p.)

THE CRUCIFIXION OF THE JEWS, Harper & Row, New York, 1975. (153 p.)

"The Evangelical Academies," *The Emory Univ. Quarterly Review*, v15, n1, March, 1959, p. 49-53.

THE FREE CHURCH, Starr King Press, Boston, 1957. (171 p.)

THE GERMAN PHOENIX, Doubleday, Garden City, N.Y., 1960. (226 p.)

ed., THE GERMAN STRUGGLE AND THE HOLOCAUST, (with Hubert G. Locke), Wayne State Univ. Press, 1974. (328 p.)

THE MACMILLAN ATLAS HISTORY OF CHRISTIANITY, Macmillan, New York, 1976. (176 p.)

"Theological Education For A Pluralistic Society," *Encounter*, 25, Summer, 1964, p. 273-282.

"Thoughts On The Church," *Brethren Life and Thought*, 8, Spring, 1963, p. 4-12.

TOTALITARIANISM, Garrett Theological Seminary Library, Evanston, 1966.

"Uprooting Antisemitism; A Call to Christians," *Journal of Church and State*, 17, Winter, 1975, p. 15-24.

Von der Freiheit der Kirche, Im Christian-Verlag, Bad Nauheim, 1957. (188 p.)

ed., Weltkirchen Lexikon, Kreuz-Verlag, Stuttgart, 1960. (3 p.)

"Who Were The Anabaptists?", *Brethren Life and Thought*, 2, Spring, 1957, p. 13-20.

"Why Don't They Understand Us," *Christianity and Crisis*, 12, No. 14, 1952, p. 106-110.

Lockwood, Rev. J. P., Memorials of the Life of Peter Bohler, Wesleyan Conference Office, London, 1868. (142 p.)

Loehr, George R., ''China's Classics and Her Need For Christ,'' *The Methodist Review,* v. 66, Oct. 1917, p. 737-742.
''Giuseppe Castiglione: Missionary Painter,'' *The Emory University Quarterly Review,* v17, n3, Fall, 1961, p. 176-184.
''Young J. Allen and Mandarins,'' *The Emory Univ. Quarterly Review,* v4, n2, June, 1948, p. 102-109.

Long, Nathaniel Guy, ''Financing the Church Budget,'' Church & Community Press, Atlanta, 1957. (61 p.)
Goal Posts, Tupper and Love (Foote & Davies, Inc.), 1953. (162 p.)
My Long Life, T.H.P., Conyers, Ga., 1978. (399 p.)
The Story of Peachtree Road Methodist Church (Atlanta) published by the History Committee of Peachtree Road Church, Atlanta, 1953. (168 p.)
The Story of Zoar, (Zoar UMC, Centerville, Ga.), 1973. (167 p.)
''The Word Became Flesh: A Christmas Meditation,'' *The Emory Univ. Quarterly Review,* v12, n4, Dec. 1956, p. 193-196.

Longstreet, Augustus Baldwin, (c.1850) — 5 folders — Ga. Papers of this author, president of Emory Univ., and Methodist clergyman include miscellaneous correspondence, reports, clippings and materials re Longstreet. Sp Cl Woodruff
A Voice From The South, Western Continent Press, Baltimore, 1847. (92 p.)
A Voice From the South, Western Continent Press, 1847 (1848), varies only in title and imprint on cover.
Address Delivered at His Inauguration, 2-10-1840. Ed. by Judson C. Ward, Jr., Emory Univ., Ga., Emory Univ. Library, 1955. Emory Publications, Sources & Reprints, Ser. 9, No. 2. (31 p.)
''Fast-Day Sermon'', delivered in Washington St. MECS, Columbia, S.C., 6-13-1861. Columbia, Townsend & North, 1861. (14 p.) CSA Biblio — Willingham
''Georgia Scenes,'' *The Magnolia,* Burges & James, Charleston, 1843, v. 2, p. 160-161; 349-355. (Pendleton, P.C., ed.)
Georgia Scenes, (2nd ed.), Harper & Brothers, New York,, copyright 1840. (214 p.)
Georgia Scenes, 1844, pub. J.O. Culpepper of Quitman, Ga. (238 p.)
Georgia Scenes, Franklin Printing and Publishing, Atlanta, 1894. (238 p.)
Georgia Scenes, Sagamore Press, New York, 1957. (208 p.) (A reprint first pub. in 1835). + Reprinted by Peter Smith, Gloucester, Mass., 1959, 198 p.
''Georgia Scenes: Julia & Clarissa,'' *The Magnolia,* Burges & James, Charleston, 1842, v. 1, p. 185-189; 216-224. (Pendleton, P.C., ed.)
''Inaugural Address,'' Southern Ladies' Book, Vol. 1, Benj. F. Griffin, printer, Macon, Ga., 1840, p. 159-164. (Pierce, G.F., ed.)
Master William Mitten, Burke, Boykin & Co., Macon, Ga., 1864. (239 p.)
Master William Mitten, J.W. Burke & Co., Macon, Ga., 1889. (366 p.)

STORIES WITH A MORAL, The John C. Winston Co., Philadelphia, 1912. (396 p.)

"The General's Horse," *The Augusta Mirror*, Wm. Tappan Thompson & James McCafferty May 5, 1838. (Magazine also included several "Georgia Scenes.")

"Valuable Suggestions Addressed to the Soldiers of the Confederate States," published by the Soldier's Tract Association, Macon, Ga., 186__. (16 p.) CSA Biblio Willingham

WILLIAM MITTEN, *Southern Field and Fireside,* James Gardner, Augusta, Stockton & Co. (Serial Story). [Magazine ran from 1859-64].

Lovejoy, Rev. W. P., A SHORT HISTORY OF METHODISM IN THE UNITED STATES, J.W. Burke & Co., Macon, 1884. (63 p.)

"Christ In Theology," *Methodist Quarterly Review,* (J.J. Tigert, ed.), Vol. 16, No. 2, July, 1894, p. 375-394.

"From Gethsemane To Calvary: An Exegetical Study," *The Methodist Review,* (J.J. Tigert, ed.), Vol. 19, No. 3, Jan.-Feb., 1896, p. 353-367.

"Is a Christian Socialism Possible?" *The Methodist Quarterly Review,* (J.J. Tigert, ed.), v. 54, Oct. 1905, p. 739-753.

No MISSIONS, NO CHRIST, (uv)

"Persecution: Catholic and Protestant," *The Methodist Review,* (J.J. Tigert, ed.), Vol. 26, No. 6, Nov.-Dec., 1900, p. 842-858.

"The Christ of the 20th Century," *The Methodist Quarterly Review,* (J.J. Tigert, ed.), Jan.-Feb., 1901, v. 50, p. 61-73.

"The Church and Education," *The Quarterly Review of the MECS,* (J.W. Hinton, ed.), Vol. 5, No. 3, July, 1883, p. 426-441.

THE GREATEST RESPONSIBILITY IN THE WORLD, The Foote and Davies Co., Printers and Binders, Atlanta, Ga., 1899. (88 p.)

"The Influence of Methodism," *The Methodist Quarterly Review,* (J.J. Tigert, ed.), May-June, 1902, v. 51, p. 367-382.

"The Italian Renaissance," *The Methodist Review Quarterly,* (Gross Alexander, ed.), v. 56, Jan. 1907, p. 115-126.

THE MISSION OF THE CHURCH, MECS Publishing House, Nashville, Tenn., 1894. (288 p.)

"The Modern Pulpit," *Southern Methodist Review,* (W.P. Harrison, ed.), Vol. 3, No. 3, Jan. 1888, p. 380-390.

"The Training of a Nation," *The Methodist Quarterly Review,* (J.J. Tigert, ed.), v. 53, Oct. 1904, p. 694-708.

"The Western Peril," *The Methodist Review Quarterly,* (Gross Alexander, ed.), v. 59, April 1910, p. 300-310.

"William McKendree, The Ecclesiastical Statesman," *The Methodist Review,* (J.J. Tigert, ed.), Vol. 21, No. 3, Jan.-Feb. 1897, p. 376-386.

Lovett, Robert W., (1787-1916) — 2 boxes — 51 BVs — Ga. Papers of Lovett, physician and preacher, member of the old Ga. Annual Conference, include correspondence, speeches and essays, diary, wills, deeds, land grants, etc. Lovett's first wife was the daughter of Bishop J.O. Andrew and some of the correspondence relates to him, to Joshua Soule, and to other churchmen and deals primarily with church matters. Sp Cl Woodruff

Lovett, W. C., ed., MINUTES OF THE 26TH SESSION OF THE SOUTH GEORGIA CONFERENCE OF THE MECS, HELD IN COLUMBUS, GA., DEC. 14-19, 1892, J.W. Burke, Stationers and Printers, 1893. (46 m.p.).
MINUTES OF THE 27TH SESSION OF THE SOUTH GEORGIA CONFERENCE OF THE MECS, HELD IN DAWSON, GA., DEC. 13-18, 1893, The Foote & Davies Co., Printers and Binders, Atlanta, Ga. 1894. (63 p.)
MINUTES OF THE 28TH SESSION OF THE SOUTH GEORLIA CONFERENCE OF THE MECS, HELD IN WAYCROSS, GA., DEC. 13-17, 1894, University Press, Nashville, Tenn., 1895. (52 m.p.)
MINUTES OF THE 29TH SESSION OF THE SOUTH GEORGIA CONFERENCE OF THE MECS, HELD IN FT. VALLEY, GA., DEC. 4-9, 1895, Thos. Gilbert, printer and stationer, Columbus, Ga., 1895. (48 m.p.)
MINUTES OF THE 30TH SESSION OF THE SOUTH GEORGIA CONFERENCE OF THE MECS, HELD IN VALDOSTA, GA., DEC. 9-14, 1896, Thos. Gilbert, Printer & Stationer, Columbus, Ga., 1897. (50 m.p.)
MINUTES OF THE 31ST SESSION OF THE SOUTH GEORGIA CONFERENCE OF THE MECS HELD IN SAVANNAH, DEC. 1-6, 1897, Thos. Gilbert, printer and stationer, Columbus, Ga., 1898. (48 m.p.)

Luccock, Halford E., and Garrison, Webb, ENDLINE LINE OF SPLENDOR, United Methodist Communications, Evanston, Ill., 1975. (112 p.)

Lunn, Arnold, JOHN WESLEY, The Dial Press, New York, 1929. (371 p.) (Ga. Ref. — 48, 49, 83, 115)

M'Anally, D. R., THE LIFE AND LABORS OF REV. E.M. MARVIN, DD, LL.D., Advocate Publishing House, St. Louis, 1878. (330 p.)

McCarty, Rev. W. A. (Ala. Conf.), and **McCarty, Rev. T. R.** (N. Ga. Conf.), DOCTRINES FOR THE TIMES, Foote & Davies, Atlanta, 1895. (251 p.)

McClintock, John, (c.1830-1870) — 16 boxes, 51 BVs — Pa. Papers of this Methodist leader (ed. of the Methodist Quarterly Review, 1848) include correspondence with prominent Methodists (Robert Emory, S. Olin, etc.) about Methodist activities. McClintock's diaries reveal much about the ME Church history. The collections also includes a ritual of the ME Church, licenses to preach, etc. Sp Cl Woodruff

McConnell, Francis J., JOHN WESLEY, Abingdon Press, New York, 1939. (355 p.) (Ga. Ref. — 41-54, 58, 60, 65, 66, 79, 81, 85, 110, 135, 257, 267).

McDaniel, Rev. S. C., The Origin and Early History of The Congregational Methodist Church, James P. Harrison and Co., Atlanta, 1881. (90 p.)

McDavid, Joel D., "An Old Call: A New Thurst," *Circuit Rider,* April, 1981,

United Methodist Publishing House, Nashville, Tenn. (J. Richard Peck, ed.). pp. 6-7.

"Getting Personal In Missions: The Advance," *The Interpreter,* April, 1981, United Methodist Communications, Evanston, Ill. (Darrell R. Shamblin, ed.). pp. 25-26.

McElreath, Walter, HISTORY OF GRACE METHODIST CHURCH (Atlanta), (24 p.) METHODIST UNION IN THE COURTS, Abingdon-Cokesbury Press, New York, Nashville, 1946. (318 p.)

McFarland, Rev. J. Buie, COUSIN EULA OR A CATHOLIC CONVERTED, Southern Methodist Publishing House, Nashville, Tenn., 1882. (195 p.)

McGehee, Rev. J. B., AUTOBIOGRAPHY, Weaver Printing Co., Buena Vista, Ga., 1915. (163 p.)

McKee, Hugh, ed., YEARBOOK AND MINUTES, NORTH GEORGIA CONFERENCE OF THE UNITED METHODIST CHURCH, HELD AT GLENN MEMORIAL UMC, EMORY UNIVERSITY, ATLANTA, GA., JUNE 21-25, 1971, The Methodist Publishing House, Nashville, Tenn. (424 p.)
YEARBOOK AND MINUTES, OF THE 106TH SESSION NORTH GEORGIA CONFERENCE OF THE UNITED METHODIST CHURCH, HELD AT GLENN MEMORIAL UMC, EMORY UNIVERSITY, ATLANTA, GA., JUNE 19-23, 1972, The Methodist Publishing House, Nashville, Tenn. (316 p.)
YEARBOOK AND MINUTES, NORTH GEORGIA CONFERENCE OF THE UNITED METHODIST CHURCH, HELD AT GLENN MEMORIAL UMC, EMORY UNIV., ATLANTA, GA., JUNE 12-16, 1973, The United Methodist Publishing House, Nashville, Tenn. (323 p.)
YEARBOOK AND MINUTES, NORTH GEORGIA CONFERENCE OF THE UNITED METHODIST CHURCH, HELD AT GLENN MEMORIAL UMC, (EMORY UNIV., ATLANTA, GA.) JUNE 11-14, 1974, The U.M. Publishing House, Nashville, Tenn. (324 p.)
YEARBOOK AND MINUTES, 1975 NORTH GEORGIA CONFERENCE OF THE UNITED METHODIST CHURCH, HELD AT GLENN MEMORIAL UMC, EMORY UNIVERSITY, ATLANTA, GA., JUNE 17-20, 1975, The United Methodist Publishing House, Nashville, Tenn. (417 p.)
YEARBOOK AND MINUTES, 1976 NORTH GEORGIA CONFERENCE OF THE UNITED METHODIST CHURCH, HELD AT GLENN MEMORIAL UMC, EMORY UNIVERSITY, ATLANTA, GA., JUNE 15-18, 1976, The United Methodist Publishing House, Nashville, Tenn. (362 p.)
YEARBOOK AND MINUTES, 1977 NORTH GEORGIA CONFERENCE OF THE UNITED METHODIST CHURCH HELD AT GLENN MEMORIAL UMC, EMORY UNIVERSITY, ATLANTA, GA., JUNE 14-17, 1977, The United Methodist Publishing House, Nashville, Tenn. (362 p.)
YEARBOOK AND MINUTES, 1978, NORTH GEORGIA CONFERENCE OF THE UNITED METHODIST CHURCH HELD AT GLENN MEMORIAL UMC, EMORY UNIVERSITY, ATLANTA, GA., JUNE 13-16, 1978, The United Methodist Publishing House,

Nashville, Tenn. (226 p.)

YEARBOOK AND MINUTES, 1979, NORTH GEORGIA CONFERENCE OF THE UNITED METHODIST CHURCH, HELD AT GLENN MEMORIAL UMC, EMORY UNIVERSITY, ATLANTA, GA., JUNE 12-15, 1979, The United Methodist Publishing House, Nashville, Tenn. (217 m.p.)

YEARBOOK AND MINUTES, 1980, NORTH GEORGIA CONFERENCE OF THE UNITED METHODIST CHURCH, HELD AT AUGUSTA, GA., JUNE 17-20, 1980, The United Methodist Publishing House, Nashville, Tenn. (351 p.)

Yearbook and Minutes, 1980, North Georgia Conference of The United Methodist Church, Held At Glenn Memorial UMC, Emory University, Atlanta, Ga., June 16-19, 1981, The United Methodist Publishing House, Nashville, Tenn. (373 p.)

McKibben, J.W.O., "Institutional Care and Placing of Dependent Children as Conducted by the North Georgia Conference." (Thesis, 1921, Emory Univ.) (50 p.)

McKoy, William A., "Church School Teaches About Death," *Christian Advocate,* v. XIV, n. 20, p. 11-12.

"Class Strengthens Church," *The Interpreter,* v. 21, n. 2, Feb. 1977, p. 47-48.

FACING DEATH FROM A CHRISTIAN PERSPECTIVE, Discipleship Resources, Nashville, Tenn., 1976.

"Get The Word Out, Get The Members Back," *The Church School,* v. 10, n. 8, April, 1978, p. 19.

"God Is Extravagent," *Pulpit Digest,* v. LVII, n. 427, Sept.-Oct. 1977, p. 14-17.

"Keys To A Christian Education Emphasis," *The Church School,* v. 5, n. 11, July, 1973, p. 3.

"Making Friends With Young People Is Preparing For Confirmation," *Christian Advocate,* -6-22-1972, p. 11-12.

"Teaching About Death," *The Church School,* v. 10, n. 6, Feb. 1978, p. 19-20.

"The Mobility of God and His People," *Pulpit Digest,* v. LII, n. 394, April, 1972, p. 21-22.

"Too Many Teachers," *Youth Leader,* v. 7, n. 1, Fall, 1974, p. 26-29.

McLeroy, Annie K., Concern Methodist Church, Putnam Co., Ga., "Sesqui-Centennial 1810-1960." (10 p.)

McMahon, William, "Letter regarding the Cherokee Mission," (dated, Huntsville, Ala., 12-7-1827), found in *The Methodist Magazine,* (Soule & Mason, eds.), Vol. 11, 1828, p. 113. A second letter on the same subject, dated 4-1-1828, found in same vol. on page 278.

McNeer, May & Ward, Lynd, JOHN WESLEY, Abingdon-Cokesbury Press, New York & Nashville, 1951. (96 p.)

McPheeters, A. A., "The Origins and Development of Clark University and Gammon Theological Seminary," University of Cincinnati, Teachers College,

Abstracts of Graduate Theses in Education, 5, 1955, p. 19-26.

McTyeire, Holland N., A History of Methodism, M.E. Church, S. Publishing House, Nashville, 1891. (692 p.) (Ga. Ref. — 72, 363).

McTier, William E., ed., The Journal of the South Georgia Annual Conference of the UMC, 1977, The United Methodist Publishing House. Part 1 — April, 1977 — (114 p.); Part 2 — Aug., 1977 — (170 p.); Part 3 — April, 1978 — (104 p.).
The Journal of the South Georgia Annual Conference of The United Methodist Church, 1978, Being the 112 Session of the South Georgia Conference, The United Methodist Publishing House, Nashville, Tenn. Part 1 (181 p.); Part 2 (112 p.).
The Journal of the South Georgia Annual Conference of the United Methodist Church, 1979, Being the 113th Session of the South Georgia Conference, The United Methodist Publishing House, Nashville, Tenn. Part 1 — (228 p.); Part 2 — (144 p.).
The Journal of the South Georgia Annual Conference of The United Methodist Church, 1980, Being the 114th Session of the South Georgia Conference, The United Methodist Publishing House, Nashville, Tenn. Part 1 — (200 p.)

MaGath, Julius, "Esperanto: The New Universal Language," *The Methodist Review Quarterly*, v. 56, Oct. 1907, p. 672-680.
Jesus Before The Sanhedrim, Southern Methodist Publishing House, Nashville, 1886. (165 p.) (2nd Ed.).
Jesus Before The Sanhedrim, Julius MaGath, Oxford, Ga., 1909. (165 p.) (7th Ed.).

Mallard, William, "A Perspective for Current Theological Conversation," in T.J.J. Altizer, ed., Toward a New Christianity, Harcourt, Brace, 1967, p. 321-341.
"Clarity and Dilemma: the Forty Sermons of John Wycliff," in Contemporary Reflections on the Medieval Christian Tradition, ed. G.H. Shriver, Duke Univ. Press, Durham, N.C., 1974, p. 19-38.
"Dating the 'Sermones Quadraginta' of John Wycliff," *Medievalia et Humanistica*, Fasc. XVII, 1966, p. 86-105.
"John Wycliff and the Tradition of Biblical Authority," *Church History*, XXX, 1 (March, 1961), p. 50-60.
"Method and Perspective in Church History: A Reconsideration," *Journal of the American Academy of Religion*, XXXVI, 4 (December, 1968), p. 345-365.
"Secularist and Traditionalist," *Religion in Life*, XLII, 4 (Winter, 1973), p. 496-507.
"Spirit and Flesh: the Way Out or the Way Through?" *Candler Review*, 1, 2 (May, 1974), p. 6-11.
"The Eclipse of Biblical Narrative," (Review Article), *Candler Review* II, 2 (May, 1975), p. 20-23.

"The Incarnation in Augustine's Conversion," accepted and in proofs for REVUE DES ETUDES AUGUSTINIENNES, Paris.
THE REFLECTION OF THEOLOGY IN LITERATURE: A CASE STUDY IN THEOLOGY AND CULTURE, Trinity University Press, San Antonio, 1977. (271 p.)
"Transcendence and Mystery in Modern Literature," in TRANSCENDENCE AND MYSTERY, ed. by Earl D.C. Brewer, IDOC, North America, Inc., New York, 1975, p. 89-105.

Mann, Harold Wilson, ATTICUS GREENE HAYGOOD: METHODIST BISHOP, EDITOR, AND EDUCATOR, Athens, Univ. of Ga. Press, 1965. (262 p.)
THE LIFE AND TIMES OF ATTICUS GREENE HAYGOOD, (dissertation), Univ. Microfilms, Ann Arbor, Mich., 1962-3. (434 p.)

(Marshallville) "On Jordan's April Banks: Excerpts from a History of the Marshallville Methodist Church, 1825-1950," *Georgia Review,* 6, Winter, 1953, p. 373-89.

Marston, Leslie R., FROM AGE TO AGE—A LIVING WITNESS, Light and Life Press, Winona Lake, Ind., 1960. (Free Methodism) (608 p.) (Ga. Ref. — p. 32-35, 38, 44, 46, 67, 69).

Martin, Emory S., HISTORY OF TAYLOR'S CREEK CAMP MEETING, LIBERTY COUNTY, GA., 1933.

Martin, Mrs. M. (of Unionville, S.C.), "A Cursory Review of Prof. Sasnett's Theory of Female Education," found in *Quarterly Review* (H.B. Bascomb, ed.), October, 1856, p. 572-582.

Martin, S. Walter, "Some Thoughts For The New Year," *The Emory Univ. Quarterly Review,* v17, n4, Winter, 1961, p. 193-195.

Martin, William, "Hon. W.C. Preston and Little Henry," *The Home Circle,* MECS Publishing House, Nashville, Tenn., 1860, p. 481. (Huston, L.D., ed.).

Maser, Frederick E., THE DRAMATIC STORY OF EARLY AMERICAN METHODISM, Abingdon Press, New York, Nashville, 1965. (109 p.) (Ga. Ref. — 13-17, 19, 46).

Mathews, Annie MacDonell, MEMORIAL STONES. (Sketch of lives of George and Annie Mathews). (66 p.)

MATHEWS, MARCIA M., RICHARD ALLEN, Helicon, Baltimore-Dublin, 1963. (151 p.)

May, James W., "Francis Asbury and Thomas White: A Refugee Preacher and His Tory Patron," *Methodist History,* v14, n3, April 1976, p. 141-164.
FROM REVIVAL MOVEMENT TO DENOMINATION: A RE-EXAMINATION OF THE

BEGINNINGS OF AMERICAN METHODISM, (thesis), Columbia Univ., 1962. (368 p.) (on Univ. Microfilms, Ann Arbor, Mich., 1972).
THE NEW EVANGELISM, Forum House, Atlanta, 1973. (cassette).

Means, Alexander, (c.1830-1880) — 2 boxes — Ga. Papers of this Methodist local preacher, who was instrumental in the establishment of a manual labor school at Covington by the Methodist Church, include correspondence, diaries, addresses, etc. Means was a noted educator (pres. of Emory College), physician, and scientist. Sp Cl Woodruff
A CLUSTER OF POEMS FOR THE HOME AND HEART, E.J. Hale & Son, Publishers, New York, 1878. (216 p.)
"A Vision of Millenium," (poem) *Southern Field & Fireside,* James Gardner, Augusta, Stockton & Co. [Magazine ran from 1859-64]. Poem also appeared in *Hygienic and Literary Magazine,* 1860, Intelligencier Power Press. (Riley, ed.).
"Address," (delivered to the Medical College of Georgia—11-8-1847), James McCafferty, printer, Augusta, 1847. (31 p.)
"An Address" delivered at the Female College at Macon, Ga., 7-13-1843, published in Macon, Ga. (22 p.) (reviewed in *The Orion,* v3, p. 188. (Penfield, Ga., 1843, Wm. C. Richards, ed.).
"Anticipations of the Latter Day Glory," SOUTHERN LADIES' BOOK, Vol. 1, Benj. F. Griffin, printer, Macon, Ga., 1840, p. 74-75. (Pierce, G.F., ed.).
"Apostrophe," (poem), *The Home Circle,* v.3., MECS Publishing House, Nashville, Tenn., 1857, p. 112. (Huston, L.D., ed.).
"Climate," TRANSACTIONS OF THE MEDICAL ASSOCIATION OF GEORGIA, 1883, p. 119-140.
"Conformity To Law In The Divine Economy," *The Quarterly Review of the MECS,* (J.W. Hinton, ed.), Vol 2, No. 2, April, 1880, p. 265-274.
"Dedication For A Friend's Album," (poem), *The Magnolia,* v.3, p. 26. (Pendleton, ed.).
DIARY FOR 1861, ed. by Ross H. McLean. Emory Univ., Ga. Emory Sources and Reprints, 1949. (46 p.)
"Epitaph of An Infant," *The Home Circle,* v.3., MECS Publishing House, Nashville, Tenn., 1857, p. 141. (poem) (Huston, L.D., ed.).
"Etherealized by Grace," *Scott's Monthly Magazine,* Vol. 1 & 2, Franklin Steam Print, Atlanta, Ga., 1866, p. 862. (Scott, W.J., ed.).
"Georgia Marble," *Southern Ladies' Book,* Vol. 1, Benj. F. Griffin, printer, Macon, Ga., 1840, p. 15-17. (Pierce, G.F., ed.).
"Hygiene," *Scott's Monthly Magazine,* Vol. 1 & 2, Franklin Steam Print, Atlanta, Ga., 1866, p. 562-565; 618-624. (Scott, W.J., ed.).
(Items printed in) *The Augusta Mirror,* William Tappan Thompson & James McCafferty, May 5, 1838.
"Meteoric Visitations," *The Quarterly Review of the MECS,* (J.W. Hinton, ed.), Vol. 4, No. 4, Oct. 1882, p. 698-704.
"Missionary Stanzas," (poem) *The Home Circle,* v.3., MECS Publishing House, Nashville, Tenn., 1857, p. 226. (Huston, L.D., ed.).
"Mount Sinai," (poem), *The Magnolia,* Burges and James, Charleston, 1842, v. 1, p. 98-99. (Pendleton, P.C., ed.).

"Ode on the Opening of the New Year 1860," *The Home Circle,* MECS Publishing House, Nashville, Tenn., 1860, p. 392-393. (poem) (Huston, L.P., ed.).

"Poetic Paraphrase of the 48th Psalm," (poem), *The Emory Univ. Quarterly Review,* v20, n1, Spring, 1964, p. 1-2.

"Revelation Sustained," *The Quarterly Review of the MECS,* Vol. 5, No. 4, October, 1883, (J.W. Hinton, ed.), p. 557-585.

"Sermons On The Resurrection," J.W. Burke & Co., Macon, Ga., 1871. (45 p.) Ga. Room

"Study of Nature and Her Laws Compatible With The Character and Functions of a Christian Minister," found in *The Quarterly Review of the MECS,* (J.W. Hinton, ed.), Vol. 1, 1879, p. 223-231.

"The Aurora Borealis," (poem), *The Magnolia,* Burges & James, Charleston, 1843, v. 2, p. 248. (Pendleton, P.C., ed.).

"The Claims of Women on the Progressive Intelligence of the Age," (address at the Annual Commencement of the Ft. Valley Institute, Houston Co., Ga., 7-1-1857). C.R. Hanleiter, Atlanta, 1857. (23 p.)

"The Falls of Ama-Colola," SOUTHERN LADIES' BOOK, Vol. 1, Benj. F. Griffin, printer, Macon, Ga., 1840, p. 102-104. (Pierce, G.F., ed.).

"The Falls of Ama-Cola," *The Home Circle,* v.1., MECS Publishing House, Nashville, Tenn., 1855, p. 491-493. (Huston, L.D., ed.).

"The First Ante-Bellum New Year's," (poem), *The Emory Univ. Quarterly Review,* v11, n1, March, 1954, p. 52-54.

"The Flood," *The Home Circle,* v.1., MECS Publishing House, Nashville, Tenn., 1855, p. 300-302. (poem), (Huston, L.D., ed.).

"The Mount of Holiness," (poem), *The Home Circle,* v.1., MECS Publishing House, Nashville, Tenn., 1855, p. 352. (Huston, L.D., ed.).

"The Rainbow Dream" (poem) *Southern Field & Fireside,* 1863, James Gardner, Augusta, Stockton & Co. [Magazine ran from 1859-64].

"The Tropes of the Bible," *Scott's Monthly Magazine,* (v.3), Franklin Steam Print, Atlanta, Ga., 1867, p. 19-27; 135-138; 302-311. (Scott, W.J., ed.).

"The Water of Life," (poem), *The Magnolia,* P.C. Pendleton, Savannah, 1842, v. 4, p. 264. (Pendleton, P.C., ed.).

Meeks, Charles M., "My Surcease," (poem), *The Methodist Quarterly Review,* v. 76, Oct. 1927, p. 546.

Mellen, George Frederick, "Bishop Pierce As A Farmer," *The Methodist Review,* v. 70, April, 1921, p. 274-287.

Methodist Episcopal Church — Georgia — Centenary Subscription Record Book, Misc. Correspondence. (23 items) Sp. Cl. Candler

JOURNALS OF THE GENERAL CONFERENCE OF THE M. E. CHURCH, VOL. 1, 1796-1836, Carlton & Phillips, New York, 1855. (504 p.)

JOURNALS OF THE GENERAL CONFERENCE OF THE M.E. CHURCH, VOL. 2, 1840-1844, Carlton & Phillips, New York, 1855. (240 p.)

MINUTES OF THE ANNUAL CONFERENCES OF THE M.E. CHURCH, 1773-1828, VOL.

1, Published by T. Mason and G. Lane for the M.E. Church, New York, J. Collord, printer, 1840. (574 p.)

Minutes of The Annual Conferences of the MEC For The Year 1828, J. Emory and B. Waugh, New York, J. Collord, Printer, 1828. (36 p.)

Minutes of the Annual Conferences of the MEC For The Year 1829, J. Emory and B. Waugh, New York, J. Collord, Printer, 1829. (41 p.)

Minutes of the Annual Conferences of the MEC For The Year 1830, J. Emory and B. Waugh, New York, J. Collord, Printer, 1830. (42 p.)

Minutes of the Annual Conferences of the MEC For The Year 1831, J. Emory and B. Waugh, New York, J. Collord, Printer, 1831. (48 p.)

Minutes of the Annual Conferences of the M.E. Church, 1829-1839, Vol. 2, Published by T. Mason and G. Lane, For the M.E. Church, New York, J. Collord, printer, 1840. (678 p.)

+ Minutes of the Annual Conferences of the M.E. Church, 1839-1840, Published by T. Mason and G. Lane, New York, J. Collord, printer, 1840.

+ Minutes of the Annual Conferences of the M.E. Church, 1841-42, Published by G. Lane and P.P. Sandford for the M.E. Church, New York, J. Collord, printer, 1842.

+ Minutes of the Annual Conferences of the M.E. Church, 1842-43, Published by G. Lane and P.P. Sandford for the M.E. Church, New York, J. Collord, printer, 1843.

+ Minutes of the Annual Conferences of the M.E. Church, 1843-44, Published by G. Lane and C.B. Tippett, for the M.E. Church, New York, J. Collord, printer, 1846.

+ Minutes of the Annual Conferences of the M.E. Church, 1844-45, Published by G. Lane and C.B. Tippett, New York, Joseph Longking, printer, 1846.

Minutes of the Annual Conferences of the M.E. Church, 1839-1845, Vol. 3, Published by T. Mason and G. Lane for the M.E. Church, New York, J. Collord, printer, 1845. (666 p.)

+ includes the following publications which were done separately.

Minutes Taken at The Several Annual Conferences of the MEC, For The Year 1821, Published by N. Bangs & T. Mason, New York, John C. Totten, Printer, 1821. (43 p.)

Minutes Taken At The Several Annual Conferences of the MEC, For The Year 1822, Published by N. Bangs and T. Mason, New York, John C. Totten, Printer, 1822. (40 p.)

Minutes Taken At The Several Annual Conferences of the MEC, For The Year 1823, Published by N. Bangs and T. Mason, New York, John C. Totten, Printer, 1823.

Minutes Taken At The Several Annual Conferences of the MEC, For The Year 1824, Published by N. Bangs and J. Emory, New York, John C. Totten, Printer, 1824. (64 p.)

Minutes Taken At The Several Annual Conferences of the MEC, For The Year 1825, Published by N. Bangs and J. Emory, Azor Hoyt, Printer, 1825. (63 p.)

Minutes Taken At The Several Annual Conferences of the MEC, For The

YEAR 1826, Published by N. Bangs and J. Emory, Azor Hoyt, Printer, 1826. (72 p.)
MINUTES TAKEN AT THE SEVERAL ANNUAL CONFERENCES OF THE MEC, FOR THE YEAR 1827, Published by N. Bangs and J. Emory, Azor Hoyt, Printer, 1827. (72 p.)

Methodist Episcopal Church, South, Annual Report of the Sunday School Society of the Methodist Episcopal Church for 1860-61. Nashville, Southern Methodist Publishing House, 1861. (52 p.) CSA Biblio Willingham
CALL OF GOD TO MEN, Papers and Addresses of the Layman's Missionary Movement Conference, 1908, M.E. Pub. House, Nashville, 1908. (302 p.)
CONFERENCE MINUTES OF THE MECS FOR 1861, Nashville, Southern Methodist Publishing House, 1862. (71 p.) CSA Biblio Willingham
Educational Commission Papers, 1914-1918. 128 items — Ga. — Tex. Papers of this commission, which was founded in 1914 to establish schools or departments of theology throughout the South and which was therefore responsible for the establishment of Emory and Southern Methodist Universities, include official correspondence, minutes, reports, etc. Correspondents include: Warren A. Candler, James Dickey, etc. Sp Cl Woodruff
General Conference Central Centenary Committee Minutes, 1883-84. (20 items) Sp Cl Candler
General Conference Committee Reports & Subscribers to Southern Methodist Review for 1887-88, 1886. Sp Cl Candler
HISTORY OF THE ORGANIZATION OF THE MECS, (OFFICIAL PROCEEDINGS OF THE GENERAL CONFERENCE, THE SOUTHERN ANNUAL CONFERENCES AND THE GENERAL CONVENTION), compiled and published by the South-Western Christian Advocate, MECS, William Cameron, printer, 1845. (267 p.) (Ga. Ref. — p. 148f.)
HISTORY OF THE ORGANIZATION OF THE MECS WITH THE JOURNAL OF ITS FIRST GENERAL CONFERENCE, MECS Publishing House, Nashville, Tenn., 1925. (518 p.) (Ga. Ref. — p. 209, 213)
HYMNS FOR THE USE OF THE M.E. CHURCH, Revised Ed., Lane & Scott, New York, Joseph Longking, printer, 1851. (714 p.) (With Supplement—Hymns for Sunday Schools, Youth, and Children).
JOURNALS OF THE GENERAL CONFERENCE OF THE MECS, HELD 1846 & 1850, John Early, for the MECS, Richmond, 1851. (602 p.) Vol. includes Journals of 1854, 1858 conferences).
Letters and Resolutions opposing Unification, 1938. (Materials distributed by Laymen's Organization for the preservation of the Southern Methodist Church), Atlanta, Ga.
MINUTES OF THE ANNUAL CONFERENCES OF THE MECS, 1845-1846, Pub. by John Early for the MECS, Sorin & Ball, T.K. and P.G. Collins, printers, 1846.
MINUTES OF THE ANNUAL CONFERENCES OF THE MECS, 1846-1847, Pub. by John Early for the MECS, Richmond, Advocate Office, C. H. Wynne, printer, 1847.
MINUTES OF THE ANNUAL CONFERENCES OF THE MECS, 1847-1848, Pub. by John Early for the MECS, Smith & Peters, printers.
MINUTES OF THE ANNUAL CONFERENCES OF THE MECS, 1848-1849, Pub. by John

Early for the MECS, Richmond Christian Advocate Office, C.H. Wynne.

MINUTES OF THE ANNUAL CONFERENCES OF THE MECS, 1849-1850, Pub. by John Early for the MECS, P.D. Bernard, printer.

MINUTES OF THE ANNUAL CONFERENCES OF THE MECS, 1850-1851, Pub. by John Early for the MECS, Chas. H. Wynne, printer.

MINUTES OF THE ANNUAL CONFERENCES OF THE MECS, 1851-1852, Pub. by John Early for the MECS, Colin & Nowlan, printers.

MINUTES OF THE ANNUAL CONFERENCES OF THE MECS, 1852-1853, Pub. by John Early for the MECS, Colin & Nowlan, printers.

MINUTES OF THE ANNUAL CONFERENCES OF THE MECS, 1853-1854, Pub. by John Early for the MECS, printed by Colin & Nowlan.

MINUTES OF THE ANNUAL CONFERENCES OF THE MECS, 1854-1855, Pub. by E. Stevenson & F.A. Owen for the MECS, Nashville, Tenn., 1855.

MINUTES OF THE ANNUAL CONFERENCES OF THE MECS, 1855-56, Pub. by E. Stevenson & F.A. Owen, for the MECS, Nashville, Tenn., 1856.

MINUTES OF THE ANNUAL CONFERENCES OF THE MECS, 1856-57, Pub. by E. Stevenson & F.A. Owen, for the MECS, Nashville, Tenn., 1857.

MINUTES OF THE ANNUAL CONFERENCES OF THE MECS, 1857-58, Pub. by E. Stevenson & F.A. Owen, for the MECS, 1858.

MINUTES OF THE ANNUAL CONFERENCES OF THE MECS, FOR THE YEAR 1858, Southern Methodist Publishing House, Nashville, Tenn., 1859.

MINUTES OF THE ANNUAL CONFERENCES OF THE MECS, 1859, Southern Methodist Publishing House, Nashville, Tenn., 1860.

MINUTES OF THE ANNUAL CONFERENCES OF THE MECS, 1860, Southern Methodist Publishing House, Nashville, Tenn., 1861.

MINUTES OF THE ANNUAL CONFERENCES OF THE MECS, 1861, Southern Methodist Publishing House, Nashville, Tenn., 1870.

MINUTES OF THE ANNUAL CONFERENCES OF THE MECS, 1862, Southern Methodist Publishing House, Nashville, Tenn., 1870.

MINUTES OF THE ANNUAL CONFERENCES OF THE MECS, 1863, Southern Methodist Publishing House, Nashville, Tenn., 1870.

MINUTES OF THE ANNUAL CONFERENCES OF THE MECS, 1864, Southern Methodist Publishing House, Nashville, Tenn., 1870.

MINUTES OF THE ANNUAL CONFERENCES OF THE MECS, 1865, Southern Methodist Publishing House, Nashville, Tenn., 1870.

MINUTES OF THE ANNUAL CONFERENCES OF THE MECS, 1866, Southern Methodist Publishing House, Nashville, Tenn., 1870.

MINUTES OF THE ANNUAL CONFERENCES OF THE MECS, 1867, Southern Methodist Publishing House, Nashville, Tenn., 1870.

MINUTES OF THE ANNUAL CONFERENCES OF THE MECS, 1868, Southern Methodist Publishing House, Nashville, Tenn., 1870.

MINUTES OF THE ANNUAL CONFERENCES OF THE MECS, 1869, Southern Methodist Publishing House, Nashville, Tenn., 1870.

MINUTES OF THE ANNUAL CONFERENCES OF THE MECS, 1870, Southern Methodist Publishing House, Nashville, Tenn., 1871.

MINUTES OF THE ANNUAL CONFERENCES OF THE MECS, 1871, Southern Methodist Publishing House, Nashville, Tenn., 1872.

Milledgeville 1st Methodist Church (Milledgeville, Ga.), "Sesqui-Centennial" Booklet — 1806-1956, Press of the Union Recorder, Milledgeville, Ga. (8 p.)

Miller, J. Maxwell, "Another Look at the Chronology of the Early Divided Monarchy," *Journal of Biblical Literature,* LXXXVI (1967), p. 276-288.

"Archaeological Survey South of Wady Mujib: Glueck's Sites Revisited," Annual of the Department of Antiquities of Jordon, 1979.

"Archaeology and the Israelite Conquest of Canaan: The Present Status of the Debate," PEQ (September, 1977).

Book Reviews found in the following Journals and Periodicals: *Religious Studies Review, Journal of Biblical Literature, Interpretation.*

"Geba/Gibeah of Benjamin," *Vetus Testamentum,* 25 (1975), p. 145-166.

"Geshur and Aram," *Journal of Near Eastern Studies,* XXVIII, 1 (1969), p. 60-61.

"In the 'Image' and 'Likeness' of God," *Journal of Biblical Literature,* XCI (1972), p. 289-304.

Israelite and Judaean History, co-edited with John Hayes, Old Testament Library Series, SCM/Westminster, London/Philadelphia, 1977.

"Jebus and Jerusalem: A Case of Mistaken Identity," *Zeitschrift des Deutschen Palastina-Vereins,* 90, (1974), p. 115-127.

"Joshua, book of," Interpreter's Dictionary of the Bible, Supplementary Volume, Abingdon, 1977, p. 493-496.

"Man in the Old Testament and Modern Science," *Juncture,* (Spring, 1968).

"Saul's Rise to Power: Some Observations Concerning 1 Samuel 9:1- 10:16; 10:26 - 11:15; and 13:2 - 14:46,;; *Catholic Biblical Quarterly,* XXXVI, (1974), p. 157-174.

"So Tibni Died," *Vetus Testamentum,* XVIII (1968), p. 392-394).

"The Descendants of Cain: Notes of Genesis 4," *Zeitschrift fur die Alttestamentliche Wissenschaft,* 86 (1974), p. 164-174.

"The Elisha Cycle and the Accounts of the Omride Wars," *Journal of Biblical Literature,* LXXXV (1966), p. 441-454.

"The Fall of the House of Ahab," *Vetus Testamentum,* XVII (1967), p. 307-324.

"The Israelite Occupation of Canaan," Chapter IV of Israelite and Judaean History, Miller & Hayes, ed. (see title), p. 213-284.

"The Korahites of Southern Judah," *Catholic Biblical Quarterly,* XXXII, 1 (1970), p. 58-68.

"The Moabite Stone as a Memorial Stela," *Palestine Exploration Quarterly,* (1974), p. 9-18.

The Old Testament and the Historian, Fortress/SPCK, Philadelphia/London, 1976.

The Omride Dynasty in the Light of Recent Literary—critical and Archaeological Research, (Dissertation — Emory Univ., 1964).

"The Patriarchs and Extra-Biblical Sources: A Response," *Journal for the Study of the Old Testament,* 1, (1977), p. 62-66.

"The Rest of the Acts of Jehoahaz," Zeitschrift fur die Alttestamentliche Wissenschaft, LXXX (1968), p. 377-342.

"W.F. Albright and Historical Reconstruction," *Biblical Archaeologists,* 42,

(1979), p. 37-47.

Miller, J. Maxwell and Tucker, Gene M., JOSHUA, CAMBRIDGE BIBLE COMMENTARY ON THE NEB, Cambridge Univ. Press, Cambridge, 1974.

Miscellaneous Pamphlets (eleven) on "Anti-Unification" including: "Who Misunderstands and Who is Misled," by Bishop Warren A. Candler.

Miscellaneous Pamphlets on "Unification," 1938, containing: "A reply to laymen opposing the plan of Methodist Union," by certain laymen of the South Georgia Conference and "The Church, the Fullness of Christ and the Hope of the Universal," by Bishop Warren A. Candler.

Mitchell, James. (member of Ga. Conference) sermon: "Thoughts On a Union of Forces", preached at Cumberland Gap, Tenn., 8-24-1873. (Candler Library)

Mitchell, Mary Edward, MEMOIRS OF JAMES MITCHELL, (44 p.) Ga. Room

Mobley, Beth, "Charles Wesley In Georgia," (essay) (typed), 4-1-1957. (29 p.) Ga. Room

Moister, Rev. William, THE FATHER OF OUR MISSIONS, (Sketch of Thos. Coke), Elliot Stock, London, 1871. (104 p.)

Mood, F. A., METHODISM IN CHARLESTON, S.C., Southern Methodist Publishing House, Nashville, Tenn., 1867.

Moore, Arthur James, (1931-1960) — 19 boxes, 7 file drawers — Ga. Collection consists of career related papers of this Methodist bishop, who served in bishoprics in the US Far West (1930), all foreign work except Latin America, Virginia, West Virginia, and Baltimore (1934), Geneva area (1952), Taiwan and Hong Kong (1958), and Atlanta (ca.1940) and as president of the Board of Missions for 20 years. Sp Cl Woodruff
BISHOP TO ALL PEOPLES, Nashville & New York, Abingdon Press, 1973. (144 p.)
CENTRAL CERTAINTIES, Abingdon-Cokesbury Press, New York, Nashville, 1952. (141 p.)
CHRIST AFTER CHAOS—THE POST WAR POLICY OF THE METHODIST CHURCH IN FOREIGN LANDS, Board of Missions and Church Extension, New York, 1944. (127 p.)
CHRIST AND OUR COUNTRY, Board of Missions and Church Extension, The Methodist Church, New York, 1945. (126 p.)
"Christ The Hope of All Nations: A Christmas Meditation," *The Emory Univ. Quarterly Review,* v5, n4, Dec. 1949, p. 193-196.
FIGHT ON! FEAR NOT!, Abingdon, Nashville, 1962. (144 p.)
"Georgia-Wide Dinner Honoring Bishop Arthur James Moore On The Occasion Of His Retirement," (booklet), The Ruralist Press, Atlanta, 1960. (16 p.) Ga. Room

IMMORTAL TIDINGS IN MORTAL HANDS, Nashville, Abingdon-Cokesbury Press, 1953. (128 p.)

"Imperishable Values," address delivered at LaGrange College, 9-7-1943. (10 p.) (Candler Library)

"Making a Faith Of Our Own," (sound recorded sermon), Druid Hills Baptist Church, 1963. 25 -m (Candler).

"Religious Vitality," (sermon) 11-27-1964, preached at Druid Hills Baptist Church.

Sound Recordings of Sermons from St. Mark Methodist Church, Atlanta, Ga., 1963, (in Candler Library). "The Anthem That Announced Him"—30 m, "Authentic Voice In A Bewildered Century"—30 m, "The Christian Home"—25 m, "The Church Mid Trial and Tribulation"—25 m, "Credentials of a Christian Life"—30 m, "The Creed of a Fool"—20 m, "The Cross Upon Which They Crucified Him"—23 m, "The Decision We Make Concerning Him"—30 m, "Eternal Life Which Christ Shares With Us"—30 m, "God's Willingness To Forgive and Forget Our Sin"—35 m, "Greatest Danger In One's Life"—31 m, "Is Life A Gift To Be Received or a Trophy To Be Won"—30 m, "Is The Christian Gospel Adequate For These Times"—40 m, "Life Takes On New Meaning"—31 m, "Life's Inevitable Choices"—30 m, "The Man Who Lost a Hero and Found God"—20 m, "The Mission That Brought Him"—20 m, "The Name That Was Given HIm"—20 m, "Our Methodist Heritage and Hope"—30 m, "The Petrifying Effect of Unsanctified Prosperity"—25 m, "The Secret of Endurance"—45 m, "Tragedy of Stopping Short"—30 m, "What Does The Church Need Most"—32 m.

THE MIGHTY SAVIOUR, Abingdon—Cokesbury Press, New York, 1952. (154 p.)

"The Prince of Peace In The Post-War World," Board of Missions and Church Extension, The Methodist Church, New York, 1944. (15 p.)

THE SOUND OF TRUMPETS, MECS General Commission on Benevolences, Nashville, 1934. (77 p.)

THE MIGHTY SAVIOR; THE HOPE THAT IS OURS THROUGH FAITH IN CHRIST, Abingdon-Cokesbury, Nashville, 1952. (154 p.)

Moore, Rev. Henry, THE LIFE OF REV. JOHN WESLEY, A.M., M.E. Church, New York, 1824. 2 Vols. Vol. 1 — (467 p.); Vol. 2 — (482 p.)

Moore, John Jamison, HISTORY OF THE A.M.E. ZION CHURCH IN AMERICA, York, Pa., 1884. (392 p.)

Moore, Mrs. Mary N., "Shall Our Methodism Accord Women The Privileges of the Laity?" *The Methodist Review Quarterly,* (Gross Alexander, ed.), v. 62, Oct. 1913, p. 733-738.

Morrison, Rev. H. M. (S. Ga. Conf.), "Election" — sermon preached at Shiloh Methodist Church, 9-26-1897, Thos. Gilbert, Columbus, 1897. (12 p.) Ga. Room

Morrow, Ralph E., THE METHODIST EPISCOPAL CHURCH, THE SOUTH, AND

Reconstruction, 1865-1880. (Dissertation) Univ. Microfilms, Ann Arbor, 1954. (356 p.)

Mossy Creek UMC, Cleveland, Ga., "A History of Mossy Creek United Methodist Church," Colonial Press, Cleveland, Ga., no date. (14 p.) Ga. Room

Mulberry St. Church (Macon, Ga.) "Memorials of Methodism In Macon, Ga. 1828-78", Semi-Centennial Exercises, J.W. Burke, Macon, 1878. (102 p.) Ga. Room

Myers, Edward H., THE DISRUPTION OF THE METHODIST EPISCOPAL CHURCH, 1844-1846, M.E. Church, South Publishing House, Nashville, Tenn., 1875. (216 p.)
ed., *The Southern School Journal,* Vol. 2, Macon, Ga., Feb., 1854, No. 2, p. 17-32. (in Wesleyan College, Macon, Ga.).

Myers, H. P., ed., MINUTES OF THE 20TH SESSION OF THE SOUTH GEORGIA CONFERENCE OF THE MECS HELD AT CUTHBERT, GA., DEC. 8-13, 1886, J.W. Burke & Co., Printers, Stereotypers, and Binders, Macon, Ga., 1886. (47 p.)
MINUTES OF THE 21ST SESSION OF THE SOUTH GEORGIA CONFERENCE OF THE MECS HELD AT SANDERSVILLE, GA., DEC. 14-19, 1887, J.W. Burke & Co., Printers, Publishers and Binders, Macon, Ga., 1887. (37 m.p.)
ed., MINUTES OF THE 22ND SESSION OF THE SOUTH GEORGIA CONFERENCE OF THE MECS, HELD AT EASTMAN, GA., DEC. 12-17, 1888, J.W. Burke & Co., Printers, Stereotypers and Binders, Macon, Ga., 1888. (46 m.p.)
ed., MINUTES OF THE 23RD SESSION OF THE SOUTH GEORGIA CONFERENCE OF THE MECS HELD AT AMERICUS, GA., DEC. 11-16, 1889, J.W. Burke & Co., Printers, Stationers and Binders, Macon, Ga., 1889. (43 m.p.)
"The Second Period of the Galilean Ministry," *The Methodist Quarterly Review,* (J.J. Tigert, ed.), v. 54, Jan. 1905, p. 39-54.

Meyers, Lewis, "Account of the Work of God in the Edisto District, S.C.," found in *The Methodist Magazine,* (Soule & Mason, eds.), Vol. 4, 1821, p. 35-36.
"Origin & Progress of Methodism In Savannah," found in *The Methodist Magazine and Quarterly Review,* (Emory & Waugh, eds.), Vol. 4, 1833, p. 246-258.
"Rise and Progress of Methodism in Savannah," found in *The Methodist Magazine,* (Soule & Mason, eds.), Vol. 4, 1821, p. 438-439.

Myers, T. Cecil, FAITH FOR A TIME OF STORM, Abingdon, Nashville, 1963. (160 p.)
HAPPINESS IS STILL HOMEMADE, Word Books, Waco, Texas, 1969. (127 p.)
LIVING ON TIPTOE, Word Books, Waco, Texas, 1972. (106 p.)
THUNDER ON THE MOUNTAIN, Abingdon, Nashville, 1965. (176 p.)
WHEN CRISIS COMES, Abingdon, Nashville, 1967. (176 p.)
YOU CAN BE MORE THAN YOU ARE, Word Books, Waco, Texas, 1976. (122 p.)

Myrick, Rev. D. J., SCRIPTURE BAPTISM; ITS DESIGN, MODE, AND SUBJECTS,

Haygood, Conference Secretary. (25 m.p.) Atlanta Intelligencer Book & Job Office, Atlanta, Ga., 1868.

MINUTES OF 1869, CONFERENCE HELD AT ROME, GA., DEC. 8-14. (50 p.)

MINUTES OF 1870, CONFERENCE HELD AT AUGUSTA, GA., NOV. 30-DEC. 6. (34 m.p.)

MINUTES OF THE 5TH SESSION OF THE NORTH GEORGIA ANNUAL CONFERENCE OF THE MECS, HELD AT ATHENS, GA., NOV. 29-DEC. 5, 1871, J.W. Burke & Co., Printers & Binders, Macon, Ga. 1872. (41 m.p.)

MINUTES OF THE 6TH SESSION OF THE NORTH GEORGIA ANNUAL CONFERENCE OF THE MECS, HELD AT ATLANTA, GA., NOV. 27-DEC. 4, 1872, J.W. Burke & Co., Book and Job Printers, Macon, Ga., 1873. (28 m.p.)

THE SEVENTH SESSION OF THE NORTH GEORGIA ANNUAL CONFERENCE OF THE MECS, HELD AT NEWNAN, GA., DEC. 10-16, 1873, J.W. Burke & Co., Macon, Ga. (41 p.)

THE MINUTES OF THE EIGHTH SESSION OF THE NORTH GEORGIA ANNUAL CONFERENCE OF THE MECS, HELD AT CARTERSVILLE, GA., DEC. 2-7, 1874. (29 m.p.) Atlanta Constitution Steam-Power Print, 1874, Atlanta, Ga.

MINUTES OF THE NINTH SESSION OF THE NORTH GEORGIA ANNUAL CONFERENCE OF THE MECS, HELD AT GRIFFIN, GA., DEC. 1-6, 1875. (19 m.p.) J.W. Burke & Co., printers and binders, Macon, Ga., 1875.

MINUTES OF THE 10TH SESSION OF THE NORTH GEORGIA ANNUAL CONFERENCE OF THE MECS, HELD AT SPARTA, GA., DEC. 6-11, 1876, J.W. Burke, Printers and Binders, Macon, Ga., 1876. (32 p.)

MINUTES OF THE 11TH SESSION OF THE NORTH GEORGIA ANNUAL CONFERENCE OF THE MECS, HELD AT GAINESVILLE, GA., NOV. 28-DEC. 4, 1877. (19 m.p.) J.W. Burke & Co., Stationers and Binders, 1877, Macon, Ga.

MINUTES OF THE 12TH SESSION OF THE NORTH GEORGIA ANNUAL CONFERENCE, HELD AT MARIETTA, GA., NOV. 27-DEC. 3, 1878, J.W. Burke, Printers and Binders, Macon. (53 p.)

MINUTES, NORTH GEORGIA CONFERENCE, HELD IN AUGUSTA, GA., 1879, Constitution Book and Job Printing Establishment, 1879. (60 p.)

MINUTES, NORTH GEORGIA CONFERENCE, HELD IN ROME, GA., 1880, Constitution Book and Job Printing Establishment, Atlanta, 1880. (41 m.p.)

MINUTES, NORTH GEORGIA CONFERENCE, HELD IN ATHENS, GA., 1881, Constitution Publishing Company, Printers, Atlanta, 1881. (47 p.)

MINUTES OF THE NORTH GEORGIA CONFERENCE, HELD IN LaGRANGE, GA., 1882, Constitution Publishing Company, Printers, Atlanta, 1882. (36 p.)

MINUTES OF THE NORTH GEORGIA CONFERENCE, HELD IN DALTON, GA., 1883, Constitution Publishing Co., Printers, Atlanta, Ga., 1883. (37 p.)

MINUTES OF THE 17TH ANNUAL MEETING OF THE WOMAN'S FOREIGN MISSIONARY SOCIETY AT GREENSBORO, GA., MAY 17-22, 1895, Richards & Shaver, Printers, Augusta, Ga., 1895. (64 p.)

MINUTES OF THE 18TH ANNUAL MEETING OF THE WOMAN'S FOREIGN MISSIONARY SOCIETY, AT WEST POINT, GA., MAY 15-19, 1896, Richards and Shaver, Augusta, Ga., 1896. (61 p.)

MINUTES OF THE 19TH ANNUAL MEETING OF THE WOMAN'S FOREIGN MISSIONARY SOCIETY OF THE N. GA. CONFERENCE, MECS, ATHENS, GA., 1897, Richards and

Shaver, print., Augusta, Ga., 1897. (63 p.)

PROCEEDINGS OF THE 20TH ANNUAL MEETING OF THE WOMAN'S FOREIGN MISSIONARY SOCIETY OF THE N. GA. CONFERENCE, MECS, FORSYTH, GA., 1898, Richards & Shaver, Augusta, Ga., 1898. (64 p.)

PROCEEDINGS OF THE 21ST ANNUAL MEETING OF THE WOMAN'S FOREIGN MISSIONARY SOCIETY OF THE N. GA. CONFERENCE, MECS, ROME, GA., 1899, Richards & Shaver, Printers and Lithographers, Augusta, Ga., 1899. (58 p.)

REPORT OF THE 22ND ANNUAL MEETING OF THE WOMAN'S FOREIGN MISSIONARY SOCIETY AT WASHINGTON, GA., MAY 16-20, 1900, Richards & Shaver, Printers and Binders, Augusta, Ga, 1900. (51 p.)

REPORT OF THE 23RD ANNUAL MEETING OF THE WOMAN'S FOREIGN MISSIONARY SOCIETY AT MADISON, GA., MAY 22-26, 1901, Richards & Shaver, Printers and Binders, Augusta, Ga. 1901. (54 p.)

REPORT OF THE 24TH ANNUAL MEETING OF THE WOMAN'S FOREIGN MISSIONARY SOCIETY AT GAINESVILLE, GA., APRIL 23-28, 1902, Richards & Shaver, printers and lithographers, August, Ga., 1902. (48 p.)

REPORT OF THE 25TH ANNUAL MEETING OF THE WOMAN'S FOREIGN MISSIONARY SOCIETY, AT MARIETTA, GA., APRIL 23-28, 1903, S.W. Murray, printer, Newnan, Ga. (61 p.)

REPORT OF THE 26TH ANNUAL MEETING OF THE WOMAN'S FOREIGN MISSIONARY SOCIETY OF THE NORTH GEORGIA CONFERENCE, MECS, HELD AT AUGUSTA, GA., APRIL 21-25, 1904, Lester Book and Stationery Co., printers, Atlanta, Ga. (65 p.)

REPORT OF THE 27TH ANNUAL MEETING OF THE WOMAN'S FOREIGN MISSIONARY SOCIETY, ELBERTON, GA., APRIL 19-24, 1904. Press of E.D. Stone, Athens, Ga. (45 m.p.)

REPORT OF THE 28TH ANNUAL MEETING OF THE WOMAN'S FOREIGN MISSIONARY SOCIETY, ATHENS, GA., APRIL 18-22, 1906, Blosser Press, W.C. Nunemacher, Manager, Atlanta, Ga. (77 p.)

REPORT OF THE 29TH ANNUAL MEETING OF THE WOMAN'S FOREIGN MISSIONARY SOCIETY, GREENSBORO, GA., APRIL 24-28, 1907. Cartersville Printing Co., Cartersville, Ga. (66 p.)

REPORT OF THE 13TH ANNUAL MEETING OF THE WOMAN'S FOREIGN MISSIONARY SOCIETY, CEDARTOWN, GA., APRIL 22-26, 1908, The Franklin-Turner Co., Atlanta, G.1. (60 p.)

REPORT OF THE 21ST ANNUAL MEETING OF THE WOMAN'S FOREIGN MISSIONARY SOCIETY, MILLEDGEVILLE, GA., APRIL 23-27, 1909, Chronicle Job Print, Augusta, Ga. (73 p.)

REPORT OF THE 32ND ANNUAL MEETING OF THE WOMAN'S FOREIGN MISSIONARY SOCIETY, NORTH GEORGIA CONFERENCE, MECS, ST. PAUL'S CHURCH, ATLANTA, GA., APRIL 27-MAY 1, 1910. (67 p.)

ANNUAL REPORT OF THE WOMAN'S PARSONAGE AND HOME MISSION SOCIETY OF THE N. GA. CONFERENCE, MECS, 1892, Barnesville Gazette Job Print. not numbered.

ANNUAL REPORT OF THE WOMAN'S PARSONAGE AND HOME MISSION SOCIETY OF THE N. GA. CONFERENCE, MECS, 1893, The Foote & Davies Co., Atlanta, Ga. (29 p.)

5TH ANNUAL REPORT OF THE WOMAN'S PARSONAGE AND HOME MISSION SOCIETY OF THE NORTH GEORGIA CONFERENCE, MECS, 1895, Methodist Book and Publishing Co., Atlanta, Ga., 1895. (35 p.)

7TH ANNUAL REPORT OF THE WOMAN'S PARSONAGE AND HOME MISSION SOCIETY OF THE N. GA. CONFERENCE, MECS, 1897, The Foote & Davies Co., Atlanta, 1898. (40 p.)

MINUTES OF THE 9TH ANNUAL MEETING OF THE WOMAN'S HOME MISSION SOCIETY OF THE N. GA. CONFERENCE OF THE MECS, HELD AT DALTON, GA., AUGUST, 1899, The A.J. Showalter Co., printers, Dalton, Ga., 1900. (57 p.)

MINUTES OF THE 10TH ANNUAL MEETING OF THE WOMAN'S HOME MISSION SOCIETY OF THE NORTH GEORGIA CONFERENCE OF THE MECS, HELD AT ELBERTON, GA., SEPT., 1900, A.J. Showalter Co., Printers, Dalton, Ga., 1900. (66 p.)

MINUTES OF THE 11TH ANNUAL MEETING OF THE WOMAN'S HOME MISSION SOCIETY OF THE N. GA. CONFERENCE, MECS, HELD AT COVINGTON, GA., MARCH, 1901, The A.J. Showalter Co., printers, Dalton, Ga. (64 p.)

MINUTES OF THE 12TH ANNUAL MEETING OF THE WOMAN'S HOME MISSION SOCIETY OF THE N. GA. CONFERENCE, MECS, HELD AT CARTERSVILLE, GA., MARCH, 1902, Record Co., St. Augustine, Fla. (71 p.)

MINUTES OF THE 13TH ANNUAL MEETING OF THE WOMAN'S HOME MISSION SOCIETY OF THE N. GA. CONFERENCE, MECS, HELD AT MADISON, GA., MAY, 1903, Record Co., St. Augustine, Fla. (72 p.)

MINUTES OF THE 14TH ANNUAL MEETING OF THE WOMAN'S HOME MISSION SOCIETY OF THE NORTH GEORGIA CONFERENCE, MECS, HELD AT FORSYTH, GA., MARCH, 1904, Richards & Shaver, Printers, Augusta, Ga. (72 p.)

MINUTES OF THE 15TH ANNUAL MEETING OF THE WOMAN'S HOME MISSION SOCIETY OF THE N. GA. CONFERENCE, MECS, HELD AT MILLEDGEVILLE, GA., MARCH, 1905, Richards & Shaver Co., Printers, Augusta, Ga. (73 p.)

MINUTES OF THE 16TH ANNUAL MEETING OF THE WOMAN'S HOME MISSION SOCIETY OF THE N. GA. CONFERENCE, MECS, HELD AT ATLANTA, GA., MARCH, 1906, Richards & Shaver Co., printers, Augusta, Ga. (79 p.)

MINUTES OF THE 17TH ANNUAL MEETING OF THE WOMAN'S HOME MISSION SOCIETY OF THE N. GA. CONFERENCE, MECS, HELD AT GRIFFIN, GA., APRIL, 1907. (79 p.) Richards & Shaver Co., printers, Augusta, Ga.

MINUTES OF THE 18TH ANNUAL MEETING OF THE WOMAN'S HOME MISSION SOCIETY OF THE N. GA. CONFERENCE, MECS, HELD AT MARIETTA, GA., APRIL, 1908, Wolfe & Lombard, printers, Augusta, Ga. (76 p.)

6TH ANNUAL REPORT OF THE WOMAN'S HOME MISSION SOCIETY OF THE N. GA. CONFERENCE, MECS, 1896. (36 p.)

8TH ANNUAL REPORT OF THE WOMAN'S HOME MISSION SOCIETY OF THE N. GA. CONFERENCE, MECS, 1898, The Mutual Printing Co., printers and publishers, Atlanta, Ga., 1899. (42 p.)

19TH ANNUAL REPORT OF THE WOMAN'S HOME MISSION SOCIETY, N. GA. CONFERENCE, DALTON, GA., 1909, Wolfe & Lombard, printers and binders, Augusta. (104 p.)

20TH ANNUAL REPORT OF THE WOMAN'S HOME MISSION SOCIETY, N. GA. CONFERENCE, GAINESVILLE, GA., 1910, Wolfe & Lombard, printers & binders,

Augusta, Ga. (99 p.)

Minutes of the 5th Annual Session of the Woman's Missionary Society of the N. Ga. Conference, MECS, Held in Athens, Ga., May 27-30u, 1883, Southern Methodist Publishing House, Nashville, Tenn. (24 p.)

Minutes of the 10th Annual Meeting of the Woman's Missionary Society Held at LaGrange, Ga., July 1-5, 1888, J.M. Richards, Book & Job Printer, Augusta, Ga. (52 p.)

Minutes of the 15th Annual Meeting of the Woman's Missionary Society, at Augusta, Ga., May 13-17, 1893, Richards & Shaver, printers, Augusta, Ga. (59 p.)

Minutes of the 16th Annual Meeting of the Woman's Missionary Society at Oxford, Ga., June 22-27, 1894, Richards & Shaver, printers, Augusta, Ga., 1894. (69 p.)

Proceedings of the 11th Annual Meeting of the Woman's Missionary Society Held at Dalton, Ga., June 29-July 3, 1889, J.M. Richards, Book & Job Printer, Augusta, Ga. (46 p.)

Proceedings of the 12th Annual Meeting of the Woman's Missionary Society held at Atlanta, Ga., June 27-July 2, 1890. Richards & Shaver, Book and Job Printers, Augusta, Ga. (47 p.)

Proceedings of the 13th Annual Meeting of the Woman's Missionary Society Held In Washington, Ga., June 18-23, 1891, Richards & Shaver, Book and Job Printers, Augusta, Ga., 1891. (55 p.)

Proceedings of the 14th Annual Meeting of the Woman's Missionary Society Held At Elberton, Ga., April 30-May 4, 1892, Richards & Shaver, Printers, Augusta, Ga. (55 p.)

1st Annual Report of the Woman's Missionary Society of the N. Ga. Conference For 1911, Held At Rome, Ga., May 12-16, 1911, Phoenix Printing Co., Augusta, Ga. (166 p.)

2nd Annual Report of the Woman's Missionary Society of the N. Ga. Conference, 1912, Held At LaGrange, Ga., May 10-14, 1912, Phoenix Printing Co., Augusta, Ga. (154 p.)

3rd Annual Report of the Woman's Missionary Society of the N. Ga. Conference, Held At Atlanta, Ga., Feb. 5-9, 1913, Phoenix Printing Co., Augusta, Ga. (160 p.)

4th Annual Report of the Woman's Missionary Society of the N. Ga. Conference, 1914, Held At Athens, Ga., Feb. 17-20, 1914, The McGregor Co., printers, Athens, Ga. (108 p.)

5th Annual Report of the Woman's Missionary Society of the N. Ga. Conference, 1915, Held At Augusta, Ga., Jan. 25-29, 1915. (99 p.)

6th Annual Report of the Woman's Missionary Society of the N. Ga. Conference, 1916, Carrollton, Ga. (106 p.)

7th Annual Report of the Woman's Missionary Society of the N. Ga. Conference, 1917, Elberton, Ga., Bartow Tribune Print, Cartersville, Ga. (89 p.)

12th Annual Report of the Woman's Missionary Society of the N. Ga. Conference, 1921, Athens, Ga., Feb. 13-17, 1922, Walton Printing Co., Augusta, Ga. (95 p.)

13TH ANNUAL REPORT OF THE WOMAN'S MISSIONARY SOCIETY OF THE N. GA. CONFERENCE, 1922, ROME, GA., JAN. 29-FEB. 2, 1923, Walton Printing Co., Augusta, Ga. (100 p.)

14TH ANNUAL REPORT OF THE WOMAN'S MISSIONARY SOCIETY OF THE N. GA. CONFERENCE, 1923, GRIFFIN, GA., MARCH 31-APRIL 4, 1924. (87 m.p.)

15TH ANNUAL REPORT OF THE WOMAN'S MISSIONARY SOCIETY OF THE N. GA. CONFERENCE, 1924, (Druid Hills, Atlanta). (99 p.)

16TH ANNUAL REPORT OF THE WOMAN'S MISSIONARY SOCIETY OF THE N. GA. CONFERENCE, 1925, (St. John, Augusta, Ga.), Banner Press, Emory Univ., Ga. (99 p.)

17TH ANNUAL REPORT OF THE WOMAN'S MISSIONARY SOCIETY OF THE N. GA. CONFERENCE, 1926, (LaGrange, Ga.), Lester Book and Stationery Co., Printers, Atlanta, Ga. (97 p.)

20TH ANNUAL REPORT OF THE WOMAN'S MISSIONARY SOCIETY OF THE N. GA. CONFERENCE, 1929, (Grace, Atlanta, Ga.), Brumby Press Inc., Marietta, Ga. (92 p.)

9TH ANNUAL REPORT OF THE WOMAN'S SOCIETY OF CHRISTIAN SERVICE, 1ST METHODIST CHURCH, GAINESVILLE, GA., MARCH 16-18, 1948, Adamson Printing Co., Atlanta, Ga. (153 p.)

N. Atlanta Dist., District Conference Record, 1869-74, 1887-91. (2v) Sp Cl Candler

N. Atlanta Dist., 1st Church, Decatur, Epworth League, Secretary's Book, 1923. Sp Cl Candler

Oxford Dist., Minutes of the District Conference, 1897-1903. (2v) Sp Cl Candler

Oxford Dist., N. Covington & Mill Charge. Qtr. Conf. meeting, 1913-14. Sp Cl Candler

Oxford Dist., Oxford Charge. (composite list of folders). 1. Church Register, 1871-80; 1891-1911. (2v); 2. Minutes of Qtr. Conf. 1903-06, 1911-14. (2v); 3. "Helping Hand" Juvenile Society" Minutes 1880-89, (2v). Misc. items (5); 4. "Helping Hands" Treasurer's Book, 1880-85; 5. Woman's Home Mission Society Minutes, 1891-1906, 1910-1911. (3v) (4 misc. items); 6. Woman's Missionary Society Minutes, 1878-86, 1901-21. 9 notebooks, 205 indiv. pieces. (2v in archives stacks); 7. Woman's Missionary Society Treasurer's Report, 1878-1914 (2v) (28 misc. items); 8. Treasurer's Account Book for Young Woman's Foreign Missionary Society, 1896.

Oxford District, Oxford Charge. "Helping Hand" Juvenile Society Minutes 1880-89, Misc. items. (5 items) Sp Cl Candler

Oxford Dist., Oxford Charge. Woman's Home Mission Society Minutes 1891-1906; 1910-11; Misc. items (4 items). Sp Cl Candler

Oxford Dist., Woman's Foreign Missionary Society, Minutes of Dist. Conference 1884-98. Sp Cl Candler

Preachers' Aid Society, Correspondence, etc. (25 items) Sp Cl Candler

Preachers' Aid Society, Minutes 1841-1943; Misc. Correspondence (17 items and 8 xerox of other items). Entry varies: Relief Society, Ga. Conf. 1838-44; Relief Society, MECS, 1844-51; Preachers' Aid Soc. Ga. Conf. MECS, 1852-66; Preachers' Aid Soc. N. Ga. 1867-1939. Sp Cl Candler

North Georgia Conference Seal. Sp Cl Candler

S. Atlanta Dist., Trinity Church. Minutes of qtr. conf., 1887-90. Sp Cl Candler

S. Atlanta Dist., Woman's Missionary Society, Minutes 1917-24. (23 items). Sp Cl Candler

Statistics, 1867-81; 1886-1905; 1931 (813 items). Sp Cl Candler

Statistics on Subscriptions to *Wesleyan Christian Advocate* & *New Century Education,* 1899. (includes Statistics for S. Ga. Conf.). Sp Cl Candler

"Sunday School Yearbook." Candler Library has 1901; 1903.

SUNDAY SCHOOL YEARBOOK, 1915, Dickert-Higgins Co., Atlanta, Ga. (45 p.)

Trustees of Fund of Special Relief Minutes, 1830-1934. (Min. for Jan. & Dec., 1836, 1846, 1851) (Missing for 1840, 1848, 1864, 1875, 1887, 1928) Sp Cl Candler

Woman's Missionary Society (composite list of folders) 1.—Executive Meeting, 1937. (2 items); 2.—List of Officers & Pledges, 1918-19; 3.—Minutes, 1878-1900 (2v) (3 copies); 4.—Treasurer's Book, 1879-86. Sp Cl Candler

Woman's Missionary Society List of Officers, 1918-19; Misc. Papers. (30 items) Sp Cl Candler

Woman's Society of Christian Service. Charter Auxiliaries, 1940. Sp Cl Candler

Woman's Society of Christian Service, 97TH ANNUAL REPORT, First Methodist Church, Gainesville, Ga., March 16-18, 1949, Adamson Printing Co., Atlanta. (153 p.)

Norwood, Frederick A., THE STORY OF AMERICAN METHODISM, Abington, Nashville, New York. 1974. (448 p.)

Norwood, John Nelson, THE SCHISM IN THE METHODIST EPISCOPAL CHURCH 1844: "A Study of slavery and Ecclesiastical Politics." Porcupine Press, Phil., 1976. (225 p.)

Nygaard, Norman E., BISHOP ON HORSEBACK, Zondervan Publishing House, Grand Rapids, Mich., 1962. (biography of Francis Asbury) (183 p.)

Olin, Stephen, "Address delivered at the Anniversary Meeting of the SC Conference Missionary Society," Charleston, January, 1824, found in *The Methodist Magazine,* (Soule & Mason, eds.), Vol. 7, 1824, p. 301-310.

THE LIFE AND LETTERS OF STEPHEN OLIN, 2 VOLS., Harper & Brothers, New York, 1854. Vol. 1 — (361 p.); Vol. 2 — (486 p.)

THE WORKS OF STEPHEN OLIN, DD, LL.D, Harper & Brothers, publishers, New York, 1852. Vol. 1 — (1,422 p.); Vol. 2 — (475 p.)

TRAVELS IN EGYPT, ARABIA, PETRAEA AND PALESTINE IN 1840, 2 Vols., Harper & Bros., New York, 1842. Review in *The Methodist Quarterly Review,* (Geo. Peck, ed.), Vol. 3, 1843, p. 303-320.

Oliver, Charles James, (1832-1868), 1 roll micro. — Ga. — Va. While serving as a Methodist minister in Savannah and Atlanta, Oliver kept a diary, 93 pages, with entries between Oct. 6, 1866 and Dec. 28, 1968, which tells of his experiences. Sp Cl Woodruff

Osborn, Hon. William A., "Reminiscences of Old First Church," (Atlanta, Ga.), 1903. (19 p.)

Outler, Albert C., JOHN WESLEY, Oxford University Press, New York, 1964. (516 p.)

Overton, J. H., JOHN WESLEY, Methuen & Co., London, 1891. (216 p.) (Ga. Ref. — 43-58)

Ozment, Robert V., BUT GOD CAN, Revell, Westwood, N.J., 1962. (126 p.)
HAPPY IS THE MAN, Revell, Westwood, N.J., 1963. (128 p.)
LOVE IS THE ANSWER, Fleming H. Revell Co., Old Tappan, N.J., 1967. (158 p.)
PUTTING LIFE TOGETHER AGAIN, Revell, Westwood, N.J., 1965. (128 p.)
THERE'S ALWAYS HOPE, Revell, Westwood, N.J., 1964. (64 p.)
WHEN SORROW COMES, Word Books, Waco, Texas; London, England, 1970. (91 p.)

Paine, Robert, LIFE AND TIMES OF WILLIAM M'KENDREE, Southern Methodist Publishing House, Nashville, Tenn., 1869. (V.1 — 491 p.); (V.2 — 483 p.)
LIFE AND TIMES OF WILLIAM McKENDREE, 2 vols., MECS Publishing House, Nashville, 1870. Vol. 1. — (491 p.); Vol. 2 — (483 p.)
LIFE AND TIMES OF WILLIAM McKENDREE, MECS Publishing House, Nashville, Tenn., 1882. (500 p.)
LIFE AND TIMES OF WILLIAM McKENDREE, In One Volume, MECS Publishing House, Nashville, Tenn., 1893. (500 p.)
LIFE AND TIMES OF WILLIAM McKENDREE, Nashville, M.E. Church, S. Publishing House, 1922. (549 p.) (Ga. Ref. — See Chapters 12, 21)

Park, Orville Augustus, Burke's Linotype Print, Macon, 1904. (109 p.)

Park St. Methodist Church, Atlanta, Ga. "Who's Who At Park St.," (Directory), 1928. (48 p.) Ga. Room

Parker, Mrs. Fitzgerald S., TWENTY-EIGHTH ANNUAL REPORT, WOMAN'S MISSIONARY COUNCIL, MECS, 1937-38, MECS Publishing House, Nashville, Dallas, Richmond, Parthenon Press, Nashville. (388 p.)

Parker, Franklin N., "A Christmas Meditation," *The Emory Univ. Quarterly Review,* v3, n3, Dec. 1947, p. 193-196.
"A Diary-Letter Written from The Methodist General Conference of 1844 by the Rev. W. J. Parks," EMORY SOURCES AND REPRINTS, Series II, (1944), No. 1, 24 p.
"The Neglect of the Atonement In Present-Day Preaching, *The Methodist Review Quarterly,* (Gross Alexander, ed.), v. 59, Jan. 1910, p. 3-15.
WHAT WE BELIEVE, Methodist Episcopal Church South Pub. House, Nashville, 1923. (143 p.)

What We Believe, MECS Publishing House, Nashville, Tenn., 1924. (rev. ed.). (143 p.)

Parks, William, Suggestions To Young Preachers, MECS Publishing House, Nashville, Dallas, 1903. (35 p.)

Parks, Rev. W. J., "A Diary Written From The Methodist General Conference of 1844," Reprint — The Library of Emory University, Atlanta, Ga., 1944. Higgins-McArthur Co., Typographers and printers, Atlanta, Ga. (24 p.)
A Short Essay On Apostasy, Southern Methodist Publishing House, Nashville, 1859. (125 p.)
A Short Essay On Apostasy, (mentioned and briefly reviewed in *Quarterly Review of the MECS,* (D.S. Doggett, ed.), January, 1858, p. 139.

Parvis, Merrill M., ed., New Testament Literature in 1942, The New Testament Club of the Univ. of Chicago, 1943. (107 p.)
ed., New Testament Manuscript Studies, Univ. of Chicago Press, 1950, (with Allen P. Wikgren). (220 p.)
The Janina Gospels and The Isle of Patmos, (thesis) Univ. of Chicago, 1944. Reprinted f. Crozer Qtly., v. 21, n. 1, Jan. 1944. (30-40 p.)

Parvis, Merrill M., and Lyons, William Nelson, New Testament Literature, Univ. of Chicago Press, 1948. (392 p.)

Paschal, Paul Holmes, This Trail of Splendor and Glory, (1st UMC, Monroe, Ga.), 1974. (140 p.)

Pate, J. Thomas, "Methodism In South Carolina," *The Quarterly Review of the MECS,* (J.W. Hinton, ed.), Vol. 7, No. 4, Oct. 1885, p. 593-603.

Patton, John, "A Dialogue On Supervision and Consultation," *The Journal of Pastoral Care,* v. XXV, n. 3, September, 1971, p. 165-175.
"The Myth of Itineracy," *Circuit Rider,* September, 1981, p. 3-4. (V.5, N.8, 1981).
History of the A. M. E. Church, AME Sunday School Union, Nashville, Tenn., 1891. (502 p.)
History of the African Methodist Episcopal Church. Arno Press & The New York Times, New York. 1969. (502 p.) (Ga. Ref. — see Chapter 7: Extinction of the Church In South Carolina.")
Recollections of Seventy Years, Arno Press and The New York Times, N.Y., 1968. (335 p.)
The Semi-Centenary and the Retrospection of the A.M.E. Church, Books for Libraries Press, Freeport, N.Y., 1972. (189 p.)

Peacock, Mary Thomas, The Circuit Rider and Those Who Followed, Hudson Printing & Lithographing Co., Chattanooga, Tenn., 1957. (465 p.)

Peck, George, ed., *The Methodist Quarterly Review,* 3rd Series, Vol. 1, Lane, G. & Sanford, P.P., New York, 1841. Periodical—MEC.

Pell, Edward Leigh, Heroes of Faith In China, MECS Publishing House, Nashville, Dallas, Richmond, 1919. (104 p.)

Pendleton, P.C., The Magnolia or Southern Monthly, V. 3, H.S. Bell, Savannah, Ga., 1841.

Pennington, Edgar Legare, "John Wesley's Georgia Ministry," found in *Church History,* American Society of Church History (?), 1939, Vol. 8, No. 3, p. 231-254. Ga. Room

Pepper, Charles W., "In Memorium—Hatton Dunnica Towson," 1919, pamphlet. (22 p.)

Peterson, Rev. P. A., Handbook of Southern Methodism—A Digest of the History and Statistics of the M.E. Church, South from 1845-1882. J.W. Fergusson & Son, Richmond, Va., 1883. (148 p.)

Phillips, Allen A., Nuggets for Happiness, Pathway Press, Cleveland, Tenn., 1959. (116 p.)

Phillips, Charles Henry, From The Farm to The Bishopric, Parthenon Press, Nashville, 1932. (C.M.E. Church) (308 p.)
The History of the Colored Methodist Episcopal Church In America, Arno Press, New York, 1972. (247 p.)

Pierce, Alfred Mann, A History of Methodism In Georgia, Feb. 5, 1736-June 24, 1955. Published by the North Georgia Historical Society, 1956. (345 p.)
Giant Against The Sky, Abingdon-Cokesbury Press, Nashville, 1948. (Biography of Warren Akin Candler). (270 p.)
Lest Faith Forget—The Story of Methodism in Georgia, Published under the authority of the North and South Ga. Conferences, 1951. (206 p.)
"Mary Slessor of Calabar," *The Methodist Review,* v. 67, Oct. 1918, p. 610f.
"The Only Social Solvent," *The Methodist Review,* v. 70, April, 1921, p. 218-236.
"W.A. Candler as a President of Emory, 1889-1898," *The Emory University Quarterly,* 1, Dec. 1945, p. 246-255.

Pierce, Bishop George F., (1872-1875) — 1 roll micro. — Ga. Collection consists of Dr. Pierce's diary kept in 1892 (during his 88th year) and of a record of his pastorship in Sparta, Ga., 1873-75. Sp Cl Woodruff
"Address Before the Few and Phi Gamma Societies of Emory College," The Family Companion, v2, 1842, p. 300-301. (Griffin, S.L., ed.).
"Address on Female Education," Southern Ladies' Book, Vol. 1, Benj. F. Griffin, Printer, Macon, Ga., 1840, p. 3-14. (Pierce, G.F., ed.).
"Character and Work of a Gospel Minister," (Discourse given 10-26, 1879 in

Abingdon, Va.,), Southern Methodist Publishing House, Nashville, Tenn., 1880. (ed. by T.O. Summers).

"Georgia Female College: Its Origin, Plan and Prospects," *Southern Ladies' Book,* Vol. 1, Benj. F. Griffin, printer, Macon, Ga., 1840, p. 65-74. (Pierce, G.F., ed.).

INCIDENTS OF WESTERN TRAVEL, Steven & Owen, Nashville, 1857. (249 p.)

"Memories of George Foster Pierce," *The Emory University Quarterly,* 8, December, 1952, p. 181-184.

"Safe Across," *The Home Circle,* MECS Publishing House, Nashville, Tenn., 1860, p. 519-521. (Huston, L.D., ed.).

Sermon delivered at Milledgeville, Ga. before the Gen. Assembly, 3-27-1863. Boughton, Nisbet & Barnes, State Printers, Milledgeville, Ga., 1863. (40 p.) Copies: Univ. of Ga., Woodruff — same sermon published by Soldier's Tract Association, MECS, Macon, Ga., 1862. (16 p.) CSA Biblio — Willingham

"The Bible," *The Family Companion,* v2, 1842, p. 345-346. (Griffin, S.L., ed.).

"The Georgia Female College, Its Origin, Plan, and Prospects," *The Wesleyan Quarterly Review,* Vol. 1, No. 2, May, 1964, p. 93-108.

Pierce, George F., and Pendleton, Philip C., *The Southern Ladies' Book,* Vol. 1, Benjamin F. Griffin, Printer, Macon, Ga., 1840. (380 p.)

Pierce, Lovick, "A Discourse Showing the Difference Between Religious Reformation & Spiritual Regeneration," Benjamin F. Griffin, Macon, Ga., 1852. (28 p.)

"A Miscellaneous Essay on Entire Sanctification," MECS Publishing House, Nashville, Tenn., 1892. (72 p.) Ga. Room

"A Sermon: Showing That In The Unity Of Faith Is The Unity Of The Church," Nashville, A.H. Redford, 1869.

"A Sermon: Showing The True Relation Ordained To Subsist Between a Pastor and His Church Members," preached at Americus, Ga., Ga. Annual Conf., 12-2-1866, J.W. Burke, Macon, 1867. (56 p.)

"Anna The Prophetess," *The Home Circle,* MECS Publishing House, Nashville, Tenn., 1860, p. 269-272. (Huston, L.D., ed.).

"Education of the Poor," *Southern Ladies' Book,* Vol. 1, Benj. F. Griffin, printer, Macon, Ga., 1840, p. 222-229. (Pierce, G.F., ed.).

"Entire Sanctification," Southern Methodist Publishing House, Nashville, Tenn., 1878. (72 p.).

"Female Biography," *The Home Circle,* MECS Publishing House, Nashville, Tenn., 1860, p. 235-240. (Huston, L.D., ed.).

"Foolish Habits," *The Home Circle,* MECS Publishing House, Nashville, Tenn., 1860, p. 161-164. (Huston, L.D., ed.).

Letters to his granddaughter, 1875-1877-1879. (3 letters). Sp. Cl. Univ. Ga.

"No Denominational Church Monopoly," J.W. Burke & Co., Macon, Ga., 1872. (41 p.)

"Music," *The Home Circle,* MECS Publishing House, Nashville, Tenn., 1860, p. 673-676; 709-712. (Huston, L.D., ed.).

"Nature and Design of Baptism," (essay), Southern Methodist Publishing

House, Nashville, Tenn., 1854. (24 p.) Reviewed in *Quarterly Review of the MECS,* (D.S. Doggett, ed.), July, 1859, p. 424.

"Obituary of..", *The Quarterly Review of the MECS,* (J.W. HInton, ed.), Vol. 2, No. 2, April, 1880, p. 231-236.

"On Female Education," *Southern Ladies' Book,* Vol. 1, Benj. F. Griffin, printer, Macon, Ga., 1840, p. 129-137. (Pierce, G.F., ed.).

"Reflections Upon Creation," *The Home Circle,* v.3., MECS Publishing House, Nashville, Tenn., 1857, p. 1-4; 153-156; 193-197. (Huston, L.D., ed.).

"Revival Report," (Athens, Ga.), found in *The Methodist Magazine,* (Soule & Mason, eds.), Vol. 10, 1827, p. 230.

SERMON ON THE OCCASION OF THE DEATH OF MRS. ANNA V. CALHOUN, Charleston, Burgess & James, 1841. (32 p.)

"The Fundamental Element of Church Government Must Be Monarchical," found in *Quarterly Review,* (H.B. Bascomb, ed.), in various installments: October, 1852, p. 34-51; January, 1853, p. 15-30; April, 1853, p. 232-253.

"The Philosophy of Family Government," *The Home Circle,* MECS Publishing House, Nashville, Tenn., 1860, p. 385-388; 449-453. (Huston, L.D., ed.).

Pierce, Lovick & G.F.), "Two Georgia Whigs of 1860," *Georgia Historical Quarterly,* 11, March, 1927, p. 31-43.

Pierce, Lovick Wilson and Maxwell, Esther Pierce, TWO BROTHERS: REDDICK AND LOVICK PIERCE; THEIR HERITAGE AND THEIR DESCENDENTS, Cherokee Publishing Company, Covington, Georgia (uv).

Pierce, Ruth Ford, "Records of Beulah Methodist Church," (Worth Co., Ga.), Jan., 1969. (typescript) (37 p.) Ga. Archives

Pilkington, James Penn, THE METHODIST PUBLISHING HOUSE, VOL. 1, Abingdon Press, Nashville, New York, 1968. (585 p.) (Ga. Ref. — 6, 7, 19).

Pinkston, Regina P., A HISTORY OF THE GREENVILLE METHODIST CHURCH, (Greenville, Ga.) Pvt. Print. (18 p.)

Pinson, W. W., "Bishop W.R. Lambuth, An Appreciation," *The Methodist Quarterly Review,* v. 71, Jan. 1922, p. 3-14.

CHINA IN ACTION, Cokesbury Press, Nashville, Tenn., 1930. (176 p.)

GEORGE R. STUART, LIFE AND WORK, Cokesbury Press, Nashville, Tenn., 1927. (276 p.)

WALTER RUSSELL LAMBUTH, PROPHET AND PIONEER, Cokesbury Press, Nashville, Tenn., 1924. (261 p.)

Pleasant Grove UMC, THE HISTORY OF PLEASANT GROVE METHODIST CHURCH, (LaGrange, Ga.), Vol. 2. (186 p.)

Pollard, Randy, HANG ON FOR DEAR LIFE, R.L. Bryan Co., Columbia, S.C., 1976. (125 p.)

THE JESUS PRINCIPLE, (uv).

Potter, Ira L., SERMONS ON VARIOUS SUBJECTS, Nashville, Tenn., J.B. McFerrin, 1858. (280 p.)
SERMONS ON VARIOUS SUBJECTS, J.B. McFerrin, Agent, Nashville, 1858. (Reviewed in *Quarterly Review of the MECS*, D.S. Doggett, ed.), January, 1859, p. 112.

Powell, Lillian Lewis, AN INFORMAL HISTORY OF THE FIRST METHODIST CHURCH OF WAYNESBORO, GA., 1812-15 — 1968, (typed copy). (213 p.)

Powell, Rev. P. W. (CME), ''Suggestive Homiletics,'' (pamphlet) (8 p.) Ga. Room

Price, Mrs. Otelia H., ''The Story of Deepstep Methodist Church,'' Deepstep, Ga. (6 p.) Ga. Room

Prussner, Frederick C., ''Form Criticism,'' Emory Univ., Atlanta, Ga. Sound Recording—1975.
''Hebrew Verb Forms,'' Emory Univ., Atlanta, Ga. Sound Recording—1974.
METHODOLOGY IN OLD TESTAMENT THEOLOGY, (thesis) Univ. of Chicago, 1952. (329-41 p.)

Pudney, John, JOHN WESLEY AND HIS WORLD, Scribner's Sons, New York. 1978. (128 p.) (Ga. Ref. — p. 40, 42, 43, 46-54, 57, 48, 65.)

Purifoy, Lewis McCarroll, NEGRO SLAVERY, THE MORAL ORDEAL OF SOUTHERN METHODISM, 1844-1861. (Dissertation) 1966. (249 p.)

Quillian, John B. C., THE GOLDEN LAMP: SKETCHES UPON THE HISTORIC SCENES, TRUTHS, AND CHARACTERS OF THE BIBLE, J.W. Burke, Macon, 1881. (150 p.)
THE GOLDEN LINKS OF THE BIBLE, C.R. Hanileiter & Co., Atlanta, 1856. (59 p.)
THE STAR OF REDEMPTION OR THOUGHTS ON THE MEDITATION AND GLORY OF THE REDEEMER, The Franklin Steam Printing Press, Atlanta, Ga., 1871. (173 p.)

Quillian, William F., (ca.1920-1950) — 1 box — Ga. Collection contains correspondence (approx. 30 pieces) relating to Wesleyan and Emory Universities, and two notebooks of this Methodist minister's sermons. Sp Cl Woodruff
HELPS TOWARD HEAVEN, Press of R.C. Ward, LaGrange, Ga., no date. (31 p.) Ga. Room

Quillian, Garnett W., REV. WILLIAM F. QUILLIAN, M.D., HIS LIFE AND SERMONS, Foote & Davies, Atlanta, 1907. (319 p.)

Radcliffe, Rev. Francis A., (S. Ga. Conf.), BAPTISM OR THE CONTROVERSY,

MECS Publishing House, Nashville, Dallas, 1908. (219 p.)

Rebisen, Mary P., "History of The First Methodist Church of Thomasville, Ga.," *The Wesleyan Quarterly Review,* Vol. 1, No. 3, Aug., 1964, p. 164-182; and Vol. 2, No. 1, Feb., 1965, p. 40-61.

Raikes, Robert, "Sunday Schools Before The Time of Robert Raikes," *The Magnolia,* V. 3, 1841, p. 509-510. (Pendleton, ed.).

Randall, Jo, WILKES COUNTY CHURCHES, Wilkes Publishing Company, Washington, Ga., 1973. (128 p.)

Range, Willard, THE RISE AND PROGRESS OF NEGRO COLLEGES IN GEORGIA, 1865-1949, The University of Ga. Press, Athens, Ga. (254 p.)

Ransom, Jim, *Words of Encouragement,* Booklet (uv),

Rawlings, E. H., WALTER RUSSELL LAMBUTH, Board of Missions, MECS, Nashville, Tenn., 1921. (47 p.)

Read, Henry O., "The Call of the Main: A Criticism," *The Methodist Review,* v. 69, July, 1920, p. 491-494.

Read, K., ed., MINUTES OF THE 24TH SESSION OF THE SOUTH GEORGIA CONFERENCE OF THE MECS HELD IN MACON, GA., DEC. 17-22, 1890, J.W. Burke & Co., Printers, Stereotypers and Binders, Macon, Ga., 1891. (28 m.p.) MINUTES OF THE 25TH SESSION OF THE SOUTH GEORGIA CONFERENCE OF THE MECS, HELD IN CORDELE, GA., DEC. 2-7, 1891, J.W. Burke & Co., Stationers and Printers, Macon, Ga., 1891. (32 m.p.)

Redford, A. H., HISTORY AND ORGANIZATION OF THE METHODIST EPISCOPAL CHURCH SOUTH, Southern Methodist Publishing House, Nashville, 1871. (660 p.)

Reichel, Rev. Levin Theodore, THE EARLY HISTORY OF THE CHURCH OF THE UNITED BRETHREN, COMMONLY CALLED MORAVIANS, IN NORTH AMERICA, 1734-1748, Moravian Historical Society, Nazareth, Pa., 1888. (241 p.) Ga. Ref. — 62, 76.

Richards, William C., THE ORION: A MONTHLY MAGAZINE, Vol. 3, W.C.R., Penfield, Ga., 1844.

Richardson, Harry V., DARK SALVATION (The Study of Methodism as it Developed Among Blacks In America). Anchor-Press, Doubleday. Garden City, N.Y., 1976. (324 p.) (Ga. Ref. — p. 5-6, 8, 9, 56-57, 159, 170, 193, 194, 196, 210).

Richardson, Rev. Simon Pater, THE LIGHTS AND SHADOWS OF ITINERANT LIFE, Methodist E. Church, South Publishing House, Nashville, Tenn., 1901. (288 p.)

Rivers, R. H., THE LIFE OF ROBERT PAINE, D.D., Southern Methodist Publishing House, Nashville, 1884. (314 p.)
THE LIFE OF ROBERT PAINE, D.D., MECS Publishing House, Nashville-Dallas-Richmond, 1916. (314 p.)

Robb, R. H., D.D., A BIOGRAPHICAL SKETCH OF REV. JAMES LOWRY FOWLER, Western Methodist Book Concern, Cincinnati, Ohio, (no date). (106 p.)

Roberts, Derrell C., "Robert Toombs: An Unreconstructed Rebel Becomes A Methodist," *The Wesleyan Quarterly Review,* Vol. 4, No. 4, Nov. 1967, p. 237-258.

Robertson, William J. (S. Ga.), "The Mode; Infant Baptism; Apostasy: Three Fresh Sermons," Methodist Episcopal Church South Publishing House, Nashville, 1897. (78 p.) Ga. Room

Robins, John B., CHRIST AND OUR COUNTRY, MECS Publishing House, Nashville, Tenn., 1889. (141 p.)
"Christian Ethics Versus Agnosticism," *The Quarterly Review of the MECS,* (J.W. Hinton, ed.), Vol. 2, No. 4, Oct. 1880, p. 662-672.
"Future Mission of Methodism," *The Quarterly Review of the MECS,* (J.W. Hinton, ed.), Vol. 6, No. 2, April, 1884, p. 324-332.
"James Clerk Maxwell," *The Quarterly Review of the MECS,* (J.W. Hinton, ed.), Vol. 7, No. 3, July, 1885, p. 477-483.
"Methodism: Positive Christianity," *The Quarterly of the MECS,* Vol. 5, No. 2, April 1883, (J.W. Hinton, ed.), p. 260-265.
"Methodist Philosophy," *The Quarterly Review of the MECS,* (J.W. Hinton, ed.), Vol. 4, No. 1, Jan. 1882, p. 59-67.
"Rational Christianity or the Young Preacher's Problem," Imon Roberts, printer, Athens, Ga., 1900. (33 p.)
THE FAMILY, A NECESSITY OF CIVILIZATION, The Foote & Davies Co., Atlanta, Ga., 1896. (317 p.)
"The Greatest Need In Human Life," Nashville, 1897. (address delivered at Webb School, 5-26-1897) (Candler Library)
THE INFLUENCE OF THE DEATH OF JESUS, Foote & Davies, Atlanta, 1894. (48 p.)
Robins was pastor of 1st Methodist, Atlanta—also author of CHRIST AND OUR COUNTRY.
"The Kingdom of the Spirit," *The Quarterly Review of the MECS,* (J.W. Hinton, ed.), Vol. 8, No. 2, April, 1886, p. 235-245.
"Three Revolutions of the 18th Century," *The Methodist Review,* (J.J. Tigert, ed.), Vol. 21, No. 1, Sept.-Oct., 1896, p. 86-91.

Robinson, Ruth Cloyd, A HISTORY OF THE WOMAN'S SOCIETY OF CHRISTIAN SERVICE AND THE WESLEYAN SERVICE GUILD OF THE S.E. JURISDICTION OF THE

METHODIST CHURCH, Parthenon Press, Nashville, 1967. (185 p.)

Rosser, George E., A NEW ERA IN PHILOSOPHICAL THEOLOGY, J.W. Burke Co., Macon, Ga., 1934. (479 p.) (Rosser was Prof. of Bib. Lit., Wesleyan College). IN A CHARIOT OF FIRE, J.W. Burke Co., Macon, Ga., 1927. (102 p.)

Rowe, Gilbert T., and Haley, Curtis B., eds., JOURNAL OF THE SPECIAL SESSION OF THE GENERAL CONFERENCE OF THE MECS HELD IN SOLDIERS' AND SAILORS' MEMORIAL AUDITORIUM, CHATTANOOGA, TENN., JULY 2-4, 1924, MECS Publishing House, Nashville, Dallas, Richmond, San Francisco, 1924. (172 p.)
JOURNAL OF THE 19TH GENERAL CONFERENCE OF THE MECS, HELD IN HOT SPRINGS, ARKANSAS MAY 3-22, 1922, MECS Publishing House, Nashville, Dallas, Richmond. (558 p.)

Rowland, J. M., THE SOUTHERN METHODIST PULPIT, Cokesbury Press, Nashville, 1927. Contains sermons: Anthony, Walter (S. Ga. Conf.) "Cohesion In Christ" p. 21; Duren, W. L. (N. Ga. Conf.) "What Is Man" p. 98.

Rowlingson, Donald T., INTRODUCTION TO NEW TESTAMENT STUDY, MacMillian, New York, 1956. (246 p.)
"Jesus In History and In Faith," JOURNAL OF BIBLE AND RELIGION, 29, June, 1961, p. 35-38.
JESUS, THE ULTIMATE, MacMillian Company, 1961. (138 p.)
"Paul's Ephesian Imprisonment," ANGLICAN THEOLOGICAL REVIEW, 32, Jan. 1950, p. 1-7.
"Pre-Seminary Studies," THE JOURNAL OF BIBLE & RELIGION, XI, 4 (Nov. 1943), p. 225-227.
"The Continuing Quest of the Historical Jesus," in Booth, Edwin P., NEW TESTAMENT STUDIES, Abingdon-Cokesbury Press, New York, Nashville, 1942. (290 p.)
"The Eloquence of Jesus," *The Emory Univ. Quarterly Review*, v3, n2, June, 1947, p. 96-103.
THE GOSPEL PERSPECTIVE ON JESUS CHRIST, Westminster Press, Philadelphia, Pa., 1968. (221 p.)
"The Message of Ephesians," *The Emory Univ. Quarterly Review*, v4, n4, Dec. 1948, p. 246-253.

Rudolph, L. C., FRANCIS ASBURY, Abingdon Press, Nashville, 1966. (240 p.) (Ga. Ref. — 72, 194).

Runyan, Theodore, Analysis of Theological Reflections," TRAINING IN THE ART OF LOVING, Gerald J. and Elisabeth Jud, Pilgrim Press, Philadelphia, Pa., 1972, p. 117-134.
"Applying the Maieutic Method to History: A Riddle in the Theology of Carl Michalson," HERMENEUTICS AND THE WORLDLINESS OF FAITH, Charles Courtney, ed., Drew Gateway Press, Madison, N.J., 1977.

"Bultmann and Preaching," *The Drew Gateway,* Vol. 26, No. 3 (Spring 1956), p. 71-74.

"Carl Michalson as a Radical Theologian," *The Drew Gateway,* Vol. 36, No. 3, (Spring-Summer 1966), p. 89-100.

"Conflicting Theological Models for God," THE LIVING GOD, Dow Kirkpatrick, ed., Abingdon Press, New York, 1971, p. 22-47.

"Friedrich Gogarten," HANDBOOK OF CHRISTIAN THEOLOGIANS, Dean G. Peerman and Martin Marty, eds., World Press, Cleveland, Ohio, 1965, p. 427-444.

"Friedrich Gogarten and Current Trends in Theology," *The Drew Gateway,* Vol. 37, No. 3, (Spring, 1967), p. 117-128.

"Hal Lindsey and Biblical Interpretation," *Adult Leader,* Vol. 11, No. 2, (Dec.-Feb. 1978, 1979), p. 15f.

ed., HOPE FOR THE CHURCH: Moltmann in Dialogue with Practical Theology, Abingdon Press, Nashville, Tenn., 1979.

"How Can We Do Theology in the South Today?" *Perkins Journal,* Vol. 29, No. 4, (Summer, 1976), p. 1-6.

"Naming the Whirlwind: To Find Order in Chaos," *Christian Advocate,* Vol. 14, No. 13 (June 25, 1970), p. 7f.

"Religion: An Anachronism in a Secularized World?" OLD MYTHS AND NEW REALITIES, U.S. Cultural Affairs Office, Munich, 1965, p. 8-11.

"Religion and soziales Gewissen in den Vereinigten Staaten," DIE AMERIKANISCHE GESELLSCHAFT HEUTE, U.S. Information Service, Frankfort, 1966, p. 1-15.

ed., SANCTIFICATION AND LIBERATION, Abingdon Press, Nashville, Tenn. 1981. (256 p.)

"Secularization and Sacrament," THE SPIRIT AND POWER OF CHRISTIAN SECULARITY, Albert L. Schlitzer, ed., Univ. of Notre Dame Press, Notre Dame, 1969, p. 123-155.

"Testing the Spirits," *Candler Review,* (May, 1974), p. 18-30.

"The Church in the World," *Christian Advocate,* Vol. 8, No. 26, (Dec. 17, 1962), p. 3.

"The Death of God—One Year Later," *Christian Advocate,* Vol. 10, No. 22, (Nov. 17, 1966), p. 7f.

"The Immediate Awareness of the Unconditioned and the Interpretation of History in the Theology of Paul Tillich," *Theologische Literaturzeitung,* Vol. 88, No. 9, (Sept. 1963), p. 712f.

"The Reality of Faith," MASTERPIECES OF CHRISTIAN LITERATURE, Frank N. Magill, ed., Salem Press, New York, 1963, p. 1167-1171.

"The Role of the Christian," ALL GOD'S PEOPLE, Board of the Laity, Evanston, 1968.

THEOLOGY FOR THE LAYMAN, Institute of Communicative Arts, Atlanta, 1966.

"Thomas Altizer and the Future of Theology," THE DEATH OF GOD DEBATE, J.L. Ice and John J. Carey, eds., Westminster Press, Philadelphia, 1967, p. 56-59. Reprinted with a reply by Prof. Altizer in THE THEOLOGY OF ALTIZER; CRITIQUE AND RESPONSE, John B. Cobb, ed., Westminster Press, Philadelphia, 1970, p. 45-76.

ed., WHAT THE SPIRIT IS SAYING TO THE CHURCHES, Hawthorn Books, New York, 1975.

Runyan, Theodore, Earl D.C. Brewer, Barbara Pittard, and Harold McSwain, PROTESTANT PARISH, Communicative Arts Press, Atlanta, 1967.

Saliers, Don E., "A Servant Church Today," *Worship,* Vol. 46, No. 8, (October, 1972), p. 473-481. (Also published in the Journal of the American Assoc. of Church Architect).
"Beauty and Holiness Revisited: Some Relations Between Aesthetics and Theology," *Worship,* Vol. 48, No. 5, (May, 1974), p. 278-293.
"Christian Worship and Contemporary Life," *Reflection,* Nov., 1974.
"Confessing Faith in God Today," guest editorial in *Ecumenical Trends,* March, 1980.
"Enmity: A Deep Emotion," in ESSAYS ON KIERKEGAARD AND WITTGENSTEIN, On Understanding the Self, ed., by R. H. Bell and R. E. Hustwit, Wooster, Ohio: The College of Wooster, 1978, p. 123-126.
"Explanation and Understanding in the Social Sciences: A Critique," *International Journal for the Philosophy of the Social Sciences,* Vol. 8, No. 4, (December, 1978), p. 367-371.
"Faith and the Comic Eye: Religious Gleanings from Comic Vision in Some Recent Fiction," *Andover Newton Quarterly,* Vol. 13, No. 4, (March, 1973), p. 259-276.
FROM ASHES TO FIRE, Abingdon, Nashville, Tenn., 1979.
"Language in the Liturgy: Where Angels Fear to Tread," *Worship,* November, 1978. Principal guest editor of this special issue.
"Liturgy and Ethics: Some New Beginnings," *Journal of Religious Ethics,* Fall, 1979. (issue delayed until March, 1980).
"New Forms of Worship," *Worship,* Vol. 46, No. 9, (November, 1972).
"On the 'Crisis' in the Language of Worship," *Music Ministry,* (Jan. 1970).
"On the 'Crisis' of Liturgical Language," *Worship,* Vol. 44, No. 7, (August-September, 1970), p. 399-411.
"Prayer and Emotion: Shaping and Expressing Christian Life," *Worship,* Vol. 49, No. 8, (October, 1975), p. 461-475. Expanded version in CHRISTIANS AT PRAYER, ed. by John Gallen, Notre Dame, 1978.
"Prayer and the Doctrine of God in Contemporary Theology, *Interpretation,* June, 1980.
"Recovering Our Spiritually," *The Circuit Rider,* Vol. 1, No. 1, (October, 1976), p. 1-5.
"Rejoice Now," Choral work commissioned by the Univ. of Notre for the dedication of the Holtkamp Organ in Sacred Heart Church. Recorded by G.I.A. and released in 1979 on *Song of David.*
"The Connection Between Worship and Healing," *Ministry and Mission,* Vol. 3, No. 3, September, 1978.
"The Ecumenical Lectionary, Rich In Musical Possibilities," *Pastoral Music,* Vol. 1, No. 3, (Feb.-March, 1977), p. 27-29.
"The Realization of Modern Liturgical Texts: Prayers We Have In Common,"

Worship, Vol. 47, No. 3, (March, 1973), p. 130-136.
"The Renewal of Worship: Pastoral Intention," *The Candler Review,* Vol. 3, No. 1, (January, 1976), p. 3-11; and "New Patterns of Worship: A Conversation," p. 19-27.
THE SOUL IN PARAPHRASE, The Seabury Press, New York, 1980. (131 p.)
"Theology and Prayer: Some Conceptual Reminders," *Worship,* Vol. 48, No. 4, (April, 1974), p. 230-235.
"Theology and Prayer: Some Notes On Seminary Learning," *Reflection,* May, 1973.
"Two Advent Homilies," (with Julian Hartt) in *Experimental Preaching,* ed. by John Killinger, Abingdon, Nashville, Tenn., 1973.
WORD AND TABLE: A BASIC PATTERN OF SUNDAY WORSHIP FOR UNITED METHODISTS, Methodist Publishing House, Nashville, Tenn., 1976.
"Worship as Central in Spiritual Formation," *Ministry and Mission,* Vol. 3, No. 4, December, 1978.
"A Critical Appraisal of the Colloquim 'Man and Symbol,' " *Worship,* Vol. 44, No. 8, (October, 1970), p. 450-457.

Samford, Thomas, "Revival Report," (Athens Dist., Ga.) found in *The Methodist Magazine,* (Soule & Mason, eds.), Vol. 10, 1827, p. 422. (reported dated 7-18-1827).

Sanders, Paul Samuel, AN APPRAISAL OF JOHN WESLEY'S SACRAMENTALISM IN THE EVOLUTION OF EARLY AMERICAN METHODISM. (Dissertation 1954), Univ. Microfilms International, Ann Arbor, 1979. (574 p.)

Sargent, David B., Jr., "Through Doubts to Faith," found in *Christian Action,* March, 1966 issue, Vol. 21, No. 7, pp. 8-13. (Monthly publication of The Methodist Publishing House, Nashville, Tenn.—Fred Cloud, ed.).

Sasnett, William J., "American Society," found in *Quarterly Review,* (H.B. Bascomb, ed.), July, 1855, p. 402-421. (name listed as Samett) (obvious misspell).
DD., DISCUSSIONS IN LITERATURE AND RELIGION, Southern Methodist Publishing House, Nashville, Tenn., 1859. (475 p.) (reviewed by President Harris in *Quarterly Review of the MECS,* D.S. Doggett, ed., July, 1860, p. 416-433.
"Evangelism," (paper written in review of John Harris' THE GREAT COMMISSION, found in 2 parts in *Quarterly Review of the MECS,* D.S. Doggett, ed., January, 1860, p. 56-69; April, 1860, p. 237-258.)
"Marriage," Commencement Address for LaGrange Female College, LaGrange, Ga., 7-6-1859, pub. by C.R. Hanleiter, Atlanta. (Reviewed in *Quarterly Review of the MECS,* D.S. Doggett, ed., January, 1860,p. 139.)
"Obstructions To The Diffusion of Higher Education," an address delivered before the Carrollton Masonic Institute, printed by C.R. Hanleiter, Atlanta. (Reviewed in *Quarterly Review of the MECS,* (D.S. Doggett, ed.), January, 1859, p. 135.

Progress: Considered With Particular Reference to the M.E. Church South, Southern Methodist Publishing House, Nashville, Tenn., 1855. (320 p.)
"The Defects of American Civilization," found in *"Quarterly Review"* (MECS), periodical listed under Bascomb, H.B. (ed.). October, 1850, p. 559-569.
"The Pulpit," found in *Quarterly Review,* (H.B. Bascomb, ed.), October, 1852, p. 544-565.
"The Relation of the Church to Missions," found in *Quarterly Review* (H.B. Bascomb, ed.) April, 1852, p. 250-279.
"Theory of Female Education," found in *Quarterly Review,* (H.B. Bascomb, ed.), April, 1853, p. 254-279.
"Theory of Female Education Vindicated," found in *Quarterly Review of the MECS,* D.S. Doggett, ed.), July, 1857, p. 380-413.
"Views of Female Education," found in *Quarterly Review,* (H.B. Bascomb, ed.), April, 1856, 245-264.
"Theory of Methodist Class Meetings," found in *"Quarterly Review"* (MECS), periodical listed under Bascomb, H.B. (ed.) April, 1851, p. 265-284.

Satterfield, Frances Gibson, "A Church Surrounded"—Pace's Ferry Methodist Church (Atlanta), 1965. (20 p.)

Savage, Horace C., Life and Times of Bishop Isaac Lane, National Publishing Company, Nashville, 1958. (240 p.) (C.M.E. Church) (Ga. Ref. — Gammon — 128, 152).

Savannah Conference, Minutes of the Savannah Conference, Central Jurisdiction, 1939-1952. Candler Library has 1939-41; 1943-45; 1947-52.

Savannah, Ga., History of Savannah Methodism from John Wesley to Silas Johnson, J.W. Burke Co., Macon, Ga., 1929. (321 p.)
"The Wesley Bi-Centenary Celebration In Savannah, Ga.," (booklet), June 25-29, 1903, The Savannah Morning News Print, Savannah, 1903. (163 p.)

Schmidt, Martin, ed., Das Zeitalter des Pietismus, Carl Schunemann, Bremen, 1965. (429 p.)
Der junge Wesley als Heiden missionar und Missions Theologie: ein Beitr. Gutersloher Verlagshaus Mohn, Gutersloh, 1973. (66 p.)
Gottheit und Trinitaet, nach dem Kommentar des Gilbert Porreta zu Bothius, De Trinitate, Verlag fur Recht und Gesellschaft, Basel, 1956. (273 p.)
John Wesley, Gotthelf-Verlag, Frankfurt, 1953.
John Wesley, A Theological Biography, The Epworth Press, London, 1962.
John Wesley—A Theological Biography, (3 vols.), Abington Press, New York, Nashville. 1962. Vol. 1 (320 p.) Ga. Ref. — 124, 126, 127, 128, 134, 135, 147, 189; Vol. 2, Part 1 (311 p.) Ga. Ref. — 14-17, 26, 28f, 38, 79, 91, 115, 130f, 145, 153, 178, 183; Vol. 2, Part 2 (320 p.) Ga. Ref. — 9, 113, 129, 156, 178, 198, 256.
John Wesley: A Theological Biography, Abingdon, New York, 1963.

PROPHET UND TEMPLE, Evangelischer Verlag, Zollikon-Zurich, 1948. (276 p.)
THE YOUNG WESLEY, MISSIONARY AND THEOLOGIAN OF MISSIONS, The Epworth Press, London, 1958. (48 p.)
URSPRUNG, GEHALT UND REICHWEITE DER KIRCHENGESCHICHTE NACH EVANGELISCHE VERTANDNIS, Josef A Kohl, Mainz, 1963. (30 p.)
WIEDERGEBURT UND NEVER MENSCH, Luther-Verlag, Witten, 1969. (439 p.)

Scomp, H. A., "A Study in New Testament Exegesis," *The Methodist Review,* (J.J. Tigert, ed.), Vol. 18, No. 2, May-June, 1895, p. 214-229.

Scott, W. J., "A Biological Thermidor," *Methodist Quarterly Review,* (W.P. Harrison, ed.), Vol. 6, No. 1, April, 1889, p. 24-38.
"A Historical Contrast: The Recluse of Lebanon and the Needlewoman of Joppa," *Methodist Quarterly Review,* (J.J. Tigert, ed.), Vol. 16, No. 2, July, 1894, p. 244-254.
BIOGRAPHICAL ETCHINGS OF MINISTERS AND LAYMEN OF THE GEORGIA CONFERENCES, Foote & Davies Co., Atlanta, 1895. (317 p.)
"Cromwell And His Times," *Methodist Quarterly Review,* (W.P. Harrison, ed.), Vol. 10, No. 2, July, 1891, p. 340-354.
FROM LINCOLN TO CLEVELAND, Jas. P. Harrison & Co., Printers and Publishers, Atlanta, 1886. (246 p.)
D.D., HISTORIC ERAS AND PARAGRAPHIC PENCILINGS, Constitution Publishing Company, Atlanta, 1892. (232 p.)
LECTURES AND ESSAYS, Constitution Publishing Co., Atlanta, Ga., 1889. (214 p.)
"Life and Genius of Sidney Lanier," *Methodist Quarterly Review,* New Series, (W.P. Harrison, ed.), Vol. 5, No. 1, Oct. 1888, p. 157-171.
"Mormanism: What Is It? What Will You Do With It?" *The Quarterly Review of the MECS,* (J.W. Hinton, ed.), Vol. 6, No. 3, July, 1884, p. 433-443.
(review of..) Life and Letters of James Osgood Andrew by G. G. Smith, Southern Methodist Pub. House, Nashville, Tenn.; J.W. Burke & Co., Macon, Ga., 1882, *The Quarterly Review of the MECS,* (J.W. Hinton, ed.), Vol. 5, No. 2, April, 1883, p. 327-337.
A.M., D.D., SEVENTY-ONE YEARS IN GEORGIA, C.P. Byrd, Atlanta, 1897. (88 p.)
SOUTH SIDE VIEWS, Jas. P. Harrison & Co., Atlanta, Ga., 1883. (80 p.)
"Story of the Magna Carta," *Methodist Quarterly Review,* (W.P. Harrison, ed.), Vol. 8, No. 2, July, 1890, p. 240-251.
"Studies In Psychology—Visions," *The Quarterly Review of the MECS,* Vol. 5, No. 3, July, 1883, (J.W. Hinton, ed.), p. 488-499.
"Transubstantiation" (paper). (23 p.) Sp Cl Candler

Scott, W.J., and Barrick, J.R., eds., *Scott's Monthly Magazine,* (1865-69), Franklin Steam Printing House, Atlanta, Ga. [latter issues designated Phillips & Crew, Atlanta, Ga., publishers]. [Sept. 1867-Jan. 1868 printed by J.W. Burke & Co., Phoenix Steam Printing House, Macon, Ga.].

Scudder, Rev. M. L., AMERICAN METHODISM, S.S. Scranton & Co., Hartford, Conn., 1868. (592 p.)

Seals, T. A., "Family Religion," *Methodist Quarterly Review,* (W.P. Harrison, ed.), Vol. 9, No. 1, Oct. 1890, p. 32-38.
"The Home Life of Nations," *Methodist Quarterly Review,* (J.J. Tigert, ed.), Vol. 16, No. 1, April 1894, p. 123-140.
"The Model Statesman," *The Methodist Review,* (J.J. Tigert, ed.), Vol. 19, No. 1, Sept.-Oct., 1895, p. 77-86.
"The True Gentleman," *Methodist Quarterly Review,* (W.P. Harrison, ed.), Vol. 13, No. 1, Oct. 1892, p. 107-122.

Sellers, Charles Coleman, LORENZO DOW: THE BEARER OF THE WORD, Milton, Balch & Co., New York, 1928. (275 p.)

Sells, James W., MESSAGES FROM THE METHODIST HOUR, S.E. Jurisdictional Council of the Methodist Church, Atlanta. 1946 (64 p.); 1947 (111 p.) Contains the following sermons: 1946, Moore, Arthur J., "New Man In A New World" (p. 29); 1947, Harris, Pierce, "The Little White Church and The Great White Way" (p. 30)

Shaw, J.B.F., THE NEGRO IN THE HISTORY OF METHODISM, The Parthenon Press, Nashville, Tenn., 1954. (234 p.)

Shaw, M. A. (S. Ga.), "What God Thinks of Missions" (pamphlet), (8 p.) Ga. Room

Sheets, Herchel H., ENEMY VERSIONS OF THE GOSPEL, The Upper Room, 1973. (72 p.)
PLACES CHRIST HALLOWED, The Upper Room, Nashville, Tenn., 1965. (125 p.)
THE ISOLATED BEATITUDES, Beacon Hill Press, Kansas City, Missouri, 1972. (71 p.)
THE LOOK THAT REDEEMED, Tidings, Nashville, 1972. (63 p.)

Shelton, William A., DUST AND ASHES OF EMPIRES, MECS Publishing House, Nashville, Dallas, 1922. (272 p.)
DUST AND ASHES OF EMPIRES, Cokesbury Press, Nashville, Tenn., 1924. (304 p.)
"Why I Said To The Methodists At Springfield, 'It's Up To You,' " (Unification pamphlet) Nashville, Tenn., 192__. (12 p.)

Shingler, J. S., LIGHTNING FLASHES AND THUNDERBOLTS (1901 SERMONS BY SAM P. JONES IN SAVANNAH, GA.), Pentecostal Publishing Co., Louisville, Ky., 1912. (288 p.)

Shipp, Rev. Albert M., THE HISTORY OF METHODISM IN SOUTH CAROLINA, Nashville, Tenn., Southern Methodist Publishing House, 1884. Reprinted by Reprint Co., Spartanburg, S.C., 1972. (652 p.)

Shockley, Grant S.; Brewer, Earl D. C.; and Townsend, Marie, BLACK PASTORS AND CHURCHES IN UNITED METHODISM, Center For Research In Social Change, Emory Univ., Atlanta, 1976. (67 p.)

Sills, John R., STUDIES IN NORTH GEORGIA METHODISM, (Town & Country Work). (39 p.)

Simmons, Rev. J. C., "A Few Plain Words on Baptism," (treatise), Southern Methodist Publishing House, Nashville, Tenn. 1881 or 1882.
"Arrows From the Quiver of Methodism," 5-1-1884. (61 p.)
"Christ In The Old and New Testament," *Methodist Quarterly Review,* (W.P. Harrison, ed.), Vol. 6, No. 2, July, 1889, p. 362-275.
"False Prophets," *Methodist Quarterly Review,* (W.P. Harrison, ed.), Vol. 12, No. 1, April; 1892, p. 18-40.
THE HISTORY OF SOUTHERN METHODISM ON THE PACIFIC COAST, Southern Methodist Publishing House, 1886, Nashville, Tenn. (454 p.)
THE KINGDOM AND COMING OF CHRIST, MECS Publishing House, Nashville, Tenn., 1891. (320 p.)

Simon, John S., JOHN WESLEY AND THE ADVANCE OF METHODISM, Epworth Press, London, 1925. (352 p.) (Ga. Ref. — 42, 77, 79, 84, 119-120, 195-196, 272, 294, 319).
JOHN WESLEY AND THE METHODIST SOCIETIES, Epworth Press, London, 1923. (381 p.) (Ga. Ref. — 12, 20, 49, 51, 53, 60, 62, 71, 72, 90, 91, 105, 248, 44).
JOHN WESLEY AND THE RELIGOUS SOCIETIES, Epworth Press, London, 1921. (363 p.) (Ga. Ref. — Chapter 7)
JOHN WESLEY, THE MASTERBUILDER, London Epworth Press, 1927. (344 p.) (Ga. Ref. — 43, 109, 148, 300).

Singleton, Rev. R. H., "Some Elements In the Life of The Successful Minister," (lecture), Atlanta, Ga., 1922. (10 p.) Ga. Room

Sisson, William Rembert, "A Statistical Study of the Circuit Churches of the M.E. Church South in the North Ga. and South Ga. Conferences for the Fiscal Year 1930-1931." (Thesis, 1934, Emory Univ.) (23 p.)

Sledd, Rev. Andrew, "Bishop Moore's Interpretation of the Plan of Unification," (pamphlet) (27 p.)
HIS WITNESS: A STUDY OF THE BOOK OF ACTS, Cokesbury Press, Nashville, Tenn., 1935. (240 p.)
"Proof or Propaganda?" (Open Letter On Unification), 1924. (27 p.)
"Reasons Why Our Colleges Fail to Educate," *The Methodist Review Quarterly,* (Gross Alexander, ed.), v. 59, Oct. 1910, p. 675-683.
ST. MARK'S LIFE OF JESUS, Cokesbury Press, Nashville, Tenn., 1927. (210 p.)
ST. MARK'S LIFE OF JESUS, Cokesbury Press, Nashville, Tenn. (rev. ed.), 1930. (210 p.)
THE BIBLES OF THE CHURCHES, Cokesbury Press, Nashville, Tenn., 1930. (220

p.)

THE BIBLES OF THE CHURCHES, Cokesbury Press, Nashville, Tenn., (rev. ed.), 1931. (220 p.)

"The Literary Woman in Rome," *The Methodist Quarterly Review*, (J.J. Tigert, ed.), Sept.-Oct., 1902, v. 51, p. 643-658.

Sledge, Robert Watson, A HISTORY OF THE METHODIST EPISCOPAL CHURCH SOUTH, 1914-1939, Univ. Microfilms, Ann Arbor, 1972. (Dissertation)

Small, Samuel W., "Deliverance From Bondage"—A Temperance Sermon, found in Jones, Rev. Sam P., *Quit Your Meanness,* Forshee & McMakin, Cincinnati, Ohio, 1886, p. 483.

FROM PRESS TO PULPIT, F. H. Revell, Chicago, Ill.

OLD SI's SAYINGS, F. H. REVELL, CHICAGO, ILL., 1886. (205 P.)

Smart, Wyatt A., "A Christmas Meditation," *The Emory Univ. Quarterly Review*, v.1, n.4., Dec. 1945, p. 193-196.

"Can We War Without Hate," *The Christian Advocate* CXVII 33, (Aug. 9, 1943), p. 6-7, 24.

"Paul and His Persecutions," RELIGION IN LIFE, XII, 2 (Spring, 1943), p. 197-204.

PREACHING IN THESE TIMES, C. Schribner's Sons, New York, 1940. (179 p.)

STILL THE BIBLE SPEAKS, Abingdon-Cokesbury Press, New York, 1948. (171 p.)

CONTEMPORARY CHRIST, Abingdon-Cokesbury Press, New York, Nashville, 1942. (164 p.)

THE SPIRITUAL GOSPEL, Abingdon-Cokesbury Press, New York, Nashville, Tenn., 1946. (134 p.)

"The Universal Gospel of Jesus," in William K. Anderson's CHRISTIAN WORLD MISSION, Com. on Ministerial Training, Nashville, Tenn., 1946 ed.

"Using The Scripture," *The Church School,* (monthly article).

Smith, Charles Spencer, HISTORY OF THE AFRICAN METHODIST CHURCH, Book Concerns of the AME Church, Philadelphia, 1922. (570 p.) Ga. Ref. — 65, 92, 94, 105, 107, 110, 112, 116, 120, 124, 352.

Smith, Miss Florine, ed., YEARBOOK & MINUTES OF THE 21ST ANNUAL CONFERENCE AND SECOND ASSEMBLY OF THE S. GA. EPWORTH LEAGUE, 1921-22, Southern Printers, Americus, Ga. (83 p.)

Smith, George, HISTORY OF WESLEYAN METHODISM, VOL. 1, WESLEY AND HIS TIMES, Longman, Brown, Green, Longmans and Roberts: London, 1857. (748 p.)

Smith, George Gilman, 1800-1859, 1860-1865, 1866-1879, 1880-1899, 1900-1919 — 523 items — Ga. — Md. — W. Va. The collection of this Methodist minister includes correspondence, writings and other miscellaneous materials. Sp Cl Woodruff

A Hundred Years of Methodism In Augusta, Ga., Richards & Shaver, Augusta, 1898. (59 p.)

Berry's Triumph, J.W. Burke & Co., Macon, Ga., 1888. (192 p.)

Childhood And Conversion, MECS Publishing House, Nashville, 1891. (116 p.)

"Freeborn Garrettson," *The Methodist Review,* (J.J. Tigert, ed.), Vol. 18, No. 1, March-April, 1895, p. 37-43.

Harry Thornton, MECS Publishing House, Nashville, Tenn., 1886. (116 p.)

"Infant's Catechism," J.W. Burke & Co., Macon, Ga., 1897. (16 p.)

Infants' Catechism, J.W. Burke & Co., Macon, 1906. (16 p.)

Intermediate Catechism on Christian Doctrine, MECS Publishing House, Nashville, Tenn., 1911. (64 p.)

"Jesse Lee," *Southern Methodist Review,* (W.P. Harrison, ed.), Vol. 3, No. 1, Sept., 1887, p. 80-95.

"John Calvin and His Correspondents," *Methodist Quarterly Review,* (J.J. Tigert, ed.), Vol. 16, No. 1, April, 1894, p. 17-35.

"John De Wickliff," *The Quarterly Review of the MECS,* (J.W. Hinton, ed.), Vol. 6, No. 4, Oct. 1884, p. 712-718.

Letter (2-7-1881)—concerning his book, History of Georgia & Florida Methodism. Sp Cl Univ Ga.

Life and Labors of Francis Asbury, MECS Publishing House, Nashville, Tenn., 1896. (311 p.)

Life and Labors of Francis Asbury, M.E. Church Publishing House, Nashville, 1898. (311 p.)

Life and Times of George Foster Pierce, D.D., LL. D., Hancock Publishing Co., Sparta, Ga., 1888. (688 p.)

Life of John W. Knight, (uv).

Mr. Hall and His Family, (uv).

The Boy In Gray, Macon Publishing Co., Macon, Ga., 1894. (267 p.)

The Child and The Savior, J.W. Burke & Co., Macon, 1883. (48 p.)

"The Colonial Church In Virginia," *Methodist Quarterly Review,* (W.P. Harrison, ed.), Vol. 14, No. 1, April, 1893, p. 46-56.

"The Colonial Church of Virginia," *Methodist Quarterly Review,* (W.P. Harrison, ed.), Vol. 13, No. 2, Jan. 1893, p. 275-290.

"The Confessions of Augustine," *Methodist Quarterly Review,* (W.P. Harrison, ed.) Vol. 10, No. 1, April, 1891, p. 59-68.

"The Georgia Life of the Oxford Methodists," *Methodist Quarterly Review,* (W.P. Harrison, ed.), Vol. 7, No. 2, Jan. 1890, p. 280-290.

The History of Georgia Methodism from 1786-1866, Atlanta, Ga., A.B. Caldwell, 1913. (430 p.)

The History of Methodism in Georgia and Florida from 1785-1865, Macon, Ga., John W. Burke & Co., 1877. (530 p.)

The Life and Letters of James Osgood Andrew, Southern Methodist Publishing House, Nashville, 1882. (562 p.)

The Life and Letters of James Osgood Andrew, Southern Methodist Publishing House, Nashville, Tenn., 1883. (562 p.)

The Story of Georgia and the Georgia People, 1732-1860, Genealogical

Publishing Co., Baltimore, 1968. (664 p.) (A reprint of the 1902 ed.)
THE YOUNG METHODIST, (A Manual) Southern Methodist Publishing House, Nashville, Tenn., 1881 or 1882.
WALK IN THE LIGHT, Southern Methodist Publishing House, Nashville, Tenn., 1880? (95 p.)
"Wherefore Shouldst Thou Doubt," (pamphlet) (27 p.)

Smith, Rev. H. Turner, BAPTISM—A REPLY TO REV. F.A. RATCLIFF OF MECS, S. GA. CONFERENCE, J.W. Burke & Co., Macon, 1907. (85 p.)

Smith, J. A., ed., MINUTES AND YEARBOOK OF THE SOUTH GEORGIA CONFERENCE OF THE MECS, 48TH SESSION, HELD IN DAWSON, GA., Nov. 25-30, 1914, The Dawson News, Dawson, Ga. (85 p.)
MINUTES AND YEARBOOK OF THE SOUTH GEORGIA CONFERENCE OF THE MECS, 49TH SESSION, HELD IN CORDELE, GA., Nov. 24-29, 1915, The Rainey Press, Dawson, Ga. (100 p.)

Smith, J. A., ed., MINUTES AND YEARBOOK OF THE SOUTH GEORGIA CONFERENCE OF THE MECS, 50TH SESSION, HELD IN THOMASVILLE, GA., Nov. 29-DEC. 4, 1916. (95 m.p.)
MINUTES AND YEARBOOK OF THE SOUTH GEORGIA CONFERENCE OF THE MECS, 51ST SESSION, HELD IN ALBANY, GA., Nov. 14-19, 1917. (97 m.p.)
MINUTES AND YEARBOOK OF THE SOUTH GEORGIA CONFERENCE OF THE MECS, 52ND SESSION, HELD IN VALDOSTA, GA., Nov. 20-25, 1918. (78 m.p.)
MINUTES AND YEARBOOK OF THE SOUTH GEORGIA CONFERENCE OF THE MECS, 53RD SESSION, HELD IN DUBLIN, GA., Nov. 19-24, 1919, Publishers' Press, Atlanta, Ga. (144 p.)
MINUTES AND YEARBOOKS OF THE SOUTH GEORGIA CONFERENCE OF THE MECS, 54TH SESSION, HELD IN MOULTRIE, GA., Nov. 17-22, 1920. (127 p.)
MINUTES AND YEARBOOK OF THE SOUTH GEORGIA CONFERENCE OF THE MECS, 55TH SESSION, HELD IN TIFTON, GA., Nov. 23-28, 1921. (125 p.)
MINUTES AND YEARBOOK OF THE SOUTH GEORGIA CONFERENCE OF THE MECS, 56TH SESSION, HELD IN WAYCROSS, GA., Nov. 22-27, 1922. (133 p.)
MINUTES AND YEARBOOK OF THE SOUTH GEORGIA CONFERENCE OF THE MECS, 57TH SESSION, HELD IN SAVANNAH, GA., Nov. 28-DEC. 3, 1923. (143 p.)
MINUTES AND YEARBOOK OF THE SOUTH GEORGIA CONFERENCE OF THE MECS, 58TH SESSION, HELD IN BAINBRIDGE, GA., Nov. 19-23, 1924, J.W. Burke Co., Macon, Ga. (135 p.)
MINUTES AND YEARBOOK OF THE SOUTH GEORGIA CONFERENCE OF THE MECS, 59TH SESSION, HELD IN MACON, GA., Nov. 25-30, 1925, J.W. Burke Co., Macon, Ga. (151 p.)
MINUTES AND YEARBOOK OF THE SOUTH GEORGIA CONFERENCE OF THE MECS, 60TH SESSION, HELD IN AMERICUS, GA., Nov. 17-22, 1926, J.W. Burke Co., Macon, Ga. (141 p.)
MINUTES AND YEARBOOK OF THE SOUTH GEORGIA CONFERENCE OF THE MECS, 61ST SESSION, HELD IN VALDOSTA, GA., Nov. 16-21, 1927, J.W. Burke Co., Macon, Ga. (139 p.)

Minutes and Yearbook of the South Georgia Conference of the MECS, 62nd Session, Held In Columbus, Ga., Nov. 8-12, 1928, J.W. Burke Co., Macon, Ga. (139 p.)

Minutes and Yearbook of the South Georgia Conference of the MECS, 63rd Session, Held In Macon, Ga., Nov. 6-10, 1929, J.W. Burke Co., Macon, Ga. (137 p.)

Minutes and Yearbook of the South Georgia Conference of the MECS, 64th Session, Held In Thomasville, Ga., Nov. 19-23, 1930, J.W. Burke Co., Macon, Ga. (124 p.)

Minutes and Yearbook of the South Georgia Conference of the MECS, 65th Session, Held In Savannah, Ga., Nov. 18-22, 1931, J.W. Burke Co., Macon, Ga. (184 p.)

Minutes and Yearbook of the South Georgia Conference of the MECS, 66th Session, Held In Albany, Ga., Nov. 16-20, 1932, J.W. Burke Co., Macon. (89 p.)

Minutes and Yearbook of the South Georgia Conference of the MECS, 67th Session, Held In Brunswick, Ga., Nov. 15-19, 1933, J.W. Burke Co., Macon, Ga. (103 p.)

Minutes and Yearbook of the South Georgia Conference of the MECS, 68th Session, Held In Macon, Ga., Nov. 14-18, 1934, Macon, Ga. (113 p.)

Minutes and Yearbook of the South Georgia Conference of the MECS, 69th Session, Held In Americus, Ga., Nov. 13-17, 1935, J.W. Burke Co., Macon, Ga. (129 p.)

Minutes and Yearbook of the South Georgia Conference of the MECS, 70th Session, Held In Columbus, Ga., Nov. 12-15, 1936, J.W. Burke Co., Macon, Ga. (131 p.)

Minutes and Yearbook of the South Georgia Conference of the MECS, 71st Session, Held In Dublin, Ga., Nov. 4-7, 1937, J.W. Burke Co., Macon, Ga. (131 p.)

Minutes and Yearbook of the South Georgia Conference of the MECS, 72nd Session, Held In Waycross, Ga., Nov. 10-14, 1938, J.W. Burke Co., Macon, Ga. (123 p.)

Year Book and Minutes of the South Georgia Conference of the Methodist Episcopal Church, 34th Session, Held in Cuthbert, Ga., Dec. 6-10, 1900, Braid & Hutton, printers and binders, Savannah, Ga., 1901. (83 m.p.)

Year-Book and Minutes of the South Georgia Conference of the MECS, 35th Session, Held In Macon, Ga., Dec. 4-9, 1901, Braid & Hutton, Printers and Binders, Savannah, Ga., 1902. (63 p.)

Year-Book and Minutes of the South Georgia Conference of the MECS, 36th Session, Held In Thomasville, Ga., Dec. 3-8, 1902, Braid & Hutton, printers and binders, Savannah, Ga., 1903. (75 p.)

Year-Book and Minutes of the South Georgia Conference of the MECS, 37th Session, Held In Sandersville, Ga., Nov. 25-30, 1903, Braid & Hutton, Printers and Binders, Savannah, Ga., 1904. (80 p.)

Year-Book and Minutes of the South Georgia Conference of the MECS, 38th Session, Held In McRae, Ga., Nov. 30-Dec. 5, 1904, Braid & Hutton,

Printers and Binders, Savannah, Ga., 1905. (87 p.)

Year-Book and Minutes of the South Georgia Conference of the MECS, 39th Session, Held In Americus, Ga., Nov. 29-Dec. 4, 1905, Braid & Hutton, Printers and Binders, Savannah, Ga., 1906. (85 p.)

Year-Book and Minutes of the South Georgia Conference of the MECS, 40th Session, Held In Valdosta, Ga., Nov. 28-Dec. 3, 1906, Braid & Hutton, Printers and Binders, Savannah, Ga. (95 m.p.)

Year-Book and Minutes of the South Georgia Conference of the MECS, 41st Session, Held In Brunswick, Ga., Nov. 27-Dec. 2, 1907 Braid & Hutton, Printers and Binders, Savannah, 1908. (93 m.p.)

Year-Book and Minutes of the South Georgia Conference of the MECS, 42nd Session, Held In Quitman, Ga., Dec. 2-7, 1908, Braid & Hutton, Printers and Binders, Savannah, Ga., 1909. (91 m.p.)

Year-Book and Minutes of the South Georgia Conference of the MECS, 43rd Session, Held In Waynesboro, Ga., Dec. 1-6, 1909, Braid & Hutton, Printers and Binders, Savannah, Ga., 1910. (80 m.p.)

Year-Book and Minutes of the South Georgia Conference of the MECS, 44th Session, Held In Columbus, Ga., Nov. 30-Dec. 5, 1910, Braid & Hutton, Printers, Savannah, Ga., 1911. (93 m.p.)

Year-Book and Minutes of the South Georgia Conference of the MECS, 45th Session, Held In Bainbridge, Ga., Nov. 29-Dec. 4, 1911, The J.W. Burke Co., Macon, Ga., 1912. (76 p.)

Year-Book and Minutes of the South Georgia Conference of the MECS, 46th Session, Held In Savannah, Ga., Nov. 27-Dec. 2, 1912, The J.W. Burke Co., Macon, Ga., 1912. (76 p.)

Year-Book and Minutes of the South Georgia Conference of the MECS, 47th Session, Held In Macon, Ga., Nov. 26-Dec. 1, 1913, Foote & Davies Co., Atlanta, Ga. (78 p.)

Smith, James Rembert Smith: Letters (29 items) to his nephew G.G. Smith. J.R. Smith was a medical doctor and Methodist minister. References concerning him are contained in Mitchell, History of Washington County. Sp Cl Univ Ga

Smith, Leon and Smith, Antoinette, "Growing Love in Christian Marriage," United Methodist Publishing House, Nashville, Tenn., 1981. (Pastor's manual).

Smith, Nellie J., Stories & Poems, MECS Publishing House, Nashville, Tenn.; Dallas, Texas, 1905. (60 p.) (a granddaughter of G.G. Smith, to whom the volume is dedicated).

Smith, Rembert Gilman, "A Vital Factor In College Life," *The Methodist Review Quarterly,* v. 60, July 1911, (Gross Alexander, ed.), p. 491-498.

"Constitutions of the Two Great American Methodist Churches," *The Methodist Review,* v. 66, Oct. 1917, p. 601-619.

"Does Protestantism Need a Bismarch?" *The Methodist Review,* (H.M. DuBose, ed.), v. 65, Oct. 1916, p. 771-774.

GARFIELD BROMLEY OXNAM, REVOLUTIONIST?, Houston, Tx., 1953. (192 p.)

IS THIS THE HOUR, Tulsa, Okla., 1947. (231 p.)

"Methodism: Miscellaneous Pamphlets," 1936-42. (Candler Library).

"Methodism's Duty To The Southern Negro," *The Methodist Review Quarterly*, (Gross Alexander, ed.), v. 57, July, 1908, p. 529-536.

METHODIST REDS, 1935. (18 p.)

MOSCOW OVER METHODISM, St. Louis, Chicago, John S. Swift Company, 1936. (280 p.)

MOSCOW OVER METHODISM?, The University Press, Houston, Texas, 1950. (182 p.)

POLITICS IN A PROTESTANT CHURCH, The Ruralist Press, Atlanta, 1930. (320 p.)

"Synthetic Authority In Religion," *The Methodist Quarterly Review*, v. 78, April, 1928, p. 259-273.

"The Church, The State, and Political Parties," *The Methodist Quarterly Review*, v. 79, April, 1930, p. 248-264.

"The Cruelty of Ignorance," *The Methodist Quarterly Review*, v. 73, April, 1924, p. 232-239.

"The Four Pillars of the Temple," *The Methodist Quarterly Review*, v. 77, April, 1928, p. 279-284.

"The Gospel and The Higher Criticism," *The Methodist Review Quarterly*, (Gross Alexander, ed.), v. 63, April, 1914, p. 348-353.

"The Maintenance of American Protestant Unity," *The Methodist Quarterly Review*, v. 75, July, 1926, p. 390-403.

"The Reflex of The Centenary Movement," *The Methodist Review*, v. 68, Jan. 1919, p. 130-139.

Smith, Warren Thomas, "Attempts At Methodist and Moravian Union: 1785-86," *Methodist History,* v8, n2, Jan. 1970, p. 36-48.

AUGUSTINE: HIS LIFE AND THOUGHT, John Knox Press, 1980. (190 p.)

HARRY HOSIER: CIRCUIT RIDER, The Upper Room, Nashville, Tenn., 1981.

"The Christmas Conference," *Methodist History,* v6, n4, July, 1968, p. 3-27.

"The Wesleys In Georgia: An Evaluation," reprint from The Journal of the Interdenominational Theological Center, Vol. VI, Spring, 1979, No. 2. Published by ITC Faculty, Atlanta, Ga. (11 p.)

"Thomas Coke and The West Indies," *Methodist History,* v3, n1, p. 1-11.

"Thomas Coke's First Trip To America," *The Wesleyan Quarterly Review,* Vol. 2, No. 3, Aug. 1965, p. 125-137.

Smith, Harmon L., "William Capers and William A. Smith," *Methodist History,* v3, n1, Octo. 1964, p. 23-32.

Smith, Whiteford, (M), "Sermon on the Occasion of the Centenary of Wesleyan Methodism," preached at Athens Methodist Church, 10-25-1839, Burges & James, Charleston, 1840. (24 p.) Ga. Room

Smithson, William T., ed., IN MEMORIAM: REV. BISHOP JAMES OSGOOD

ANDRED, D.D.; REV. AUGUSTUS B. LONGSTREET, D.D., LL.D.; REV. WILLIAM A. SMITH, D.D., compiled & published by Wm. T. Smithson, New York, (no date). (139 p.)

THE METHODIST PULPIT SOUTH, Henry Polkinhorn, Washington, D.C., 1858. (314 p.) Containing the following sermons: Pierce, G.F., "Devotedness To Christ" (p. 56); Means, Rev. A., "God In Christ Jesus," (p. 105); Smith, Whitefoord, "Man Subjected To The Law of Suffering," (p. 123); Pierce, Lovick, "Paul's Commission To Preach" (p. 188); Anderson, Josephus, "Religious Principle," (p. 280). (This work reviewed in *Quarterly Review of the MECS,* D.S. Doggett, ed., Jan. 1859, p. 138.

THE METHODIST PULPIT, SOUTH, 3rd ed., published by W.T. Smithson, Washington, D.C., 1859. (440 p.)

Sneed, James J., ed., YEARBOOK AND MINUTES OF THE 14TH SESSION OF THE NORTH GEORGIA CONFERENCE, METHODIST CHURCH, WESLEY MEMORIAL METHODIST CHURCH, ATLANTA, GA., JUNE 17-20, 1952, Scanland's Inc., Printers, Tampa, Fla. (139 p.)

YEARBOOK AND MINUTES OF THE 15TH SESSION, NORTH GEORGIA CONFERENCE OF THE METHODIST CHURCH, HELD IN WESLEY MEMORIAL METHODIST CHURCH, ATLANTA, GA., JUNE 22-26, 1953, The Decatur News Publishing Co., Decatur, Ga. (153 p.)

YEARBOOK AND MINUTES OF THE 88TH SESSION OF THE NORTH GEORGIA CONFERENCE, THE METHODIST CHURCH, HELD IN WESLEY MEMORIAL METHODIST CHURCH, ATLANTA, GA., JUNE 21-25, 1954. (153 p.)

YEARBOOK AND MINUTES OF THE 89TH SESSION, NORTH GEORGIA CONFERENCE OF THE METHODIST CHURCH, HELD IN 1ST METHODIST CHURCH, ATHENS, GA., JUNE 20-24, 1955. (187 p.)

YEARBOOK AND MINUTES OF THE 90TH SESSION, NORTH GEORGIA CONFERENCE OF THE METHODIST CHURCH, HELD IN 1ST CHURCH, ATHENS, GA., JUNE 18-22, 1956. (207 p.)

YEARBOOK AND MINUTES OF THE 91ST SESSION, NORTH GEORGIA CONFERENCE, OF THE METHODIST CHURCH, HELD IN 1ST METHODIST CHURCH, ATLANTA, GA., JUNE 17-21, 1957. (211 p.)

YEARBOOK AND MINUTES OF THE 92ND SESSION, NORTH GEORGIA CONFERENCE, OF THE METHODIST CHURCH, HELD IN 1ST METHODIST CHURCH, ATLANTA, GA., JUNE 16-20, 1958. (244 p.)

Snelling, William Amos, (1873-1950) — 4 boxes — Ga., Ark., Texas. Family papers of this Central Ga. businessman and Methodist layman include correspondence that reveals much of everyday life—crops and business conditions, social customs, and church activities. Sp Cl Woodruff

Soule, Joshua and Mason, T., eds., *The Methodist Matazine,* published for the Methodist Episcopal Church, John C. Totten, printer, New York, 1818. Vol. 1 (monthly periodical).

South Carolina Conference, "Proceedings of the Methodist Sunday School

Convention of Ministers & Delegates from within the bounds of the S.C. Conference.'' (held in Columbia, May 5-7, 1859, printed by J.C. Morgan, Columbia, S.C. (52 p.) (reviewed in *Quarterly Review of the MECS*, (D.S. Doggett, ed.), October, 1859, p. 609.) Sermon on that occasion: by Whitefoord Smith, whose paper, ''Influence of the Sunday School'' was adopted.

South Carolina Missionary Society, ''Third Annual Report,'' found in *The Methodist Magazine,* (Soule & Mason, eds.), Vol. 7, 1824, p. 196-198.

South Carolina Conference, ''Annual Report of the Conferences Staff to the Board of Christian Education.'' Candler Library has 1938; 1939.

South Georgia Conference, Epworth League of the MECS, South Georgia, 5th Annual Conference, Atlanta, held April 22-25, 1897, Foote & Davies, Atlanta. (88 p.) Ga. Room

''Methodism in South Georgia,'' Report of the Survey Conducted by the Town & Country Commission of the S. Ga. Conf., 1954. (62 p.)

Minutes of the Epworth League, S. Ga. Conf., 1902-? Candler Library has 1922.

MINUTES OF THE 9TH SESSION OF THE SOUTH GEORGIA ANNUAL CONFERENCE OF THE MECS, HELD AT AMERICUS, GA., DEC. 15-21, 1875. (55 p.) [prob. printed by J.W. Burke & Co.]

MINUTES OF THE 10TH SESSION OF THE SOUTH GEORGIA ANNUAL CONFERENCE OF THE MECS, HELD AT SANDERSVILLE, GA., DEC. 13-18, 1876. (43 m.p.) [Prob. printed by J.W. Burke & Co.].

MINUTES OF THE 11TH SESSION OF THE SOUTH GEORGIA CONFERENCE OF THE MECS HELD AT TALBOTTON, GA., DEC. 12-17, 1877. (31 p.)

MINUTES OF THE 12TH SESSION OF THE SOUTH GEORGIA CONFERENCE OF THE MECS HELD AT THOMASVILLE, GA., DEC. 11-16, 1878. (35 p.)

MINUTES OF THE 13TH SESSION OF THE SOUTH GEORGIA CONFERENCE OF THE MECS HELD AT PERRY, GA., DEC. 10-15, 1879. (40 p.)

MINUTES OF THE 14TH SESSION OF THE SOUTH GEORGIA CONFERENCE OF THE MECS HELD AT HAWKINSVILLE, GA., DEC. 8-12, 1880. (48 p.)

MINUTES OF THE 15TH SESSION OF THE SOUTH GEORGIA CONFERENCE OF THE MECS HELD AT COLUMBUS, GA., DEC. 7-11, 1881. (47 p.)

MINUTES OF THE 16TH SESSION OF THE SOUTH GEORGIA CONFERENCE OF THE MECS HELD AT ALBANY, GA., DEC. 13-19, 1882. (49 p.)

MINUTES OF THE 17TH SESSION OF THE SOUTH GEORGIA CONFERENCE OF THE MECS, HELD AT MACON, GA., DEC. 12-17, 1883. (33 p.)

MINUTES OF THE 18TH SESSION OF THE SOUTH GEORGIA CONFERENCE OF THE MECS HELD AT SAVANNAH, GA., DEC. 17-22, 1884. (44 p.)

MINUTES OF THE 19TH SESSION OF THE SOUTH GEORGIA CONFERENCE OF THE MECS HELD AT BRUNSWICK, GA., DEC. 9-14, 1885. (40 m.p.)

MINUTES OF THE SOUTH GEORGIA CONFERENCE, MECS, HELD IN SAVANNAH, GA., DEC. 11-16, 1867. (29 p.)

MINUTES OF THE SOUTH GEORGIA CONFERENCE, MECS, HELD IN ALBANY, GA., DEC. 16-21, 1868. (34 m.p.)

MINUTES OF THE SOUTH GEORGIA CONFERENCE OF THE MECS HELD IN CUTHBERT, GA., DEC. 1-7, 1869. (30 p.)

MINUTES OF THE SOUTH GEORGIA CONFERENCE OF THE MECS HELD IN FT. VALLEY, GA., DEC. 14-19, 1870, J.W. Burke & Co., Printers and Binders, Macon, Ga. (31 m.p.)

MINUTES OF THE SOUTH GEORGIA CONFERENCE OF THE MECS HELD IN THE CITY OF COLUMBUS, GA., DEC. 13-18, 1871, J.W. Burke & Co., Printers and Binders, Macon, Ga., 1872. (35 m.p.)

MINUTES OF THE SOUTH GEORGIA CONFERENCE OF THE MECS HELD AT THOMASVILLE, GA., DEC. 11-16, 1872, J.W. Burke & Co., Printers and Binders, Macon, Ga., 1873. (36 p.)

Mulberry Street Methodist Church, Macon, Ga.—(bound volume of pamphlets and programs—in Wesleyan College Library, Macon, Ga.).

OFFICIAL JOURNAL AND YEARBOOK OF THE SOUTH GEORGIA ANNUAL CONFERENCE OF THE METHODIST CHURCH, (81st Session, Bainbridge, Ga., Nov. 6-10, 1946). (150 p.)

OFFICIAL JOURNAL AND YEARBOOK OF THE SOUTH GEORGIA ANNUAL CONFERENCE OF THE METHODIST CHURCH, (82nd Session, Brunswick, Ga., June 25-29, 1947). (151 p.)

OFFICIAL JOURNAL AND YEARBOOK OF THE SOUTH GEORGIA ANNUAL CONFERENCE OF THE METHODIST CHURCH, (83rd Session, Cordele, Ga., June 23-27, 1948). (145 p.)

OFFICIAL JOURNAL AND YEARBOOK OF THE SOUTH GEORGIA ANNUAL CONFERENCE OF THE METHODIST CHURCH, (84th Session, June 8-12, 1949, Columbus, Ga.). (155 p.)

OFFICIAL JOURNAL OF THE 3RD SESSION OF THE SOUTH GEORGIA CONFERENCE OF THE METHODIST CHURCH, HELD AT VALDOSTA, GA., Nov. 5-9, 1941. (94 p.)

OFFICIAL JOURNAL OF THE 4TH SESSION OF THE SOUTH GEORGIA CONFERENCE OF THE METHODIST CHURCH, Nov. 5-8, 1942, HELD IN TRINITY METHODIST CHURCH, SAVANNAH, GA. (93 m.p.)

OFFICIAL JOURNAL OF THE SOUTH GEORGIA ANNUAL CONFERENCE OF THE METHODIST CHURCH, (5th Session, Nov. 3-7, 1943, at Tifton, Ga.) (92 m.p.)

THE OFFICIAL JOURNAL OF THE SOUTH GEORGIA ANNUAL CONFERENCE OF THE METHODIST CHURCH, (79th Session, Macon, Ga., Nov. 7-10, 1944). (106 p.)

THE OFFICIAL JOURNAL OF THE SOUTH GEORGIA ANNUAL CONFERENCE OF THE METHODIST CHURCH, (80th Session — Waycross, Ga. — Nov. 6-9, 1945). (78 m.p.)

THE 7TH SESSION OF THE SOUTH GEORGIA ANNUAL CONFERENCE OF THE MECS HELD AT MACON, GA., DEC. 17-23, 1873, J.W. Burke & Co., Macon, Ga. (29 p.)

THE EIGHTH SESSION OF THE SOUTH GEORGIA ANNUAL CONFERENCE OF THE MECS, HELD AT SAVANNAH, GA., DEC. 9-14, 1874, J.W. Burke & Co., Macon, Ga. (31 p.)

WESLEY MONUMENTAL M.E. CHURCH SOUTH-SEMICENTENNIAL CELEBRATION— 1878-1928. (pamphlet) (8 p.)

MINUTES OF THE 1ST ANNUAL SESSION OF THE WOMAN'S PARSONAGE AND HOME MISSION SOCIETY HELD AT VINEVILLE, MACON, GA., Nov. 29-DEC. 3, 1894,

News Printing Co., Macon, Ga., 1895. (12 p.)

MINUTES OF THE 17TH ANNUAL MEETING OF THE WOMAN'S FOREIGN MISSIONARY SOCIETY OF THE S. GA. CONFERENCE, HELD AT ALBANY, GA., 1896, J.W. Burke Co., Macon, Ga., 1896. (31 p.)

MINUTES OF THE 18TH ANNUAL MEETING OF THE WOMAN'S FOREIGN MISSIONARY SOCIETY OF THE S. GA. CONFERENCE, HELD AT MACON, GA., JUNE 11-15, 1897, J.W. Burke Co., Books, Stationary, Printing & Binding, Macon, Ga. (32 p.)

MINUTES OF THE 20TH ANNUAL MEETING OF THE WOMAN'S FOREIGN MISSIONARY SOCIETY OF THE S. GA. CONFERENCE, HELD AT VALDOSTA, GA., APRIL 7-11, 1899, Press of J.W. Burke Company, Macon, Ga., 1899. (33 p.)

Cook, Mrs. Ed F., ed., MINUTES OF THE 26TH ANNUAL MEETING OF THE WOMAN'S FOREIGN MISSIONARY SOCIETY OF THE S. GA. CONFERENCE, HELD AT CORDELE, GA., JUNE 9-14, 1905, Jas. J. and Thos. Gilbert, Printers and Manufacturing Stationers, Columbus, Ga., 1905. (44 p.)

Glass, Miss Loula Evans, ed., MINUTES OF THE 28TH ANNUAL MEETING OF THE WOMAN'S FOREIGN MISSIONARY SOCIETY OF THE S. GA. CONFERENCE, HELD AT SAVANNAH, GA., APRIL 12-16, 1907, Gilbert Printing Co., Columbus, Ga., 1907. (63 m.p.)

MINUTES OF THE 31ST ANNUAL MEETING OF THE WOMAN'S FOREIGN MISSIONARY SOCIETY OF THE S. GA. CONFERENCE, MECS, HELD AT CUTHBERT, GA., APRIL 1-5, 1910, Gilbert Printing Co., Columbus, Ga., 1910. (50 m.p.)

REPORT OF PROCEEDINGS OF 18TH CONFERENCE OF THE WOMAN'S HOME MISSION SOCIETY OF THE S. GA. CONFERENCE, BRUNSWICK, GA., MAY 12-16, 1911, The Anderson Printing Co., Macon, Ga. (52 p.)

WOMAN'S HOME MISSION SOCIETY, S. GA. CONFERENCE, 13TH ANNUAL REPORT, WRIGHTSVILLE, GA., MAY 10-15, 1906, Byck's Print, Savannah, Ga. (83 p.)

15TH ANNUAL REPORT OF THE WOMAN'S HOME MISSION SOCIETY OF THE S. GA. CONFERENCE, FITZGERALD, GA., MAY 7-12, 1908, M.S. and D.A. Byck Co., Savannah, Ga. (80 p.)

16TH ANNUAL REPORT OF THE WOMAN'S HOME MISSION SOCIETY OF THE S. GA. CONFERENCE, AMERICUS, GA., APRIL 30-MAY 4, 1909, Press—Braid & Hutton, Savannah, Ga. (82 m.p.)

MINUTES OF THE 3RD ANNUAL MEETING OF THE WOMAN'S MISSIONARY SOCIETY OF THE S. GA. CONFERENCE, MECS, HELD AT DUBLIN, GA., FEB. 6-11, 1914, Press of Southern Printers, Americus, Ga. (89 m.p.)

MINUTES OF THE 7TH ANNUAL MEETING OF THE WOMAN'S MISSIONARY SOCIETY OF THE S. GA. CONFERENCE, MECS, HELD AT SAVANNAH, GA., MARCH 1-5, 1918, Gilbert Printing Co., Columbus, Ga. (81 p.)

MINUTES OF THE 8TH ANNUAL MEETING OF THE WOMAN'S MISSIONARY SOCIETY OF THE S. GA. CONFERENCE, MECS, HELD AT MACON, GA., GEB. 7-11, 1919, Gilbert Printing Co., Columbus, Ga. (68 p.)

WOMAN'S MISSIONARY SOCIETY OF THE S. GA. CONFERENCE, 19TH ANNUAL MEETING, AMERICUS, GA., 1ST CHURCH, APRIL 1-4, 1930, Lyon, Harris & Brooks, Macon, Ga. (99 p.)

WOMAN'S MISSIONARY SOCIETY, 20TH ANNUAL SESSION AND THE 52ND ANNUAL MEETING OF THE WOMAN'S MISSIONARY ORGANIZATION, S. GA. CONFERENCE, MECS, BAINBRIDGE, GA., APRIL 6-9, 1931. (102 p.)

Wesleyan Collection, ca.1770-1970 — 3 boxes. Collection includes letters and other papers of Methodist ministers. Letters of Conference presidents, letters to Rev. Joseph Hutton, and miscellaneous letters from a number of Methodists over a long period of years. Also included are various broadsides, circulars, brochures, photographs, and other printed material. Sp Cl Woodruff

West, Sam Carroll, THE METHODIST EPISCOPAL CHURCH SOUTH AND THE EDUCATION OF SOUTHERN NEGROES FROM 1861-1900, (thesis), Emory Univ., Atlanta, Ga., 1944. (69 p.)

Wheeler, Mary Sparkes, FIRST DECADE OF WOMAN'S FOREIGN MISSIONARY SOCIETY, Phillips & Hunt, New York; Walden & Stowe, Cincinnati, 1881. (346 p.)

White, Goodrich C., "Higher Education," *The Emory Univ. Quarterly Review,* v10, n2, June, 1954, p. 121-129.
TEACHING IN THE SUNDAY SCHOOL, Cokesbury Press, Nashville, Tenn., 1926. (211 p.)
"The Courage That Endures," *The Emory Univ. Quarterly Review,* v2, n3, Oct. 1946, p. 170-175.

White, Mary Culler, JUST JENNIE, THE LIFE STORY OF VIRGINIA M. ATKINSON, Tupper and Love, Atlanta, (Foote & Davies, Inc.), 1955. (104 p.)

Whitehead, John, M.D., THE LIFE OF THE REV. JOHN WESLEY, M.A. (Two vol. inone), Hill & Brodhead, Boston, 1846. (Vol. 1 — 308 p.; Vol. 2 — 313 p.)

Whitehead, Paul, "Bishop Pierce," *Methodist Quarterly Review,* (W.P. Harrison, ed.), Vol. 7, No. 1, Oct. 1889, p. 72-92.

Whiting, Thomas A., BE GOOD TO YOURSELF, Abingdon Press, Nashville, Tenn. (Parthenon Press), 1981. (128 p.)
SERMONS ON THE PRODIGAL SON, Abingdon Press, Nashville, 1959. (111 p.)

Wight, Rev. J. B., TOBACCO, ITS USE AND ABUSE, MECS Publishing House, Nashville, Tenn., 1889. (232 p.)

Wightman, Rev. William M., "Biographical Sketch of Bishop Capers," found in *Quarterly Review,* (H.B. Bascomb, ed.), April 1855, p. 161-179. Additional sketch on Bishop Capers by Wightman found in *Quarterly Review of the MECS,* (D.S. Doggett, ed.), July 1859, p. 321-333.
LIFE OF WILLIAM CAPERS, D.D., Methodist Publishing House, Nashville, Tenn., 1858. Reprint, 1902. (516 p.)
LIFE OF WILLIAM CAPERS, Southern Methodist Publishing House, Nashville, Tenn., 1859. (516 p.)

Williams, Rev. C. C., THE STORY OF ST. PAUL'S CLHURCH, AUGUSTA, GA., 1750-1906, Chronicle Job Printing Office, Augusta, Ga. (46 p.)

Williams, George Walton, ADVICE TO YOUNG MEN AND NACOOCHEE AND ITS SURROUNDINGS, Walker Evans & Cogswell, Co., Charleston, S.C., 1896. (127 p.)
LETTERS TO YOUNG MEN; SUCCESS AND FAILURE, MAKING & SAVING, Charleston, 1885.

Williams, Katharine S., A HISTORY OF THE CANDLER SCHOOL OF THEOLOGY LIBRARY, (thesis), 1961, Emory Univ., Atlanta, Ga.

Williams, N. H., "Belief In Miracles," *The Methodist Quarterly Review,* v. 72, Oct. 1923, p. 643-652.
FOUR LECTURES TO PREACHERS, Florida Methodist Publishing Co., Lakeland, Fla., no date. (48 p.) Ga. Room
"The Numinous Value of the Holy," *The Methodist Quarterly Review,* v. 76, Jan. 1927, p. 46-55.
"The Universal and Unequivocal Message of Deeds," *The Methodist Quarterly Review,* v. 73, Oct. 1924, p. 592-605.
"Theology As The Interpretation of A New Order of Life," *The Methodist Quarterly Review,* v. 78, July 1929, p. 408-419.

Williamson, Robert F., (1846-1962) — 6 folders — Ga. Schley Co. Collection of this itinerant minister of the Georgia Conference, Methodist Church, South, includes his journal (1855-1867) and diary (1846-1862), a picture of the S. Ga. Annual Conference, MECS (1896), and information on Williams on Methodist Church history and Red Oak Methodist Church in Williamson, Ga. Sp Cl Woodruff

Wilson, Robert L., THE EFFECT OF RADICALLY CHANGING COMMUNITIES ON METHODIST CHURCHES IN 32 CITIES IN THE SOUTHEAST, Board of Missions of the Methodist Church, National Bindary Co. of Ga., 1966. (71 p.)

Winchester, C. T., THE LIFE OF JOHN WESLEY, MacMillan Co., New York, 1906. (301 p.) (Ga. Ref. — 40-50)

Winter, Lovick P., "Charles Wesley In America," *The Methodist Review,* (H.M. DuBose, ed.), v. 65, Jan. 1916, p. 71-84.

Winton, Rev. G. B., "Sketch of Bishop Atticus G. Haygood," 1915. (24 p.)

Wiseman, F. Luke, CHARLES WESLEY, Abingdon Press, New York, 1932. (231 p.) (Ga. Ref. — Chapter 1)

Women's Foreign Missionary Society, The Cherokee Corner Women's Foreign Missionary Society (Oglethorpe Co.), Minutes, rosters, financial reports, misc. data. 1881-1898. Sp Cl Univ. Ga.

Wood, A. S., THE BURNING HEART, Wm. B. Eerdmans Publishing Co., Grand Rapids, Mich., 1967. (302 p.) (Wesley biog.).

Woodlawn Methodist Church, Augusta, Ga. "Woodlawn Methodist Church News" (bulletins bound), 1965-66. Ga. Room

Worley, Lynda F., "A History of Centenary Institute, Selma, Alabama," *The Wesleyan Quarterly Review*, Vol. 2, No. 1, Feb. 1965, p. 21-39.

Wray, J. E., "Another View of Thomas Carlyle," *The Methodist Review*, (J.J. Tigert, ed.), Vol. 26, No. 4, July-August, 1900, p. 578-586.

Wright, Richard R., 87 YEARS BEHIND THE BLACK CURTAIN, Rare Book Co., Philadelphia, Penn., 1965. (351 p.) (Ga. Ref. — chapter 21).
THE BISHOPS OF THE AME CHURCH, A.M.E. Sunday School Union, 1963. (225 p.) (Ga. Ref. — Gammon — 27, 88, 170, 192.)

Yarbrough, George W., "A Diamond From the Rubbish," *The Methodist Review*, v. 66, Jan. 1917, p. 93-99.
BOYHOOD AND OTHER DAYS IN GEORGIA, Publishing House of the M.E. Church, South, Nashville, Dallas, Richmond, 1917. (248 p.)

Yarbrough, John F., ed., YEAR-BOOK AND MINUTES OF THE 53RD SESSION OF THE NORTH GEORGIA CONFERENCE, MECS, HELD AT WESLEY MEMORIAL CHURCH, ATLANTA, GA., Nov. 12-17, 1919, Emory University, Ga. (176 p.)

Young, Rev. James, A HISTORY OF THE RISE AND PROGRESS OF METHODISM, Daniel McLeod, New Haven, 1831. (468 p.)

Young, William James, WHEN GOD AND MAN MEET, Geo. H. Doran Co., New York, 1922. (275 p.)

www.ingramcontent.com/pod-product-compliance
Lightning Source LLC
Chambersburg PA
CBHW071131280326
41935CB00010B/1177